# CHURCH HISTORY
## IN BLACK AND WHITE

**Sacred Grove,** *Manchester, New York, 13 August 1907, Anderson Collection, LDSCA. The cover and frontispiece view is Anderson's most famous, artistically stunning photograph, that of a young boy standing in the grove of trees traditionally identified as the place of Joseph Smith's first vision in the spring of 1820. The grove, about one-fourth mile west of Joseph and Lucy Mack Smith's home, is part of a four-hundred-year-old forest that covered much of western New York at the time of the Smith family's arrival in the area in 1818 or 1819. The large trees, including beech, elm, hickory, maple, and oak, had diameters of six feet or more and reached heights of up to 125 feet. Under this natural canopy grew ash, hornbeams, and wild cherry. The woodland floor was carpeted with clumps of chokecherry and dogwood, ferns, grasses, and wildflowers.*

# CHURCH HISTORY
## IN BLACK AND WHITE

George Edward Anderson's Photographic Mission
to Latter-day Saint Historical Sites
—⟨⟩ 1907 Diary, 1907-8 Photographs ⟨⟩—

EDITED BY

Richard Neitzel Holzapfel

T. Jeffery Cottle

Ted D. Stoddard

RELIGIOUS STUDIES CENTER
BRIGHAM YOUNG UNIVERSITY
PROVO, UTAH

Copyright © 1995 by Religious Studies Center
Brigham Young University

Library of Congress Catalog Card Number: 95–79001
ISBN 0–88494–998–2

First Printing, 1995

Distributed by BOOKCRAFT, INC.
Salt Lake City, Utah

Printed in the United States of America

*For*

*Zachary Holzapfel*
*Madeliene Cottle*
*and*
*Mary Louise Stoddard*

# Contents

Acknowledgments

*ix*

List of Photographs

*xi*

Preface

*xv*

Map:
George Edward Anderson's Photographic Mission Through the U.S., 1907–8

*xxi*

Introduction: From Golden Plates to Glass Plates

*1*

1907 Diary and 1907–8 Photographs of George Edward Anderson

*19*

Appendix One:
George Edward Anderson's Notes Made from *An Illustrated Historical Atlas of Caldwell County, Missouri*

*213*

Appendix Two:
George Edward Anderson's Notes at the End of His Diary
*215*


Bibliography
*221*


Index
*229*

# Acknowledgments

The Religious Studies Center (RSC) at Brigham Young University (BYU) in Provo, Utah, funded our initial efforts to work on this project through the help of Donald Q. Cannon and Barbara Crawley. The RSC's continued support and encouragement have been most helpful, especially the efforts of Kent P. Jackson, Heidi Gassman, Jason Roberts, LeGrande W. Smith, Cord M. Udall, and Charlotte Pollard. Richard O. Cowan, H. Dean Garrett, and Verna Wolfgramm of the Department of Church History at BYU also supported our research during the 1994–95 academic year.

Edith Mena of the Daughters of Utah Pioneers (DUP) Museum at Salt Lake City, Utah, provided access to the original 1907 Anderson diary. The Archive Division, Church Historical Department, The Church of Jesus Christ of Latter-day Saints (LDSCA), in Salt Lake City, Utah, provided copies of Anderson's photographs from its collection, including, for use in this book, copies of Anderson's famous "Sacred Grove" images from the original glass-plate negatives. Randall Dixon and William Slaughter (LDSCA) have been longtime supporters of our work in the past, and their efforts on this project have been particularly helpful. The BYU Harold B. Lee Library Archives provided copies of Anderson photographs from its collection and, through the kind assistance of Thomas R. Well, provided a photograph of an original Anderson glass-plate negative.

Richard S. Van Wagoner provided a copy of an original Anderson postcard, which is found in the photographic collection of the Lehi Library Historical Archives in Lehi, Utah. Homer Ellsworth provided access to an Anderson photograph that is found in the Ellsworth family history.

Additional efforts by Cory Maxwell, Jana Erickson, and Rebecca Taylor have contributed to the final design and editing of this work.

We also appreciate the efforts of Paul Anderson, Richard L. Anderson, Alex Baugh, Barbara Bernauer, Jeffery S. Bird, Susan Easton Black, Danielle Bradford, Carl Camp, Chris Charles, David Charles, Annette Curtis, Micheala Voss Cottle, Larry E. Dahl, Larry Draper, Homer Ellsworth, Don Enders, Rell G. Francis, Jeni Broberg Holzapfel, Robert W. Holzapfel, Zachary Holzapfel, Dorothy Horan, Diana Johnson, Susannah Broberg Langehiem, James Kimball, Robert Lowe, Lachlan Mackay, Matthew Moore, Shelly Neiderman, Venesse Nelson, Steve Olson, Julie Place, Larry C. Porter, Ronald E. Romig, David R. Seely, Stephen H. Smoot, Mary O. Stoddard, John Telford, and Mike Trapp for their individual contributions to this project.

# List of Photographs

1. *Sacred Grove*, Manchester, New York, 13 August 1907 .................................... ii
2. *George Edward Anderson's 1907 Diary* ........................................ xvi
3. *"Church History in Photograph" Album* ...................................... xviii
4. *An Anderson Glass-Plate Negative* ......................................... xix
5. *George Edward and Olive Lowry Anderson Family*, Springville, Utah, about 1907 .............. 2
6. *Anderson Postcard* ................................................... 11
7. *Anderson Family*, Springville, Utah, 1907 ................................... 11
8. *The Liahona Office Building*, Independence, Missouri, 25 April 1907 ................... 24
9. *The Examiner Printing Company Building*, Independence, Missouri, 25 April 1907 ........... 25
10. *The Stone Church (RLDS)*, Independence, Missouri, 25 April 1907 ...................... 26
11. *The Independence Temple Property*, Independence, Missouri, 26 April 1907 .................. 28–29
12. *South Pleasant Street*, Independence, Missouri, 26 or 27 April 1907 ...................... 30
13. *LDS Central States Mission Leaders and Bennion Family*, Independence, Missouri, 26 April 1907 . 31
14. *LDS Central States Mission Leaders and Staff*, Independence, Missouri, 26 April 1907 ......... 32
15. *Temple Lot*, Independence, Missouri, 26 April 1907 ............................. 33
16. *Temple Lot*, Independence, Missouri, 26 April 1907 ............................. 33
17. *Temple Lot*, Independence, Missouri, 26 April 1907 ............................. 34
18. *The Church of Christ (Temple Lot)*, Independence, Missouri, 26 April 1907 .................. 36–37
19. *A Group of Latter-day Saints Gathered on the Temple Lot*, Independence, Missouri,
     28 April 1907 .................................................... 38
20. *Quincy*, Adams County, Illinois, 1 May 1907 ................................. 40
21. *Nauvoo*, Hancock County, Illinois, 2 May 1907 ............................... 42
22. *Printing Office, Ivins–Smith–Taylor Home, and Post Office*, Nauvoo, Illinois, 2 May 1907 ..... 43
23. *Smith Family Cemetery*, Nauvoo, Illinois, 2 May 1907 ........................... 44
24. *Mansion House*, Nauvoo, Illinois, 2 May 1907 ................................ 46
25. *Nauvoo House (Riverside Mansion)*, Nauvoo, Illinois, 2 May 1907 .................... 47
26. *Carthage Jail*, Carthage, Illinois, 3 May 1907 ............................... 48

27. *WATER STREET,* Nauvoo, Illinois, 4 May 1907 . . . . . . . . . . . . . . . . . . . . . . . . . . . . . *50–51*
28. *CORNER OF WATER AND BAIN STREETS,* Nauvoo, Illinois, 4 May 1907 . . . . . . . . . . . . . . . . . . . . . . . . . *52*
29. *RED BRICK STORE FOUNDATION,* Nauvoo, Illinois, 4 May 1907 . . . . . . . . . . . . . . . . . . . . . . . *52*
30. *NAUVOO TEMPLE BLOCK,* Nauvoo, Illinois, 4 May 1907 . . . . . . . . . . . . . . . . . . . . . . . . . *53*
31. *CHARLES AND EMMA DAVIDSON PITT HOME,* Nauvoo, Illinois, 4 May 1907 . . . . . . . . . . . . . *54*
32. *NAUVOO HOUSE CORNERSTONE,* Nauvoo, Illinois, 4 May 1907 . . . . . . . . . . . . . . . . . . . . . . . . . *55*
33. *WINE CELLAR,* Nauvoo, Illinois, 4 May 1907 . . . . . . . . . . . . . . . . . . . . . . . . . . . . . *56*
34. *NAUVOO,* Hancock County, Illinois, 4 May 1907 . . . . . . . . . . . . . . . . . . . . . . . . . . . . . *56*
35. *SNOW–ASHBY DUPLEX,* Nauvoo, Illinois, 4 May 1907 . . . . . . . . . . . . . . . . . . . . . . . . . *57*
36. *CULTURAL AND MASONIC HALL,* Nauvoo, Illinois, May 1907 . . . . . . . . . . . . . . . . . . . . . . . . . *58*
37. *WILFORD AND PHOEBE CARTER WOODRUFF HOME,* Nauvoo, Illinois, May 1907 . . . . . . . . . . *59*
38. *NAUVOO EXPOSITOR BUILDING,* Nauvoo, Illinois, May 1907 . . . . . . . . . . . . . . . . . . . . . . . *59*
39. *JOHN D. AND AGATHA WOOLSEY LEE HOME,* Nauvoo, Illinois, May 1907 . . . . . . . . . . . . . . *60*
40. *NAUVOO,* Hancock County, Illinois, May 1907 . . . . . . . . . . . . . . . . . . . . . . . . . . . . . *62–63*
41. *BIG BLUE RIVER,* Jackson County, Missouri, 9 May 1907 . . . . . . . . . . . . . . . . . . . . . *66*
42. *RICHMOND,* Ray County, Missouri, 10 May 1907 . . . . . . . . . . . . . . . . . . . . . . . . . . . *68*
43. *PIONEER CEMETERY,* Richmond, Missouri, 10 May 1907 . . . . . . . . . . . . . . . . . . . . . . . *68*
44. *JACOB WHITMER'S TOMBSTONE,* Pioneer Cemetery, Richmond, Missouri, 10 May 1907 . . . . . . . . . . . *69*
45. *DAVID WHITMER'S TOMBSTONE,* Richmond City Cemetery, Richmond, Missouri, 10 May 1907 . . . . . . *69*
46. *ALEXANDER DONIPHAN HOME,* Richmond, Missouri, probably May 1907 . . . . . . . . . . . . . . . *71*
47. *PETER AND MARY MUSSELMAN WHITMER HOME,* Richmond, Missouri, probably May 1907 . . . . . . . . . . *71*
48. *DAVID AND JULIA ANN WHITMER HOME,* Richmond, Missouri, probably May 1907 . . . . . . . . . . . . . . . *73*
49. *CROOKED RIVER BATTLEGROUND SITE,* Ray County, Missouri, 15 May 1907 . . . . . . . . . . . . . *77*
50. *CROOKED RIVER BATTLEGROUND SITE,* Ray County, Missouri, 15 May 1907 . . . . . . . . . . . . . *79*
51. *FAR WEST TEMPLE SITE,* Caldwell County, Missouri, 16 May 1907 . . . . . . . . . . . . . . . . . . . . . . . *81*
52. *FAR WEST TEMPLE SITE,* Caldwell County, Missouri, 16 May 1907 . . . . . . . . . . . . . . . . . . . . . . . *81*
53. *SITE OF JOSEPH AND EMMA HALE SMITH HOME,* Far West, Missouri, 16 May 1907 . . . . . . . . . . . . . . *83*
54. *ELIZABETH ANN WHITMER COWDERY PAINTING,* Kerr Home, Caldwell County, Missouri, 17 May 1907. . *84*
55. *RLDS SUNDAY SCHOOL GROUP,* Far West, Missouri, 19 May 1907 . . . . . . . . . . . . . . . . . . . . . . . *86*
56. *JOHN WHITMER'S TOMBSTONE,* Kingston City Cemetery, Kingston, Missouri, 19 May 1907 . . . . . . . . . *87*
57. *"POOR FARM,"* Kingston, Missouri, 19 May 1907 . . . . . . . . . . . . . . . . . . . . . . . . . . . *88*
58. *T. B. BUZZARD HOME,* near Adam-ondi-Ahman, Daviess County, Missouri, 20 May 1907 . . . . . . . . . *89*
59. *LYMAN AND HARRIET BENTON WIGHT HOME,* Adam-ondi-Ahman, Missouri, 20 May 1907 . . . . . . . . . *90*
60. *LYMAN AND HARRIET BENTON WIGHT HOME,* Adam-ondi-Ahman, Missouri, 20 May 1907 . . . . . . . . . *91*
61. *THE VALLEY OF ADAM-ONDI-AHMAN,* Adam-ondi-Ahman, Daviess County, Missouri, 20 May 1907 . . . *92*
62. *DAVIESS COUNTY COURTHOUSE CORNERSTONE-LAYING CEREMONY,* Gallatin, Missouri, 21 May 1907 . . . *94*
63. *CORNERSTONE OF DAVIESS COUNTY'S NEW COURTHOUSE,* Gallatin, Missouri, 21 May 1907 . . . . . . . . . *94*
64. *JOHN B. MCLALLEN,* Breckenridge, Missouri, 22 May 1907 . . . . . . . . . . . . . . . . . . . . . . . *96*
65. *HAUN'S MILL SITE,* Caldwell County, Missouri, 23 May 1907 . . . . . . . . . . . . . . . . . . . . . . . *98–99*
66. *MILLSTONE AT HAUN'S MILL,* Caldwell County, Missouri, 23 May 1907 . . . . . . . . . . . . . . . . . . . . . . . *100*
67. *MILLSTONE AT HAUN'S MILL,* Caldwell County, Missouri, 23 May 1907 . . . . . . . . . . . . . . . *100*
68. *HAUN'S MILL,* Caldwell County, Missouri, 23 May 1907 . . . . . . . . . . . . . . . . . . . . . . . *102*
69. *H. ELMER PARKER HOME,* Caldwell County, Missouri, 25 May 1907 . . . . . . . . . . . . . . . . . . . . . . . *103*
70. *POTTER'S SLOUGH,* near Montrose, Lee County, Iowa, 29 May 1907 . . . . . . . . . . . . . . . . . . . . . . . *105*

71. *POTTER'S SLOUGH*, near Montrose, Lee County, Iowa, 29 May 1907 . . . . . . . . . . . . . . . . . . . . . . . . . . . . *105*
72. *BRIGHAM AND MARY ANN ANGELL YOUNG HOME*, Nauvoo, Illinois, May 1907 . . . . . . . . . . . . . . . . . . . . . *107*
73. *CHAUNCEY AND ELIZA JANE CHURCHILL WEBB AND JOSEPH AND JANE BICKNELL YOUNG HOMES*,
    Nauvoo, Illinois, May 1907 . . . . . . . . . . . . . . . . . . . . . . . . . . . . *110*
74. *HEBER CHASE AND VILATE MURRAY KIMBALL HOME*, Nauvoo, Illinois, May 1907 . . . . . . . . . . . . . . . . . . *111*
75. *GROUP OF LDS CHURCH CENTRAL STATES MISSIONARIES*, Chicago, Illinois, probably 5 June 1907 . . . . . *114*
76. *RACHEL SMITH ELLSWORTH AND DAUGHTER*, Chicago, Illinois, 11 June 1907 . . . . . . . . . . . . . . . . . . . . *117*
77. *UNION PARK*, Chicago, Illinois, 17 June 1907 . . . . . . . . . . . . . . . . . . . . . . . . . . . . *121*
78. *MISS POST, MR. FOSTER, AND MISS CHICAGO*, Chicago, Illinois, June or July 1907 . . . . . . . . . . . . . . . *127*
79. *GERMAN EDGAR AND RACHEL SMITH ELLSWORTH FAMILY*, Chicago, Illinois, 31 July 1907 . . . . . . . . . . *138*
80. *JEFFERSON PARK*, Chicago, Illinois, 2 August 1907 . . . . . . . . . . . . . . . . . . . . . . . . . . . . *140*
81. *KIRTLAND TEMPLE*, Kirtland, Ohio, August 1907 . . . . . . . . . . . . . . . . . . . . . . . . . . . . *142*
82. *KIRTLAND TEMPLE*, Kirtland, Ohio, August 1907 . . . . . . . . . . . . . . . . . . . . . . . . . . . . *145*
83. *KIRTLAND TEMPLE*, Kirtland, Ohio, August 1907 . . . . . . . . . . . . . . . . . . . . . . . . . . . . *146*
84. *INTERIOR OF THE KIRTLAND TEMPLE*, Kirtland, Ohio, August 1907 . . . . . . . . . . . . . . . . . . . *148*
85. *INTERIOR OF THE KIRTLAND TEMPLE*, Kirtland, Ohio, August 1907 . . . . . . . . . . . . . . . . . . . *148*
86. *SIDNEY AND PHEBE BROOK RIGDON HOME*, Kirtland, Ohio, 6 August 1907 . . . . . . . . . . . . . . . . *149*
87. *PARLEY PARKER AND THANKFUL HALSEY PRATT HOME*, Kirtland, Ohio, 7 August 1907 . . . . . . . . . . *150*
88. *WILLIAM AND CAROLINE AMANDA GRANT SMITH HOME*, Kirtland, Ohio, 6 August 1907 . . . . . . . . . . *151*
89. *HYRUM AND JERUSHA BARDEN SMITH HOME*, Kirtland, Ohio, 7 August 1907 . . . . . . . . . . . . . . . *151*
90. *KIRTLAND TEMPLE*, Kirtland, Ohio, 7 August 1907 . . . . . . . . . . . . . . . . . . . . . . . . . *153*
91. *KIRTLAND, LAKE COUNTY (GEAUGA COUNTY IN 1830s), OHIO*, 6 or 7 August 1907 . . . . . . . . . . . . . . *154–55*
92. *NEWEL KIMBALL WHITNEY STORE*, Kirtland, Ohio, 7 August 1907 . . . . . . . . . . . . . . . . . . . . *156*
93. *NEWEL KIMBALL AND ELIZABETH ANN SMITH WHITNEY HOME*, Kirtland, Ohio, 7 August 1907 . . . . . . . *157*
94. *JOSEPH AND EMMA HALE SMITH HOME*, Kirtland, Ohio, 7 August 1907 . . . . . . . . . . . . . . . . . . *158*
95. *KIRTLAND TEMPLE AND CEMETERY*, Kirtland, Ohio, 7 August 1907 . . . . . . . . . . . . . . . . . . . *159*
96. *KIRTLAND HOTEL*, Kirtland, Ohio, August 1907 . . . . . . . . . . . . . . . . . . . . . . . . . . . . *160*
97. *H. E. HARRISON HOME*, Cleveland, Ohio, 9 August 1907 . . . . . . . . . . . . . . . . . . . . . . . . *161*
98. *SACRED GROVE*, Manchester, New York, 13 August 1907 . . . . . . . . . . . . . . . . . . . . . . . . *165*
99. *JOSEPH AND LUCY MACK SMITH FARM*, Manchester, New York, 13 August 1907 . . . . . . . . . . . . . . *166*
100. *HILL CUMORAH*, Manchester, New York, August 1907 . . . . . . . . . . . . . . . . . . . . . . . . . *168*
101. *HILL CUMORAH*, Manchester, New York, August 1907 . . . . . . . . . . . . . . . . . . . . . . . . . *169*
102. *HILL CUMORAH*, Manchester, New York, August 1907 . . . . . . . . . . . . . . . . . . . . . . . . . *169*
103. *A VIEW FROM THE HILL CUMORAH*, Manchester, New York, August 1907 . . . . . . . . . . . . . . . . . *170*
104. *MAIN STREET*, Palmyra, Wayne County, New York, August 1907 . . . . . . . . . . . . . . . . . . . . *171*
105. *BOOK OF MORMON PROOF SHEETS*, Palmyra, New York, August 1907 . . . . . . . . . . . . . . . . . . *172–73*
106. *EGBERT B. GRANDIN BOOKSTORE AND PRINTING OFFICE*, Palmyra, New York, August 1907 . . . . . . . . *174*
107. *JOSEPH AND LUCY MACK SMITH HOME*, Manchester, New York, 19 August 1907 . . . . . . . . . . . . . . *176–77*
108. *JOSEPH AND LUCY MACK SMITH HOME*, Manchester, New York, 19 August 1907 . . . . . . . . . . . . . . *178*
109. *INTERIOR OF JOSEPH AND LUCY MACK SMITH HOME*, Manchester, New York, August 1907 . . . . . . . . . *179*
110. *INTERIOR OF JOSEPH AND LUCY MACK SMITH HOME*, Manchester, New York, August 1907 . . . . . . . . . *179*
111. *SMALL COUNTRY LANE LEADING TO THE SACRED GROVE*, Manchester, New York, 17 August 1907 . . . . . *180*
112. *HATHAWAY BROOK, JOSEPH AND LUCY MACK SMITH FARM*, Manchester, New York, August 1907 . . . . . . *181*
113. *JOSEPH AND LUCY MACK SMITH FARM*, Manchester, New York, 18 August 1907 . . . . . . . . . . . . . . *182*

114. *Joseph and Lucy Mack Smith Farm*, Manchester, New York, August 1907 . . . . . . . . . . . . . . . . . . . . . *183*

115. *Joseph and Lucy Mack Smith Farm*, Manchester, New York, August 1907 . . . . . . . . . . . . . . . . . . . . . *183*

116. *Near Joseph and Lucy Mack Smith Home, Manchester Road*, Manchester, New York,
August 1907 . . . . . . . . . . . . . . . . . . . . . . . . . . . . . . . . . . . . . . . . . . . . . . . . . . . . . . . . . . . . . . . . . . . . . . . . *184*

117. *District No. 10 Schoolhouse*, Manchester, New York, 17 August 1907 . . . . . . . . . . . . . . . . . . . . . . *184*

118. *Martin and Lucy Harris Farm*, Palmyra, New York, 18 August 1907 . . . . . . . . . . . . . . . . . . . . . . *185*

119. *Martin and Lucy Harris Farm*, Palmyra, New York, 18 August 1907 . . . . . . . . . . . . . . . . . . . . . . *185*

120. *The Hill, Martin Harris Farm*, Palmyra, New York, 18 August 1907 . . . . . . . . . . . . . . . . . . . . . . . *186*

121. *Crossing of the New York Central Railroad*, Palmyra, New York, 18 August 1907 . . . . . . . . . . . *187*

122. *Wallace and Margaret Cavanaugh Miner Farm*, Manchester, New York, 19 August 1907 . . . . . . . *188*

123. *Cave Hill*, Manchester, New York, 19 August 1907 . . . . . . . . . . . . . . . . . . . . . . . . . . . . . . . . . . . . . . *188*

124. *Peter and Mary Musselman Whitmer Farm*, Fayette, New York, 1907 . . . . . . . . . . . . . . . . . . . . . . *189*

125. *Peter and Mary Musselman Whitmer Farm*, Fayette, New York, 1907 . . . . . . . . . . . . . . . . . . . . . . *189*

126. *Seneca Lake*, Seneca County, New York, 1907 . . . . . . . . . . . . . . . . . . . . . . . . . . . . . . . . . . . . . . . . . . . *190*

127. *Harmony*, Susquehanna County, Pennsylvania, 1907 . . . . . . . . . . . . . . . . . . . . . . . . . . . . . . . . . . . . *191*

128. *Joseph and Emma Hale Smith Home*, Harmony, Pennsylvania, 1907 . . . . . . . . . . . . . . . . . . . . . . . *192*

129. *Harmony Property Deed Signed by Joseph and Emma Hale Smith* . . . . . . . . . . . . . . . . . . . . . . . *193*

130. *Joseph and Emma Hale Smith Home*, Harmony, Pennsylvania, 1907 . . . . . . . . . . . . . . . . . . . . . . . *194*

131. *A Young Woman*, Harmony, Pennsylvania, 1907 . . . . . . . . . . . . . . . . . . . . . . . . . . . . . . . . . . . . . . . . *194*

132. *Isaac and Elizabeth Hale Tombstones*, Harmony, Pennsylvania, 1907 . . . . . . . . . . . . . . . . . . . . . *195*

133. *Alvin Smith Tombstone*, Harmony, Pennsylvania, 1907 . . . . . . . . . . . . . . . . . . . . . . . . . . . . . . . . . . *196*

134. *Susquehanna River*, Harmony, Pennsylvania, 1907 . . . . . . . . . . . . . . . . . . . . . . . . . . . . . . . . . . . . . . *197*

135. *Susquehanna River*, Harmony, Pennsylvania, 1907 . . . . . . . . . . . . . . . . . . . . . . . . . . . . . . . . . . . . . . *197*

136. *"Money Hole,"* Harmony, Pennsylvania, 1907 . . . . . . . . . . . . . . . . . . . . . . . . . . . . . . . . . . . . . . . . . . *198*

137. *New York–Pennsylvania State Line*, 1907 . . . . . . . . . . . . . . . . . . . . . . . . . . . . . . . . . . . . . . . . . . . . . *198*

138. *Nineveh (Colesville Township)*, Broome County, New York, 1907 . . . . . . . . . . . . . . . . . . . . . . . . *199*

139. *Pickerel Pond, Joseph and Polly Peck Knight Farm*, Colesville, New York, 1907 . . . . . . . . . . . . *199*

140. *Tunbridge Gore*, Orange County, Vermont, 1907 . . . . . . . . . . . . . . . . . . . . . . . . . . . . . . . . . . . . . . . *200*

141. *Tunbridge Gore*, Orange County, Vermont, 9 February 1908 . . . . . . . . . . . . . . . . . . . . . . . . . . . . . . *201*

142. *Tunbridge Hill Cemetery*, Orange County, Vermont, 1908 . . . . . . . . . . . . . . . . . . . . . . . . . . . . . . . *202*

143. *Schoolhouse*, Royalton, Vermont, 1907 . . . . . . . . . . . . . . . . . . . . . . . . . . . . . . . . . . . . . . . . . . . . . . . . *202*

144. *Harvey Smith Home*, South Royalton, Vermont, 13 November 1907 . . . . . . . . . . . . . . . . . . . . . . . *203*

145. *Solomon and Lydia Gates Mack Homesite*, Sharon, Vermont, 1907 . . . . . . . . . . . . . . . . . . . . . . . *203*

146. *Memorial Cottage and Joseph Smith Memorial Monument*, Sharon, Vermont, 31 October 1907 . . . *204–5*

147. *Joseph Smith Memorial Monument*, Sharon, Vermont, 1907 . . . . . . . . . . . . . . . . . . . . . . . . . . . . . . *206*

148. *Joseph Smith Memorial Monument*, Sharon, Vermont, 1907 . . . . . . . . . . . . . . . . . . . . . . . . . . . . . . *207*

149. *Interior of Joseph Smith Memorial Cottage*, Sharon, Vermont, 1907 . . . . . . . . . . . . . . . . . . . . . . . *208*

150. *Lebanon, New Hampshire*, 6 January 1908 . . . . . . . . . . . . . . . . . . . . . . . . . . . . . . . . . . . . . . . . . . . . . *209*

151. *Squire Murdock Farm*, Norwich, Vermont, 23 January 1908 . . . . . . . . . . . . . . . . . . . . . . . . . . . . *210–11*

152. *George Edward Anderson's 1907 Diary* . . . . . . . . . . . . . . . . . . . . . . . . . . . . . . . . . . . . . . . . . . . . . . *243*

153. *Joseph and Lucy Mack Smith Farm*, Manchester, New York, August 1907 . . . . . . . . . . . . . . . . . . . . . *243*

# Preface

To capture the transitory forms of life, to stay the onrushing hands of time, to memorialize the living and remember the dead—these have been the desires of humankind from time immemorial. During the long period of human history before the invention of photography in 1839, this desire to capture shadows was satisfied only partially by art in its various forms.

Following the spectacular announcement by Louis Jacques-Mande Daguerre in France and William Henry Fox Talbot in Great Britain (the two principal inventors of the art of photography), photographers swiftly became the popular reporters not only of the world's happenings but also of individual, family, and community life. Photographers helped transmit history as they documented wars, politics, disasters, feats of engineering, and special celebrations.

The portrait was instantly democratized, each family maintaining its thick albums of tintypes, *cartes de visite*, or cabinet photographs and collecting the passing shadows of the inexorable progress from birth to death.

The stereograph's imitation of three-dimensional space astonished and delighted the general populace, with Oliver Wendell Holmes bestowing upon photography the ultimate accolade: it was the "Recording Angel," seeing all, even the faintest imprint of a withering vine or the fleeting smile of a bemused child. With photography, there seemed to be the chance of seizing life in all its variety and setting it down for study and reflection.

Photographers during the Civil War and the expeditionary photographers of U.S. government surveys raised photography to a new level—documentary—in the latter half of the nineteenth century.

George Edward Anderson, known as "Ed" or "Eddy" throughout his life, carried with him the heavy camera and glass plates of his trade across the United States in a momentous trip in 1907–8 where he photographed sites of important and transcendent events for the Latter-day Saints—the First Vision, the restoration of the priesthood, the publication of the Book of Mormon, the dedication of the Kirtland Temple, the establishment of the City of Zion, and the martyrdom of Joseph and Hyrum Smith.

The photographs included in this book represent a portion of those images preserved from the historic trip across the United States by this LDS missionary-photographer. His 1907 diary, which is the focus of this book, allows us for the first time to appreciate more fully his photographic efforts in their historical, cultural, and religious setting. Anderson's mission to England began in April 1907 when he left his family in Springville, Utah. He took a year to reach Great Britain, as he took the time to photograph Church history sites along the way. When Anderson was released from his mission, he continued his photographic work in England and in the United States, arriving home in November 1913—almost seven years from the time he initially left Springville.

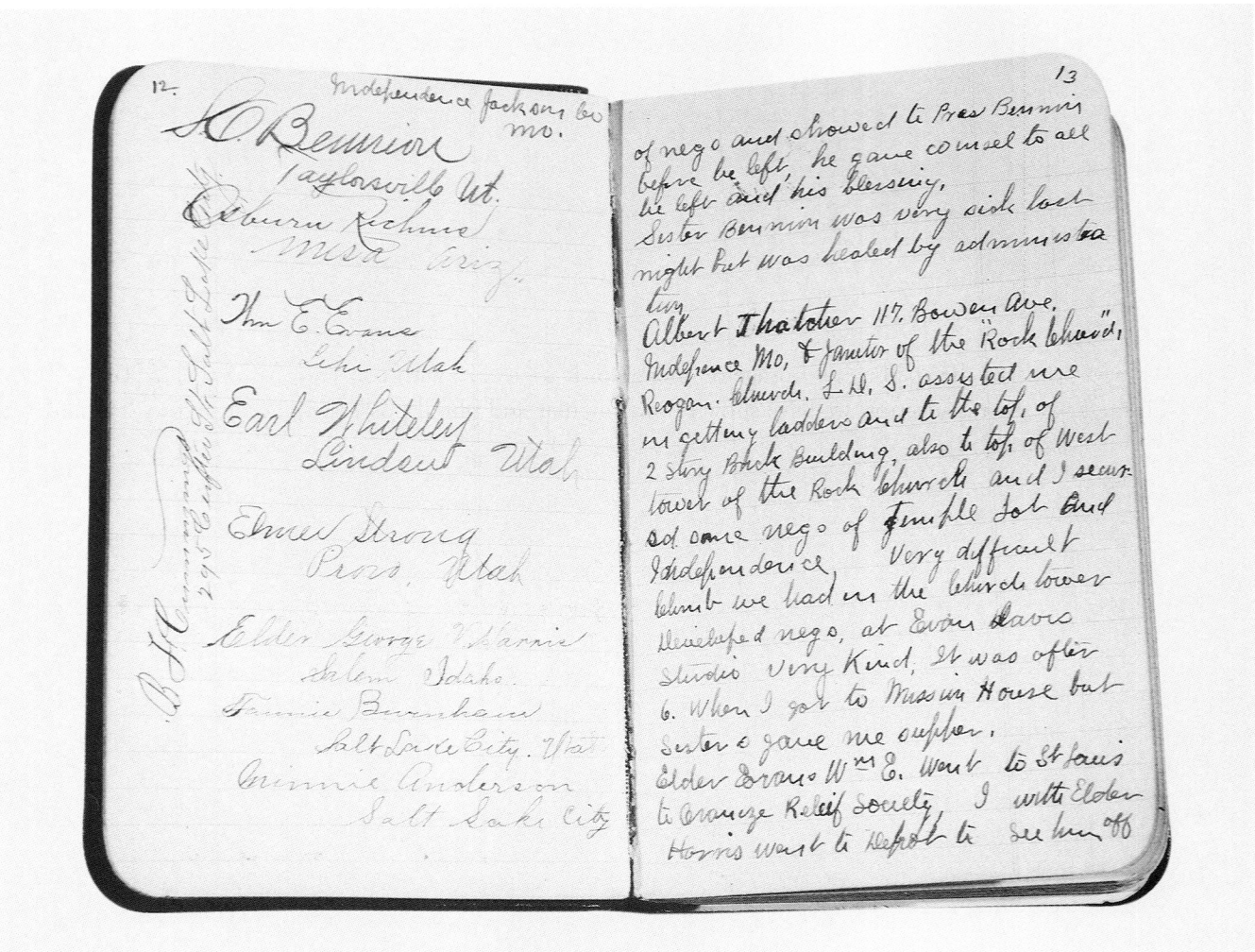

***George Edward Anderson's 1907 Diary,*** *courtesy of the DUP. Shows a page of autographs and a partial diary entry for 26 April 1907, when Anderson was in Missouri.*

## Description of the 1907 Diary

The 1907 diary of George Edward Anderson is located in the Daughters of Utah Pioneers (DUP) Museum in Salt Lake City, Utah. Physically, the diary is very small, consisting of about two hundred pages that measure only 3¾ inches by 6 inches. Anderson penned numbers in the upper corners beginning with the first entry, dated 20 April 1907, and concluding with his notes on page 183 (the last diary entry is dated 21 August 1907). The diary was a gift from his sister and brother-in-law as he prepared to begin his mission for the LDS Church in 1907.

Anderson wrote on the inside front cover: "Geo. Ed Anderson, Springville, Utah Co., Utah, P.O. Box 177." The majority of the pages are filled with his diary entries, but several pages are dedicated to notes on historical topics, background information on the places he planned to visit or had visited, autographs, and, in one case, a chemical formula used in a photograph-developing procedure.

## Editorial Procedures

As we prepared Anderson's diary for publication, we standardized certain items in the manuscript to make it more readable. At the same time, we made no changes that would distort Anderson's writing style or that would mar the feelings his style fosters in the minds of readers of his diary. We made the following editorial decisions:

- Anderson did not always introduce a new topic with a new paragraph. We have attempted to organize the material into paragraphs to reflect general paragraph unity.
- Anderson usually wrote in thought-phrases that are not complete sentences. We have not attempted to turn his thought-phrases into complete sentences, but we have placed a period at the end of what we perceive each thought-phrase to be.
- We have adjusted the spelling and usage of most words to accord with conventions of the 1990s.
- Throughout the manuscript, we have shown both singular and plural possessives according to standard English of the 1990s.
- Anderson's writing is often very difficult to decipher. We have done our best to decipher every word correctly. Where we could not decipher a word or part of a word, we have used brackets to show our intent. If we could not read a letter or letters within a word, we show a period inside brackets ([.]). If we could not read a word, we use a dash inside brackets ([—]). If we were not sure we had read or spelled a word correctly, we show a question mark inside brackets ([?]) following the word. Whenever Anderson left out a word or words, we show that omission with "blank" inside brackets ([blank]).
- We have followed conventions of the 1990s in standardizing Anderson's capitalization.
- Wherever appropriate, we have changed singular nouns and courtesy titles to plural forms.
- Anderson often associates the time of day with activities he was involved in throughout the day. We have added the designations *a.m.* and *p.m.* to pinpoint whether events occurred during the morning, afternoon, or evening hours.
- Anderson occasionally crossed out words to reflect his own editing of his diary. We have not included any of the crossed-out words in our manuscript.
- Anderson occasionally used a caret (^) to show an insertion during his editing of his diary. We have included, without notation, all of Anderson's insertions.
- Anderson used several ways to show amounts of money. We have consistently followed conventions of the 1990s in all references to amounts of money.
- We have standardized all references to dates in the diary by showing them in the order of month, day, and year (e.g., April 20, 1907).
- Anderson frequently abbreviated words and names of people and places. Wherever possible or appropriate, we have spelled out his abbreviations.
- Anderson sometimes used his diary for an autograph book. We have not included the autographs in the diary itself because we feel that doing so would cause a distraction for the reader. We have, however, included the autographs in footnotes that coincide with the pages in the diary.
- At the end of his diary, Anderson made a list of the photographs he planned to take or had already taken. This information is included in Appendix Two. We have exhausted our resources in finding as many of Anderson's pictures as we believe exist, and we have included many of them at the appropriate places in the manuscript. The reader who compares the photographs in this book with Anderson's list of photographs will see that some are missing. We were limited in the number we could include in the project, and we hope that copies of any missing photographs can be located at some point in the future.
- Anderson numbered the pages in his diary. Throughout our manuscript, we have shown each Anderson page break by placing the new page number in brackets immediately in front of the first word on a new

page (e.g., "[**p. 7**] a nickel, which I gave him"). With bracketed page numbers, we have also shown the page number where each new day's entry begins.

- We have included numerous footnotes to clarify events in the diary or to give additional information about the events.

## *The Photograph Collections*

The majority of Anderson's photographs taken during his 1907–8 journey are located in the Archive Division, Church Historical Department, The Church of Jesus Christ of Latter-day Saints (LDSCA), Salt Lake City, Utah, in two separate collections: the George Edward Anderson Glass Negative Collection (1897–1927) and the George Edward Anderson Photograph Collection.

Another important part of Anderson's work is preserved in a photographic album presented to LDS Church

**"Church History in Photograph" Album,** *courtesy of LDSCA. This album was presented to President Joseph F. Smith by Olive Lowry Anderson in 1909. The album contains photographs taken by George Edward Anderson in 1907–8 while traveling through the United States on his way to England to begin his proselytizing mission.*

***An Anderson Glass-Plate Negative***, *courtesy of BYU. This original five-by-seven-inch glass-plate negative of John B. McLallen was taken near Haun's Mill, Missouri (see p. 96). Anderson's glass plates are precious treasures of historic and artistic value, and they can be duplicated endlessly with the same quality as the first print Anderson made from them.*

President Joseph F. Smith by Anderson's wife, Olive, sometime in 1909, also located in the LDSCA. The 7 January 1909 issue of the *Springville Independent* noted, under a section entitled "Items of Interest," that Olive Anderson recently displayed "an exquisite work of art, being an album containing photographs taken by her husband in and about the historic localities connected with L.D.S. history." The article further noted that "the album is to be presented to Joseph F. Smith by Mrs. Anderson, at the request of her husband."

This album is important because it helps us document Anderson's activities after he completed the 1907 diary on 21 August and before he began his 1908 diary in England following his arrival there on 27 April 1908.

The album measures 13¾ inches by 10 inches and has "Church History in Photograph by Geo. E. Anderson" printed in gold letters on the front and also has Joseph F. Smith's name imprinted in the lower right-hand corner. To the photographs in the album, Anderson added captions (either typed or handwritten) that identify the locations and significance of each photograph. Included in the album are a number of photographs not found in the Anderson glass negative and print collections.

We also identified a single Anderson photograph of Brigham Young's Nauvoo home in a separate LDSCA collection, which presumably will eventually be placed in an Anderson collection in the future.

Another collection of Anderson photographs in the Harold B. Lee Library Archives at Brigham Young University (BYU), Provo, Utah, also includes several views taken during the 1907–8 journey.

Sometimes Anderson inscribed either a name, date, location, and/or catalog number on the emulsion of the original glass-plate negative by writing on the negative with India ink, in reverse, on the edge of the emulsion so that, on the contact print, the writing would be reversed to normal. Some of the writing was for Anderson's information only and therefore does not appear on the print.

On the glass-plate negative of the copy that we have provided in this work and that is housed at BYU, Anderson wrote "John B. McLallen Breckenridge RFD R#I." When the entire image is printed, the writing can be seen on the outer edge. Of course, the writing is backwards and is therefore difficult to read. Typically, Anderson did not use the entire image for his final print, thus eliminating the distraction. We assume he wrote the name and address on Mr. McLallen's portrait so that he could print photographs at some time in the future and then send a copy to McLallen at the address indicated on the negative.

An original Anderson postcard from this period is found in the Lehi Library Historical Archives, Lehi, Utah. The Ellsworth family has also provided us a copy of another Anderson photograph taken during this trip. Obviously, many more Anderson photographs taken during the trip are located in personal family collections or in institutional repositories. We hope that this book will stimulate people to look in old scrapbooks and trunks for letters, photographs, and other historically important items that could increase our knowledge of this period and of Anderson's work.

# GEORGE EDWARD ANDERSON'S PHOTOGRAPHIC MISSION THROUGH THE U.S., 1907–8

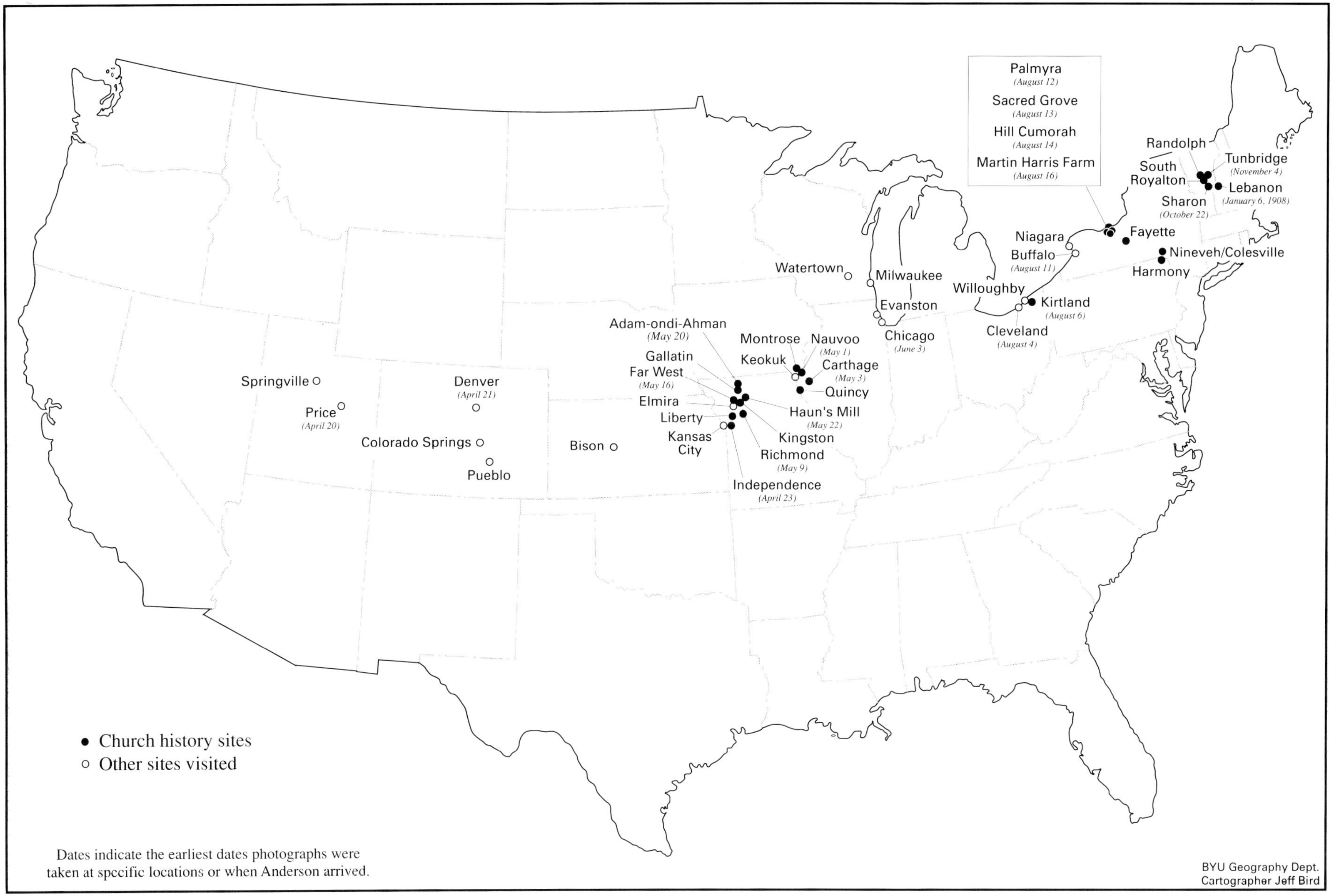

BYU Geography Dept.
Cartographer Jeff Bird

Tunbridge
*(November 4)*

Lebanon
*(January 6, 1908)*

Randolph

South Royalton

Sharon
*(October 22)*

Fayette

Nineveh/Colesville

Harmony

| Palmyra *(August 12)* |
| Sacred Grove *(August 13)* |
| Hill Cumorah *(August 14)* |
| Martin Harris Farm *(August 16)* |

Niagara

Buffalo
*(August 11)*

Kirtland
*(August 6)*

Cleveland
*(August 4)*

Willoughby

Milwaukee

Evanston

Chicago
*(June 3)*

Watertown

Montrose

Nauvoo
*(May 1)*

Carthage
*(May 3)*

Quincy

Haun's Mill
*(May 22)*

Keokuk

Kingston
*(May 9)*

Richmond

Independence
*(April 23)*

Adam-ondi-Ahman
*(May 20)*

Gallatin

Far West
*(May 16)*

Elmira

Liberty

Kansas City

Bison

Denver
*(April 21)*

Colorado Springs

Pueblo

Price
*(April 20)*

Springville

● Church history sites
○ Other sites visited

Dates indicate the earliest dates photographs were taken at specific locations or when Anderson arrived.

# From Golden Plates to Glass Plates

## Richard Neitzel Holzapfel

*I*n a 1928 letter to LDS Church historian and Apostle Joseph Fielding Smith, Junius F. Wells (an assistant LDS Church historian) described the nature and value of a photographic collection being offered for sale by a poor widow in Springville, Utah.[1] The collection of negatives and prints belonged to an almost-forgotten Utah landscape and portrait photographer, George Edward Anderson, who had recently died.[2]

That there are in this collection negatives of Church scenes, groups of historic gatherings, views of notable celebrations, parades and pageants, of almost inestimable interest and value to the Historian's Office. . . . That George Ed Anderson performed a very remarkable mission while traversing the scenes of the Church History—the missions at the East and abroad, visiting hundreds of homes and neighborhoods where he bore a faithful testimony of the Truth and made countless friends for the Church, I personally know; and that he did so without adequate recompense in poverty at times to the distress of his family. The increment of his life's work should now come to them.[3]

The collection, numbering more than thirty thousand negatives, was purchased by the LDS Church for $2,500 from Anderson's widow, Olive Lowry Anderson, through Wells's efforts.

## Anderson and Photography

Photography was still considered magical at the turn of the century. Wells understood the significance of a collection of photographs taken over a period of several decades, especially for unborn generations who could see—through these photographs—people, places, and a world that was quickly being transformed beyond recognition.

Anderson's photographs captured the past intact, miraculously frozen in time and space by the most ephemeral of substances—photons of reflected light.

When the packet *British Queen* docked in New York City's harbor on Friday afternoon, 20 September 1839, following a transatlantic voyage, one of western civilization's most astonishing and versatile discoveries arrived in America—photography. What arrived was a seventy-nine-page booklet of instructions by Louis Daguerre, inventor of the first practical permanent photographic process. The booklet was immediately translated from French into English, thus allowing inventors in the United States to replicate the photographic process that he had announced to an astonished crowd in Paris earlier that year.[4]

By the time George Edward Anderson (born 28 October 1860) began practicing this art form as a young apprentice in Salt Lake City, photography had made several significant advances from the first daguerreotypes. During his professional career, Anderson was compelled to purchase new equipment to keep up with the fast-moving field. While Anderson, out of financial necessity, practiced a wide variety of photographic skills, including portraiture, he became increasingly interested in one branch of the art: documentary photography.

Anderson was not the first photographer to dream of a complete photographic record of the rise of the Church, but he was the first professional Latter-day Saint to travel from the West to the East to begin the effort. He is arguably the most important photographer of LDS historical sites to date, both numerically and artistically. Anderson wrote the following in his journal, on 20 April 1907, as he departed for his mission:

Rose about 6:00 a.m. . . . Bid Father and Mother Lowry good-bye. Brother Thornburg got grips etc. from depot, and Olive [Anderson] assisted me in packing up. Bid all good-bye and left Springville on No. 6 about 10:15 a.m.

Snow in canyon and all the way up. . . . Off at Price and took next section of No. 6, which left Price about 7:00 p.m. Dinner with Joseph Jones. Gave me sack of apples and $2.[5]

**George Edward and Olive Lowry Anderson Family,** *Springville, Utah, about 1907, Anderson Collection, BYU. Left to right: Olive Lowry, Edda, G. Lowry, George Edward, Eva. This photograph was taken sometime before Anderson left on his mission to England in April 1907.*

The sack of apples and the $2 were long gone by the time Anderson reached his final destination—England—but his appetite to capture the Latter-day Saint past through the medium of photography never subsided. At forty-six years of age, he was beginning a mission for the LDS Church—a mission that would eventually occupy nearly seven years of his life.[6]

## Service to the Church

This mission to England was not the first time Anderson had been called to give lay service in the Church. He had already been a bishop in Springville, Utah, for four years, serving at his own expense like all Mormon lay leaders, as he was likewise financing this mission.

Dedicated to building a new chapel in Springville, Utah, along with his other Church duties, Anderson incurred a heavy personal debt in his own business, which took second place to his ecclesiastical assignment. His debt increased when he completed a new studio, the G. E. Anderson Art Bazaar, following his release as bishop.

In March 1907, shortly before his mission departure, another national depression caused widespread unemployment, resulting in a steady decline in Anderson's business. After all, when a family had to choose between providing the basic necessities of life or having a portrait taken, the choice almost always went against a photograph. Olive, his wife, had already become a major financial contributor to the family budget by working in a local cannery. Now, as she gave her husband a final embrace before he left for England, she assumed complete responsibility for feeding and clothing their three children, ages four through sixteen years.

## The Photographic Mission

Though Anderson was bound for England, he took almost a year to reach his destination. En route, he systematically visited LDS historical sites in Missouri, Illinois, Ohio, New York, Pennsylvania, and New England to make a photographic record of the sites for a Utah-born generation who had heard the stories of the early Saints but who generally were unable to visit the sites of the events.

At several points, Anderson asked William C. Spence, the transportation agent for the LDS Church, to reschedule his departure date to England so he could have more time to continue his photographic efforts in the United States. "[T]elegraphed W. C. Spence," he noted. " 'Have fine views. Need more time. Can steamer ticket be extended? Wire G. Ed. Anderson.' "[7] At first, this passion was a personal calling; but two months later, in Chicago, he encountered LDS Church Apostle George Albert Smith, a grandson of Joseph Smith's cousin, George A. Smith, and everything changed. Elder Smith was in Chicago on Church business when Anderson recorded:

> Apostle George A. Smith came into priesthood meeting. Brother Smith told me to meet him 1:30 to 2:00 p.m. and he would look at views and give me what information he could about Palmyra, [New York], Sharon, [Vermont]. I made notes of the points he gave. I ask him if I should sail on the vessel that sails on the third. He said, "No. Keep on with the work."[8]

Anderson carried his heavy eight-by-ten view camera, supplies, and personal belongings and traversed the midwestern plains, the wooded forests of New York and New England, and the grain-ripened fields of early Restoration country, often finding the only lodging to be under a tree with merely his camera cloth for covering. He noted on one occasion: "I rested under a tree near the road and concluded to sleep there, which I did. Cool before morning, so covered with camera cloth."[9]

Anderson's photographic apparatus and processing methods were typical of the period. His view cameras, which he usually referred to as *instruments*, were equipped with rapid rectilinear lenses and were of various sizes. A bulky collection of glass plates (of various sizes up to fourteen by seventeen inches) weighing between three and four tons was accumulated during his photographic career.

We know that many more Anderson original glass negatives and prints exist beyond what has been found in private and public repositories. Only recently, for example, we were asked by an Anderson family member to examine a crate that was found in an abandoned barn and that contained a number of glass-plate negatives belonging to Anderson. Also, the 1907 diary reveals a large number of photographs, such as his photographs of Niagara Falls, that were taken during Anderson's 1907–8 trip and that are not found in any Anderson collection.

Seeking the most telling views of LDS historical sites, Anderson recorded, "Would like to get the views I can see in my mind's eye."[10] At one point, he regretfully wrote, "Need the painter's hand to do it justice and fix the colors."[11] He later added, "Could not get the effect of light and shade I wished."[12] Although his photographs should be prized for their value as historic documents, they nevertheless should also be highly valued for their aesthetic qualities, despite Anderson's concerns regarding his inability to replicate perfectly the natural colors of the world in his black-and-white photographs.

## Photographic Success

A few examples of Anderson's 1907–8 work first appeared in the *Boston Sunday Globe* on 10 May 1908, along with a balanced article about the LDS Church—a surprising development in light of the Reed Smoot hearings that had just concluded in Washington before a senatorial subcommittee.[13] The press's gleeful and sensational treatment of Mormon polygamy, political "interference," and temple ceremonies marked a deterioration in a public image that had never been very positive, to say the least.

Springville residents learned about the article when George Edward Anderson's brother handed [the *Springville Independent* newspaper] a copy of the *Boston Globe* of May 10 which contains a fine write up of the Prophet Joseph Smith and his old home in Vermont. It gives a brief account of his work and of the recent efforts of the Saints at improving that sacred spot. There are pictures of the Prophet and Hyrum, their mother, the monument, etc. all of which are from photos taken by the brother of Mr. Anderson.[14]

In July 1908, the *Boston Sunday Globe* article with Anderson's illustrations was reprinted in the *Juvenile Instructor*.[15] Shortly thereafter, the LDS Sunday School organization published a more complete collection of Anderson's photographs in *The Birth of Mormonism in Pictures: Scenes and Incidents in Early Church History*, written by LDS Church author and teacher John Henry Evans.[16]

## Experiences in Missouri

Anderson's first stop to photograph historical sites was Missouri, and the sixty-two extant views he made there are memorable and noteworthy.[17] It is not clear how much detailed information he had about Missouri and its Latter-day Saint past, but surely he would have known the historical outline, the folk traditions, the promises, and the tragic sufferings the Saints had experienced there.

"I feel so impressed," Anderson wrote in his diary, "with the necessity of making the views. I can see what a blessing they would be to our people in arousing an interest in this land and the work that is before us."[18] The "land" was Missouri, and documenting Church historical sites was a dream, almost an obsession, and certainly a religious mission in his eyes. Missouri, however, played a special part in the drama because it was not simply an experience of the past but of the future. Latter-day Saints sang about, prayed about, discussed, and planned for their return to the promised land to establish their model city in preparation for the Second Coming.[19]

When Anderson first arrived in Missouri, he wrote, "I selected points that I thought would make good views and show the temple ground so that a person from the outside could see how it was situated."[20] This attitude seems to have been his constant concern. His diary and photographs reflect his feeling of the sacredness of the places on which he walked. "I feel it a privilege," he recorded, "to be in this land which the Prophet of the Lord designated as the center stake of Zion and where the great temple of our God should be raised."[21] While in Independence, he made other views, including the LDS Church mission home, which had just been established in March 1907, and the RLDS Stone Church.

Later, Anderson "made negative of Richmond, [Missouri], from hill northwest of town. Also of the tombstone of one of Eight Witnesses, Jacob Whitmer, in the old cemetery."22 As he moved from one historical site to the next, he continued to feel that he "should have more time to get views of the important points in Church history."23

Anderson arrived at Far West, Missouri, on 16 May 1907. Where once a thriving community of hundreds of homes and farms had stood, he found a few homes and a small, white frame church. "Just southwest and across the street from temple block," he wrote, "is the Reorganized Church [building], dedicated November 18, 1906."24 Like the modern visitor, Anderson had to imagine what the 1838 Latter-day Saint capital had once looked like. He also visited Haun's Mill a few days later and, utilizing an old millstone, some paint, and a brush, made his famous sign to identify the site: "In memory of the victims of Haun's Mill Massacre, Oct. 30th, 1838."25

## Experiences in Illinois

Like Joseph Smith and the early Saints, Anderson left Missouri and arrived in Illinois. At about 4:30 p.m. on 1 May 1907, he "made a view of Quincy while waiting for train. On east side of Mississippi, on the bluffs, presents a striking appearance from the west side of the Mississippi."26 Anderson then left Quincy and headed north via Montrose, Iowa, to Nauvoo, the former city of the Saints. While there, like the modern-day pilgrim, he walked through the town that once boasted a much larger population. There he saw the grave of Emma Smith and the homes of Wilford Woodruff and Heber C. Kimball. And, like most visitors, he was eventually drawn from Nauvoo to Carthage—the county seat and location of the Carthage Jail.

On 3 May, Anderson noted: "Rose before 6:00 a.m. Decided to go to Carthage with Elders Rassmussen and Ralphs. Brother Charles R. Pitt took us over in surrey. . . . Cloudy and cold. Reached Carthage

about 1:00 p.m."27 Anderson, the photographer par excellence, always noted weather conditions that would affect his work. When he arrived at Carthage, he "visited the jail where the Prophet and Patriarch were killed."28 He reflected later in the day, when he took time to write in his journal, that he "saw the hole in the door made by the bullet, [and] the window from which the Prophet jumped. The well has been filled up and is marked by some flowers put out in a circle." He took the opportunity to make one view of the jail "in a snowstorm."29

## Experiences in Ohio

Eventually, Anderson made his way to the Western Reserve—an area in northeastern Ohio. There he found the first Latter-day Saint temple—the Kirtland Temple, dedicated on 27 March 1836. While in the Kirtland area, he visited and photographed important sites and recorded information that gave a unique view of Kirtland at the turn of the century. As he approached the small village near Cleveland, he noted: "[Went] within one-half mile of Kirtland and where I could plainly see the first temple erected to our God in this dispensation."30 He made particular note of his approach to the sacred spot on the hill: "Crossed the east branch of the Chagrin River and soon came to Chillicothe Road, which leads south to the temple."31

He continued his description: "On reaching the temple, I set my load down and rested on the grass for three-fourths of hour."32 After the brief but much-needed rest, he continued: "Elder Albert E. Stone of the Reorganized Church showed me through the temple. From the tower, we get a beautiful view and an idea of the situation of Kirtland. It is decidedly a pretty place—one of the most beautiful I have ever seen."33

## Experiences in New York

After several rewarding days in Kirtland, Anderson moved farther east to the birthplace of the Restoration—western New York. There, he sought out the significant sites of the early Latter-day Saint story—the location of the First Vision in 1820, the hill where the golden plates lay hidden for centuries, and the building where the Book of Mormon was first published in 1830. Anderson arrived at the Smith farm during harvest time in August 1907. The 1907 diary and a later reminiscence published in 1920 blend together to give us details about this event—details that otherwise would have had to come from secondhand accounts given by Anderson's family and neighbors.

Anderson's well-known image of the Sacred Grove is really two separate photographs taken during this particular visit. They show the silhouettes of the backlighted trees with a twelve-year-old boy standing in the scene to remind us that Joseph Smith was a young boy when he entered the grove to offer his first vocal prayer. The young boy stands in different positions in each photograph, and Anderson has numbered them "3" and "3A," indicating that they are two distinct images. As one leading photographic scholar asserted regarding these photographs, they are among "the most striking and dramatic images of [Anderson's] entire career."[34]

Anderson later recalled the episode and added details to his 1907 diary account of his experience in the Sacred Grove. As Anderson recalled in his 1920 article, young Hugh Austin, the son of a local farmer, approached the missionary-photographer and asked, "Mr. Anderson, are you going down in the grove to take pictures?" Anderson said that he was. The boy then asked, "Please, may I go with you?" Again Anderson responded affirmatively. When the missionary asked the young boy why he wanted to go, the boy replied, "I wanted to show you the tree where they said Joseph Smith prayed. I thought you would like to make a picture of it!"[35]

The man and the boy entered the grove near the southeast corner, and Hugh led Anderson to a place the boy identified as the spot where Joseph F. Smith, along with a group of Saints, knelt and prayed on their return trip from the dedication of the Joseph Smith Memorial in 1905. Anderson said, "Now I am going to make a picture of the grove, looking toward the house, and I would like to have you in the picture.

So go out that way and I will tell you when to stop. That will remind us that Joseph Smith was a boy. . . . The figure of the boy is seen between the trees in my picture."[36] The two photographs taken on that occasion (13 August 1907) may be the most famous and inspiring photographs in the LDS Church.

Along with the Smith farm in Manchester, Anderson visited other significant Church historical sites in the area, including the Hill Cumorah (known as "Mormon Hill" in 1907) and the Martin Harris farm. On a Sunday morning in August 1907, Anderson "rose about 6:00 a.m.," worked on his camera, and then

> found Martin Harris farm. Now owned by Mr. Bush, and for upwards of fifty-one years known as the "Mormon Hill" farm. Recently came into possession of Mr. Shaw. Beautifully located, running north and south and immediately north of the New York Central [Railroad], about two miles northwest from Palmyra on the state road running to Manchester.[37]

Although the diary ends abruptly on 21 August 1907, while Anderson was in the Palmyra area, he continued to make a photographic record of his travels through important Church history sites until he left for England in April 1908.

## Preserving Tradition Through a Diary

Anderson's diary preserves early traditions about people and places that have been lost through the deaths of those who were intimately acquainted with these things. For example, during Anderson's visit to Missouri, he spent time with the Himes family, local residents of Independence. Andrew Himes, the father of the family, provided information about Independence and its history for the missionary-photographer during an evening conversation following dinner. One of these stories, recorded in Anderson's diary, was unknown to LDS, RLDS, and Hedrickite scholars.[38] Joseph Smith Lee, apparently known as "Buckskin Joe," lived in the Independence area in 1871 and made a prediction regarding any attempt to build the temple on the original temple lot. An incident in May 1872, which resulted in the death of John H. Hedrick, a member of the Hedrickite movement, apparently fulfilled his prediction. Although just a footnote to Restoration history, Anderson's diary preserves an early 1870s tradition about Jackson County that would otherwise be lost to us.

Another significant contribution of Anderson's diary is the information recorded during his visits with descendants of the Book of Mormon witnesses in Missouri. He is, therefore, an important source for the preservation of the witnesses' family traditions from their descendants. His diary adds biographical information and confirms earlier interviews. His visits to Kingston and Richmond, while members of the second generation of Whitmers and Pages were still alive, allowed him to record their stories of the deathbed experiences of the witnesses.[39]

From a communication perspective, Utah was still a long way from Missouri in 1907. People still were bound to the land, and few had opportunity to travel extensively to seek historical facts such as the information Anderson gleaned from his interviews. He, like others who traveled to Missouri to interview the witnesses of the Book of Mormon, wanted to hear for himself what the witnesses had said.

Another reason the diary is important is that it is a valuable window into the lives of Latter-day Saints at the turn of the century, when the Church made a significant transition from the pioneer period to the twentieth century.

Anderson began keeping a diary in 1895. The collection of Anderson diaries covers nearly twenty-five years.[40] More than his earlier or later diaries, the 1907 diary reveals Anderson's feelings and contains long entries atypical of his other diaries. He is candid about his struggles and his joys. Through this diary, we are able to see the world as he saw and understood it. As we read the journal over and over again, it becomes like one of Anderson's photographs—a picture develops that at first is somewhat unclear but then eventually results in contours that become distinct, well-defined shades.

People keep diaries for several different reasons—some to record their deeds for future generations, especially family members; some to capture their lives in a concrete way; and others to play the role of a confidant.

Although we cannot be sure why Anderson wrote in his diary—it may be simply the result of a nineteenth-century LDS record-keeping tradition—we can appreciate the difficulty of his taking precious time to record his experiences. Stealing a few moments in a crowded home or on a busy train, Anderson, time and again, took pen and paper in hand to preserve aspects of his life. To be sure, they are selective aspects. Nevertheless, they allow us to appreciate his life in a fresh way.

In Ed Anderson's 1907 diary, we hear the voice of a unique Latter-day Saint bound together with others in a common faith and tradition. His perspective on the world is different, however, both in style and content, from the perspectives of other Latter-day Saints who also kept diaries at this time. Like a quilt maker, Anderson sewed together the patchwork of his daily experiences into a larger pattern. Certainly he, like other diarists, is the designer of the quilt and therefore ultimately selects what he will discuss and what he will not discuss. In that sense, a diary is never a complete picture of someone's world but is only a partial view.

## Identifying and Dating Photographs

A significant contribution made by Anderson's 1907 diary is the proper identification and dating of Anderson photographs found in various archives. Since 1989, T. Jeffery Cottle and I have been involved in a three-volume project that attempts to collect a visual record of early Church historical sites.[41] We had limited access to some of Anderson's diary entries through the courtesy of Rell G. Francis. Mr. Francis had been able to copy a few entries from the 1907 diary but was unable to copy the entire diary or to make a complete transcript of it. These diary entries have circulated for some time with numerous copy errors not found in Francis's original notes.

Having access to the original diary has allowed us to compare the original with the various sets of notes and to correct errors in these diary extracts that have been circulating for some time. The complete diary has also allowed us to date many of Anderson's photographs. Because some publishers and scholars have not had access to the diary, the dating of photographs used in their publications has been problematic—in some cases, misdating the photographs by several years.[42]

We have now corrected some of the site identifications and dating found in some of our previous work. For example, in an early publication, Jeff Cottle and I incorrectly identified an Anderson photograph taken in Nauvoo as the temple block.[43] The diary gives a detailed description of this image and places the location two blocks south of the temple.[44]

## Preserving a Vanishing World

Along with the bulky glass-plate negatives that so richly detail the sites of Church historical significance, the diary also richly details Anderson's experiences as he traversed the dew-laden fields, the dusty village lanes and roads, and the busy streets of America's largest metropolitan cities. Both the photographs and the diary preserve a sense of the reality of a now-vanished world that would be difficult to reconstruct without clues left by such chroniclers of the period.

The modern reader may not be able to imagine accurately the transportation revolution that occurred between Anderson's birth in 1860 and his mission in 1907. The revolution began in the first decades of the nineteenth century, but for those not near the major waterways of North America and for those living in the West, the revolution would not come until the second half of the century.

The railroad reached across the United States by 1869. From the main line, branches spread across the landscape. In Utah, Anderson documented this expansion of the iron highway. The development of a viable railway system throughout the United States was significant. Railroads ran year-round and could easily traverse hills and mountains. In the cities and major towns of Utah, another advancement—electric streetcars—made a significant impact on daily transportation.

From the time Anderson began his apprenticeship with C. R. Savage in the late 1870s until he returned to Springville, Utah, in 1913 from his photographic and proselytizing mission, the mileage of railways increased from fewer than ninety thousand miles to over a quarter million miles. In the cities throughout North America, streetcar lines expanded to serve the needs of a society on the move. Anderson's 1907 diary and the 1907–8 photographs reveal this forgotten world when trains and streetcars played a significant role.

Through Anderson's photographs, we see this world of steel, steam, iron, and electricity in the streetcar tracks, the electric streetcar lines overhead, the railway tracks, and trains that sped by (blurred in some cases) as he took his views. The 1907 diary reveals the ever-present train and streetcar as his major means of transportation. Of course, he traveled on foot and in horse-drawn vehicles to those areas still without the new means of transportation. Only on a few occasions does Anderson mention the automobile. His world was bound, like that of so many other Americans of the period, to public transportation in the cities and to the use of trains for travel across the great distances of North America.

The modern reader may have a difficult time imagining this world, but Anderson provides written and photographic evidence of its almost pervasive influence on America. The period was a time before airplanes filled the skies and private automobiles filled the concrete and asphalt highways. For the most part, streetcars have now disappeared in America, and the railways have become of minor importance in the transportation of people.

## The LDS Church in Transition

Anderson's world was changing rapidly in other ways as he made his way across the North American continent in 1907–8. The LDS Church had undergone significant and abrupt changes as it confronted a complex and often hostile world. The changing political, economic, and religious landscape in America and the world required Church leaders to move forward in dramatic ways in fulfilling their mission.

During the presidencies of Lorenzo Snow (1898–1901) and Joseph F. Smith (1901–18), the Church made the transition from the pioneer period of the nineteenth century to the modern period of the twentieth century. In the Rocky Mountain kingdom, the Latter-day Saints moved from a society that was naturally influenced by the institutional Church in politics, economics, education, and society when they first settled, to a society in which the Church played less of a role in secular concerns.

The period between 1900 and 1920 saw the cessation of Church-authorized plural marriages, the integration of Utah into the large American market-economy and two-party political system, the birth of the Church Educational System, the issuance of statements by the First Presidency and the Quorum of the Twelve to define and explicate basic Church doctrine, the expansion of missionary efforts, the modernization of Church administrative procedures, the correlation of Church auxiliary organizations, and a new image of the Church, not only in the United States but also throughout the world.

The Smoot hearings (1904–7) were a traumatic period for the LDS Church, as the history and doctrine (including temple ordinances) were discussed openly and often ridiculed in the press. As Anderson prepared to leave on his mission in April 1907, the First Presidency issued an "Address to the World," which answered charges stemming from the Smoot hearings.[45] This document was significant, as it was voted upon by the Church membership during a general conference session.

## America in Transition

Anderson's 1907 diary reflects this period of transition within the Church. The diary also acts as a window to the larger American society as well. The growth of the population and of the industrial and agricultural production of the United States during this period was phenomenal. The population of the U.S. in 1880 was just a little over fifty million people. By 1900, it had grown to nearly ninety million, and by 1920, it stood at 118 million. A crucial factor in this growth of population was another feature of the New World: the large-scale emigration from Europe. Nearly fourteen million emigrated between 1900 and 1914 alone. America's explosive growth of native population and immigrant population was not achieved, however, without severe political and social tensions.

Traveling to LDS Church historical sites between April and August 1907, Anderson encountered a society much different from the generally homogenous society of the rural valleys of Utah. He was unacquainted with the social realities of the larger American society divided by class, gender, ethnicity, and race. Outside his beloved home, for example, he encountered firsthand the division between black and white America. On one occasion, he attempted to find lodging in a large city. The hotel he chose, however, was "for colored folks" only. A "poor" black gentleman Anderson met at the place wanted to help carry his bags and heavy photographic equipment. "[He] was hungry," Anderson noted with a sense of sympathy, and "wished a nickel, which I gave him."[46]

Beginning in the late 1880s, many local and state laws were passed that legalized long-customary, discriminatory practices, including those related to public accommodations. The U.S. Supreme Court held that such separation was constitutional as long as both races received equal treatment. A combination of white discrimination and other factors produced widespread segregation.

In the large cities, Anderson discovered much of America that was not good. After a brief period of frustration, he sought some contact with his Utah roots and decided to leave a big midwestern city for what he hoped would be a more familiar place where he would be welcomed with open arms. In Independence, he wrote, "Sister McCarthy made me welcome. I was thankful to get out of the noise, bustle, dust, and smoke of Kansas City."[47] Anderson always sought out the community of Saints wherever he found himself. He met people he knew from Utah, he visited Church leaders, and he made new friends among brothers and sisters of the Church.

His hometown of Springville had fewer than thirty-three hundred people. The county seat, Provo, had fewer than nine thousand. And Salt Lake City, the largest city in Utah, had fewer than ninety thousand inhabitants. Anderson's first major stop on his trip to the East was Denver, with nearly 213,000 people—the third largest city in the western United States (only San Francisco and Omaha were larger). During the next few months, he visited four of the largest American cities, including the largest and the second largest: New York City with more than 3.5 million people and Chicago with nearly 2 million. Even Cleveland and Buffalo had more than 400,000 people each.

## Natural and Man-Made Wonders

Anderson's diary reflects his amazement at the natural wonders he encountered along the way as he moved from one city to another. The railway routes from Springville to western New York allowed him to see some of North America's most interesting scenery. After seeing Horseshoe Falls at Niagara, for example, he wrote: "The greatest sight I ever beheld in nature."[48]

Along with these natural wonders, Anderson also noted man-made wonders that he witnessed. In Chicago, he wrote: "What a sight it is to get in town among those great skyscrapers."[49] While traveling across America, he saw an escalator for the first time: "Revolving stairways—see people going up and down. It was a strange sensation."[50] He saw a small boat powered by an outboard motor and said, "They had a small skiff, which was propelled by gasoline engine, and they towed along a small, flat-bottom boat. . . . Astonished to see the speed at which the boats go propelled by these gas motors."[51]

Anderson also visited the Union Stockyards in Chicago, just a year after novelist Upton Sinclair published *The Jungle* (1906), a novel that exposed the corruption of the meat-packing industry there. While Anderson marveled at the technology that enabled Armour and Company to process large numbers of animals, he was disgusted by the conditions and slaughter of the animals.[52]

## Financing the Mission

As with most missionaries of the period, Anderson was careful with his money. Throughout the diary, readers will regularly find entries such as "Fixed up cash account."[53] Only after a careful examination does a reader discover that Anderson was recording his expenses for the day. He began his mission with some cash, as was typical of many missionaries at the turn of the century. He was given a farewell in Springville before leaving. The farewell activity was not only a time for friends and family to say good-bye but also an opportunity for community members to help him get started financially:

> You are requested to attend a Farewell Testimonial in the 1st Ward Meeting House Friday January 18, 1907 at 7 P.M. in honor of Elder Geo. Ed. Anderson, who leaves for a mission to Great Briton.
>
> A splendid program has been arranged for the occasion. A voluntary contribution will be accepted to assist Bro. Anderson to his field of labor. Your Brothers, O. B. Huntington, J. H. Manwaring, W. E. Strong.[54]

Anderson faithfully recorded all the help he received before he began his missionary travels. The 18 January 1907 First Ward social yielded $32.80. Two days later, at church services, he received an additional $8.40. A sister gave him a suit that he estimated cost $10.50. John Hafen hosted a social that added an additional $13.25 to the missionary fund.[55]

Anderson's diary reveals his efforts to finance his mission through his photography. In Chicago, for example, he photographed the laying of the cornerstone of a new Salvation Army building. On 25 June, he noted, "Out and sold two views of Salvation Army laying cornerstone."[56] He took pictures of various people he met along the way and traded the pictures for kindnesses and services rendered, such as a night's lodging or free use of photographic facilities. His skill not only helped pay his way as he proceeded toward his mission in England but also served as a tool to preach the gospel to those he met along the way. "Showed the pictures and talked the gospel to

## POST CARD

CORRESPONDENCE HERE   |   FOR ADDRESS ONLY

G. ED. ANDERSON, PHOTOGRAPHER, SPRINGVILLE, UTAH.

*Anderson Postcard, courtesy of Lehi [Utah] Library Historical Archives. Like many photographers of the period, George Edward Anderson provided customers with photographs on postcards that could be sent to friends and family members.*

Mr. Smith," he noted in his diary on one occasion.[57] The pictures were the images he had recently taken of Church historical sites in Missouri and Illinois.

Following his arrival in England, Anderson reproduced his photographs on postcards, tracts, and lantern slides, all in an effort to further his proselytizing activities. Along with LDS Church historical sites, Anderson also showed view books of Chicago, Niagara Falls, and other places of interest to the people he met during his travels in Britain.[58]

### Missionary Mail

Like other missionaries far away from home, Anderson also demonstrates through his diary his concern for family, his relationships with other missionaries, and the approbation of Church leaders with whom he came in contact during his travels. Letters from family and friends were appreciated and read. While in Chicago, Anderson wrote: "Received pictures of my family tonight, which gave me much satisfaction."[59] When an expected letter did not arrive, he noted: "Surprised that I got no letter from home."[60] He was a prodigious letter-writer. He not only wrote letters but kept copies and made copious references to those with whom he corresponded and to the dates he

*Anderson Family, Springville, Utah, 1907, Elfie Huntington, courtesy of Rell G. Francis. Anderson notes in his diary on 27 June 1907, "Received pictures of my family tonight, which gave me much satisfaction."*

sent his letters. The diary is full of references to post-cards, sometimes called *postals*. Evidently, these postcards were illustrated with Anderson photographs, and the reverse side of the postcards had Anderson's business name and address. For example, on one occasion Anderson noted, "Finished a batch of postals and views."[61] Two days later he wrote, "5:00 p.m., developed postal cards."[62]

## Anderson as a Record Keeper

Anderson saw himself in a tradition of recording sacred history, carefully recording long entries in his journal about the historical significance of his views and detailing background information gleaned from several sources. In one exceptionally long journal entry, he quoted extensively from *An Illustrated Atlas of Caldwell County, Missouri*, published in 1876. As he discussed his work in Caldwell County, he included page references to particular quotes.[63] Besides making notes from historical accounts he came across, he also took photographs of historical documents. For example, while in Harmony, Pennsylvania, he took a photograph of a deed signed by Joseph Smith Jr. when Joseph sold his property in Harmony.[64]

As Anderson moved from one historical site to the next, he often sent copies of his historical notes and photographs to Andrew Jenson, the LDS Church assistant historian, who himself had traversed these sites nearly twenty years earlier. Apparently, Jenson had provided Anderson with an itinerary: "From Kansas City go to Independence; then to Lexington Junction (30 miles) where you may branch off to DeWitt, Carroll County, return to Lexington Junction, and then go north to Richmond."[65] The diary seems to indicate that Anderson was unable to visit all the sites Jenson outlined. The instructions directed him to "visit Mentor, Hiram, Mantua etc.," all sites Anderson did not visit and for which he therefore did not leave a photographic record.

The period from 1892 to 1915 was one of unequaled interest in the LDS past. Church leaders wanted the rising generation to gain an improved collective memory and personal appreciation for Latter-day Saint heritage. The Church Historian's Office was the center of this activity. Numerous historical works were prepared and published during this singular period. Church leaders were also interested in contemporary history and inaugurated an expansive record-keeping program. Individual members were encouraged to keep personal records, and missionaries were instructed to keep diaries. Andrew Jenson stated, "We want to make you all historians."[66] Anderson fulfilled this dual goal, recording his own life in his diary and recapturing the past through his photographs of Church historical sites and personal research of the Mormon past.

## The RLDS Church

The diary of the missionary-photographer also reveals the unexpected help and friendship he received from local professional photographers as well as from old-timers—former enemies of the Saints and their children—and, more significantly, from members of the RLDS faith. At a period when LDS and RLDS relations were not as courteous as they now are, Anderson found a common ground of faith as well as a concern for preserving a common, collective heritage. Probably in somewhat of a different situation from other LDS missionaries laboring in Missouri, Illinois, and Ohio, he out of necessity reached out to the non-LDS community—including families of former antagonists of the LDS Church and members of the RLDS Church—in his efforts to document the early history of the Restoration.

For example, an RLDS bishop in Independence, Missouri, loaned Anderson a map so he could copy a "plot of temple lot and vicinity."[67] As Anderson sought out such people to find information or to get help in identifying certain locations, the people extended themselves—not only as they offered insights into the past but also as they opened their homes and gave hospitality to this missionary from the Rocky Mountains. In some respects, they shared his goal of capturing the past—not only of the place but also of the spirit of a time when mistrust and misunderstanding guided the events of history. Now they, along with George Edward Anderson, were willing to go beyond past difficulties and forge new relationships based on mutual respect.

## Other Christian Groups

Anderson's exposure to other religions and forms of worship yielded surprises as he confronted a totally new experience—Christian evangelical fundamentalism. By 1907, more than forty percent of Americans lived in urban areas. With the growth of the city, political, social, economic, and religious leaders became greatly concerned with urban poverty, disease, and crime. Numerous organizations, like the Salvation Army and the Volunteers of America, became very active in helping the poor with food, shelter, clothing, and, of course, spiritual renewal. With the generous support of wealthy businesspeople like Cyrus McCormick, George Armour, Cornelius Vanderbilt II, and J. P. Morgan, Chicago reformers, particularly the evangelical groups, were active and visible. Along the street, Anderson heard their pleas for souls and donations. He listened to their fiery talks and beautiful music. On one occasion, after attending a Salvation Army gathering where people stood on chairs, knelt on the floor, and shouted "Glory to God" and "Hallelujah," he noted in his diary, "I never saw such a meeting."[68]

The *Chicago Tribune* contrasted the Latter-day Saint street meetings and the evangelical Protestant groups that Anderson had stopped to observe: "When [the Latter-day Saints] offer prayer it is a short, simple recital, rather than a noisy, senseless imprecation. . . . Theirs is not the loud 'God bless this and God bless that' of the average street preacher."[69] The favorable article continued: "The Mormon missionaries preach equality. That suits the persons who gather in the street crowds. Theirs is not a long, loud harangue, ending with pleas for pennies. They do not want help. Rather they want to help those who listen to them."[70]

Anderson always felt the need to attend a worship service on Sundays, and when he could not find an LDS congregation, he walked into other churches. His first Sunday in Cleveland he wrote: "Could not find [LDS] Sunday School, so at service in the Catholic Church."[71] Even though he spent time listening to and experiencing other faiths and traditions, along with his own, he always remembered that he was on his way to a proselytizing mission himself.

## The Challenges of Missionary Work

The diary reveals the same apprehensions and struggles that current missionaries experience as they make the attempt to preach the gospel in public for the first time. Following Anderson's first street meeting with local missionaries in Chicago, he wrote, "I spoke at street meeting on the corner of Paulina and Grand. My first experience, and it was difficult."[72] He noted on another occasion, "I find it a hard task to speak to a moving audience."[73] The rewards came, however, as he shared his testimony and taught the gospel in the homes of those who would listen.

His travels crossed four LDS missions: the Western States Mission, headquartered in Denver; the Central States Mission, in Independence; the Northern States Mission, in Chicago; and the Eastern States Mission, in New York City. The period was an exciting one for missionary work in the United States.

Beginning in 1906, the missionary force increased to a thousand elders and sisters in the field. The missionaries still provided themselves with the books and tracts they needed in their work. Anderson's diary reveals his efforts to sell Church literature to interested persons. It also reveals the importance of music, not only in local LDS meetings but also in the street meetings. The diary reveals his personal struggles in this aspect of missionary work. On one occasion, he reflected: "Tried to sing with Elder Rasmusson." He added plaintively, "I may learn."[74] On another occasion, he recorded: "Practiced singing with the elders."[75] He sang on the street, at Church meetings, and in the homes of those he visited, always hoping to improve.

## Health Concerns and the Word of Wisdom

Anderson was a vegetarian who placed a great deal of emphasis on his diet. His missionary diary begins in Springville as he boards a Rio Grande and

Western train to start his journey across the United States. He recorded that Joseph Jones, a resident of Price, Utah, gave him a "sack of apples" to eat on the train as he took the next leg of his journey to Denver, Colorado.[76] This notation is the first clue that he was concerned about food. In fact, he listed fastidiously the foods he ate and made numerous references to the LDS code of health known as the "Word of Wisdom" (D&C 89).[77] These entries reveal another period of transition, not only for the LDS Church but also for the larger American society at the time.

Within the larger American society, the Battle Creek Toasted Corn Flake Company, managed by William Keith Kellogg, precursor of the W. K. Kellogg Company, had just introduced its now-famous breakfast cereal, cornflakes, in 1906. It was considered a health food. While in Chicago, Anderson noted: "Made a strawberry shortcake with *cornflakes* and berries."[78] His diary demonstrates a concern for and an abiding interest in information coming out of Battle Creek, Michigan.[79]

Kellogg's efforts to provide America with a nutritious substitute for the diet of salt beef and pork, hominy, condiments, and alkali-raised white bread prevalent at the time were not only medical but also moral.[80] These efforts to reform American lifestyles began in Battle Creek. John Henry Kellogg, brother of William K. Kellogg, was a physician, a health-food pioneer, a committed Seventh-day Adventist, and a practicing vegetarian when he supervised his church's Western Health Reform Institute (Battle Creek Sanitarium). In founding their cereal companies, both W. K. Kellogg and C. W. Post were influenced by John Henry Kellogg's work at the sanitarium.

Another health-food pioneer was Sylvester Graham, a clergyman who advocated a health regimen emphasizing temperance and vegetarianism. He believed that the use of an unsifted, coarsely ground wheat (graham) flour would improve the health of American citizens. This flour was named after him, and the modern "graham cracker" reminds us of his efforts. Anderson was determined to find graham bread whenever he could. For example, he recorded in his diary that he had been invited to eat at a local restaurant but "thought better [to] buy a lunch, which we did—fruit, bananas, cheese, and *graham* bread—which we ate in the public park."[81]

During this period of transition, LDS Church leaders prayerfully discussed the principles explicated in the Word of Wisdom. Most general authorities insisted upon complete abstinence from tea, coffee, liquor, and tobacco. In 1900, President Lorenzo Snow emphasized the centrality of not eating meat, which his predecessor, Wilford Woodruff, had also advocated. President Snow believed members should be encouraged, but not forced, to refrain from eating meat except in dire necessity, particularly since Joseph Smith taught that animals have spirits.[82]

Beginning during the first years of President Joseph F. Smith's administration (1901–18), the Church pursued a course that would ultimately require basic compliance to a narrow interpretation of the law—the abstinence of tobacco, alcohol, tea, and coffee, and dropping the emphasis on abstaining from meat. Evidently, Anderson sought to keep the counsel provided by Presidents Woodruff and Snow. His diary clearly reflects a Latter-day Saint who wanted to do what was right and who was committed to living a "clean life." Throughout the diary, he took time to mention what he ate. Following his tour of the Armour meat-processing facilities in Chicago, he reflected: "Will be glad when man does not have to satisfy his appetite on meat."[83]

Anderson's diary reveals the long hours of work and strenuous efforts he made to obtain and to develop his views of Church historical sites. For example, he recorded on 19 May 1907, "Bed about 11:00 p.m."[84] On the following day, he wrote: "Rose soon after 5:00 a.m."[85] Ironically, Anderson seemed almost overly concerned about most dimensions of the Word of Wisdom (D&C 89), yet he seemed to ignore the health directive to "retire to thy bed early, that ye may not be weary" (D&C 88:124), thereby pushing himself to near physical exhaustion on numerous occasions. Following a bout with the flu, he was forced to carry his heavy photographic equipment as he moved on to the next historical site: "Carried the instrument about mile when Mr. Gooley overtook me and a ride of two miles on a surrey was very acceptable, for when on my feet, I am in distress."[86]

A full day of activity was often followed with a long night of developing the negatives taken during the day. On one such occasion, Anderson rose before 6:00 a.m. and worked past midnight: "[D]eveloped about sixty-five prints on Azo. Numbered and spotted negatives; printed by gaslight. Elder Harris assisted me in washing the prints. It was after 12:00 midnight, nearly 1:00 a.m., when we got to bed."[87]

## Conclusion

The 1907 diary of George Edward Anderson reveals the experiences of an interesting person and a truly human missionary. The sense of wonder and holiness of the places he visited and the struggles, frustrations, joys, satisfactions, and experiences of the journey make this diary a classic. The diary ends before he finished his photographic mission in the United States and months before he sailed to Europe to begin his labors there among the people of Great Britain. He did finally arrive in England on 27 April 1908, a year after beginning his travels from a small town in Utah County, Utah.[88] Eventually, Anderson completed his proselytizing mission in Europe and sailed for America in August 1911; but he did not return home immediately. He stayed in South Royalton, Vermont, continuing his quest to photograph Church historical sites. After ending his nearly seven-year "mission" in 1913, he returned home to Utah.

For Anderson, the incredible capacity of this modern miracle to record the reality of life with factual precision characterized photography and separated it from all other media. Furthermore, prints from his plate negatives of Church historical sites could be enlarged with fidelity and then endlessly duplicated or preserved in publications. Thus, from

Joseph Smith's gold plates to Anderson's own glass plates, George Edward Anderson undoubtedly found a continuum and a focus for his 1907–8 photographic mission.

A full-page, pro-LDS article, illustrated with Anderson's views and printed in the 10 May 1908 issue of the *Boston Sunday Globe*, gave the following testimony concerning Anderson's photographic efforts:

> Recently a photographer from Utah spent several weeks in New England making pictures of scenes connected with the life of Joseph Smith to be used in a history. He had been away from home more than a year, picturing the scenes connected with the life of the prophet, chief of which are those connected with his death, at the hands of a mob, in Carthage, Ill.; his home as a youth in Palmyra, N.Y., where he announced his first revelations, and finally his birthplace in Vermont.
>
> These views will make a record in photography to be handed down through generation after generation of Mormon believers, as the illustrated pictures of the pious monk were handed down in the earlier days of Christianity.[89]

George Edward Anderson died on 9 May 1928 of complications from heart disease while he was in Arizona documenting the LDS Mesa Temple dedication. Like many of the early Saints, Anderson felt an urge to record history. But unlike the diaries, letters, and reminiscences of others, he chose the unique combination of photography and a written record to document the story of the Restoration.

George Edward Anderson, a village photographer from Utah, should be remembered as an important chronicler of LDS Church history. Through his 1907–8 photographs and his 1907 diary, he reminds the Latter-day Saint community of its collective past and heightens individual appreciation of a unique heritage.

# Notes

1. I am indebted to Rell G. Francis for suggesting the title of this essay and for his willingness to share, both in printed form and through conversations, information about George Edward Anderson. I have also benefited from the published works of Nelson B. Wadsworth. Francis and Wadsworth have each contributed significantly to preserving Anderson's work (see bibliography for a listing of their publications) and have helped to stimulate in me an insatiable interest in documentary photographs. Before he died in 1990, G. Lowry Anderson, Anderson's son, also shared with me, on several occasions, stories and insights about his father.

2. Anderson's efforts seem to have been appreciated by only a few farsighted individuals. Anderson's name does not appear in the Journal History of The Church of Jesus Christ of Latter-day Saints (Archive Division, Church Historical Department, The Church of Jesus Christ of Latter-day Saints, Salt Lake City, Utah); in Andrew Jenson, *Latter-day Saint Biographical Encyclopedia: A Compilation of Biographical Sketches of Prominent Men and Women in The Church of Jesus Christ of Latter-day Saints*, 4 vols. (1901–36, reprinted, Salt Lake City: Western Epics, 1971); or in Frank Esshom, *Pioneers and Prominent Men of Utah* (Salt Lake City: Utah Pioneers Book Publishing, 1913). Since the first publications of Anderson's LDS Church historic sites images in 1908, many of his photographs were published without any acknowledgment of his creative efforts in providing these dramatic black-and-white views. Even today, his images grace the pages of articles, essays, and book-long treatments of LDS Church history without any reference to his unique contribution in preserving the past. Only through the recent efforts of a few individuals, including Rell G. Francis and Nelson Wadsworth, has this injustice been reversed. Hopefully, Anderson's photographic efforts will be properly credited in the future by historians and publishers who have a moral obligation to credit his contributions.

3. Junius F. Wells to Joseph Fielding Smith, 16 October 1938, LDSCA.

4. See *Images of America: A Panorama of History in Photographs* (Washington, D.C.: Smithsonian Books, 1989).

5. George Edward Anderson Diary, 20 April 1907, the Daughters of Utah Pioneers Museum, Salt Lake City, Utah.

6. Anderson was set apart on 29 November 1906 for a mission to Great Britain by President Seymour B. Young (1837–1922), one of the first seven presidents of the Seventy. "Missionary Registers" (1860–1959), Missionary Department Collection, LDSCA.

7. Anderson Diary, 26 April 1907.

8. Ibid., 29 June 1907.

9. Ibid., 15 August 1907.

10. Ibid., 16 August 1907.

11. Ibid., 14 August 1907.

12. Ibid., 17 August 1907.

13. *Boston Sunday Globe*, 10 May 1908. Reed Smoot, a member of the LDS Council of the Twelve Apostles since 1900, was elected to the U.S. Senate representing the state of Utah in 1903. In January 1904, the Senate Committee on Privileges and Election began a long investigation regarding Smoot's seating. Eventually, in January 1907, he took his seat in Washington, D.C.

14. *Springville Independent*, 1908, newspaper clipping found in George Edward Anderson Manuscript Collection, LDSCA.

15. "Shrine for Mormon Pilgrims in Vermont," *Juvenile Instructor* 43 (1 July 1908): 246–53.

16. John Henry Evans, *The Birth of Mormonism in Picture: Scenes and Incidents in Early Church History* (Salt Lake City: Deseret Sunday School Union, 1909).

17. See Richard Neitzel Holzapfel and T. Jeffery Cottle, "Capturing the Past: G. E. Anderson's 1907 Photographic Mission to Missouri," *Restoration Studies* 5 (1993): 216–39.

18. Anderson Diary, 25 April 1907.

19. For an overview of Latter-day Saint interest in Missouri, see Holzapfel, "Establishing Zion in Preparation for the Second Coming," in *Watch and Be Ready: Preparing for the Second Coming of the Lord* (Salt Lake City: Deseret Book, 1994), 105–34.

20. Anderson Diary, 24 April 1907.

21. Ibid.

22. Ibid., 10 May 1907.

23. Ibid., 26 April 1907.

24. Ibid., 16 May 1907.

25. See ibid., 23 May 1907.

26. Ibid., 1 May 1907.

27. Ibid., 3 May 1907.

28. Ibid.

29. Ibid.

30. Ibid., 6 August 1907.

31. Ibid.

32. Ibid.

33. Ibid.

34. Nelson Wadsworth, "A Village Photographer's Dream," *Ensign,* September 1973, 55.

35. George Ed. Anderson, "Boy in the Picture of the Sacred Grove," *Improvement Era* 23 (May 1920): 638–40.

36. Ibid.

37. Anderson Diary, 18 August 1907.

38. Ibid., 28 April 1907.

39. Ibid., 10–13 May 1907.

40. Anderson diaries may be found in DUP, LDSCA, and BYU libraries. Obviously, some diaries have not been placed in a repository at this time and appear to be in private possession or lost.

41. See Holzapfel and Cottle, *Old Mormon Nauvoo and Southeastern Iowa: Historic Photographs and Guide; Old Mormon Palmyra and New England: Historic Photographs and Guide;* and *Old Mormon Kirtland and Missouri: Historic Photographs and Guide* (Santa Ana, Calif.: Fieldbrook Productions, 1991).

42. See, for example, Holzapfel and Cottle, "The City of Joseph in Focus: The Use and Abuse of Historic Photographs," *BYU Studies* 32 (winter/spring 1992): 249–68.

43. See Holzapfel and Cottle, *Old Mormon Nauvoo and Southeastern Iowa: Historic Photographs and Guide,* 39.

44. See Anderson Diary, 4 May 1907.

45. See "Address to the World," *Improvement Era* 10 (May 1907): 481–95.

46. Anderson Diary, 23 April 1907.

47. Ibid.

48. Ibid., 11 August 1907.

49. Ibid., 7 June 1907.

50. Ibid., 10 June 1907.

51. Ibid., 29 May 1907.

52. See ibid., 14 June 1907.

53. Ibid., 6 May 1907.

54. "Printed letter," George Edward Anderson Manuscript Collection, LDSCA.

55. "Cash Account Received to Aid Me with Mission," George Edward Anderson Manuscript Collection, LDSCA.

56. Anderson Diary, 25 June 1907.

57. Ibid., 16 June 1907.

58. See George Edward Anderson Diary, 5 August 1909 and 27 December 1909, Harold B. Lee Library, BYU, Provo, Utah.

59. Anderson Diary, 27 June 1907.

60. Ibid., 11 July 1907.

61. Ibid., 20 July 1907.

62. Ibid., 22 July 1907.

63. See ibid., 16 May 1907.

64. "Church History in Photograph," LDSCA.

65. George Edward Anderson Manuscript Collection, LDSCA.

66. Cited in James B. Allen and Glen M. Leonard, *The Story of the Latter-day Saints* (Salt Lake City: Deseret Book, 1992), 453.

67. Anderson Diary, 26 April 1907.

68. Ibid., 25 June 1907.

69. *Chicago Tribune*, 8 September 1907.

70. Ibid.

71. Anderson Diary, 4 August 1907.

72. Ibid., 14 June 1907.

73. Ibid., 19 July 1907.

74. Ibid., 19 June 1907.

75. Ibid., 30 June 1907.

76. Ibid., 20 April 1907.

77. The Doctrine and Covenants (D&C) is one of the official scriptures of the LDS Church and is divided into sections and verses.

78. Ibid., 21 June 1907, emphasis added.

79. See ibid., 20 June 1907.

80. John Harvey Kellogg once noted, "A man that lives on pork, fine-flour bread, rich pies and cakes, and condiments, drinks tea and coffee, and uses tobacco, might as well try to fly as to be chaste in thought." In Harold McGee, *On Food and Cooking: The Science and Lore of the Kitchen* (New York: Charles Scribner's Sons, 1984), 246.

81. Anderson Diary, 8 July 1907, emphasis added.

82. See Thomas G. Alexander, *Mormonism in Transition: A History of the Latter-day Saints, 1890–1930* (Urbana, Ill.: University of Illinois Press, 1986), 259–60.

83. Anderson Diary, 14 June 1907.

84. Ibid., 19 May 1907.

85. Ibid., 20 May 1907.

86. Ibid., 26 May 1907.

87. Ibid., 29 April 1907.

88. For Anderson's arrival and mission assignment information, see *Millennial Star* 70 (30 April 1908): 284.

89. *Boston Sunday Globe*, 10 May 1908.

# 1907 Diary and 1907–8 Photographs
# of George Edward Anderson

*April 20, 1907, Saturday, Springville, Utah, Train to Denver [p. 1]*

Cold. Think must have been frost. Rose about 6:00 a.m. Called on Sister [Martha Jane] Alleman and told her why I had not taken trunk and cake to son John [Alleman],[1] who is in Chicago. Bid Father and Mother Lowry[2] good-bye. Brother [Walter W.] Thornburg got grips[3] etc. from depot, and Olive [Anderson][4] assisted me in packing up. Bid all good-bye and left Springville on No. 6 about 10:15 a.m.[5]

Snow in canyon and all the way up. Fixed up Bingham Canyon business[6] and wrote to Olive. Disappointed not to find Brother J. B. Fairbanks[7] on the train. Off at Price, [Utah], and took next section of No. 6, which left Price about 7:00 p.m. Dinner with Joseph Jones. Gave me sack of apples and $2. Fixed up pictures etc. for Emily, Lowry, and Nadalsey [?] and straightened up other business. See letters and statements.

---

1. John W. Alleman (1885–1936) was a resident of Springville, Utah, and was serving in the Northern States Mission at the time. Anderson visited him in Chicago. See 3 June 1907 diary entry.

2. John Lowry (1829–1915) and Sarah Jane Brown Lowry (1834–1920), Anderson's father-in-law and mother-in-law.

3. A common word at the turn of the century for *luggage*.

4. Olive Lowry Anderson (1862–1946), Anderson's wife.

5. The western terminus of the Rio Grande Western Railway was Ogden, Utah. It connected with the Denver and Rio Grande Railway at Grand Junction, Colorado. From this point travelers could proceed to Denver and points east.

6. Bingham Canyon is located in the Oquirrh Mountains approximately twenty-five miles southwest of Salt Lake City. By the turn of the century, the small, individual mining claims were consolidated into the hands of several copper giants. Anderson accepted on-call assignments from several railway companies, including the Rio Grande Western Railway Company, to document their expansion throughout Utah. His 1907 photographic work in the canyon has been preserved in the train photograph collection of Robert W. Edwards of Salt Lake City.

7. John B. Fairbanks (1855–1940), "art missionary" sent to Paris by the Church in preparation for completing the Salt Lake Temple murals.

Brother Fairbanks not on train. Invited Mr. Nelson of Utah Fuel Company[8] to lunch with me.[9]

## *April 21, 1907, Sunday, Train to Denver [p. 2]*

Pillow Susie Boyer gave me helped make me rest very comfortable. Sleep soon after 9:00 p.m. Awake about 12:00 midnight at Grand Junction, [Colorado]. Wrote to Olive and woke just before Glenwood Springs, [Colorado]. Posted letter. Snow at Eagle, [Colorado], and up canyon. Tennessee Pass about 9:30 a.m. All covered with recent snow, which I understand has been quite general in this part of Colorado. Bread, eggs, butter, prunes, honey, and nut butter cake and apples made a good breakfast at 7:30 a.m., Minturn, [Colorado]. Cold.

Old couple, Graham, going to Iowa behind me. Gave them apples. Also to Mr. Je[.], the conductor last night.

Wrote R. D. Adams, Cedar City, Utah, asking him to send twenty [—] $5 to Boston. Wrote above on train. Pueblo, about 1:30 p.m.; Denver, 6:30 p.m.[10]

Colorado Springs[11] beautiful town, thirty-five thousand. No saloons. General [William J.] Palmer had this in the charter. Pike's Peak and mountains to the west of us. Snow everywhere.

Room, two streets from Union Depot [Denver] and to the left of Seventeenth. After some trouble to policeman[12] and others, located LDS chapel at 622 West Sixth Avenue. Met and shook hands with number of elders and sisters. Among them [p. 3] Daniel Webster of Taylorsville, Salt Lake County, Utah; Rachel Lathern, Mattie Lagenbocker. All inquired about Ida Alleman[13] when they learned I was from Springville. Elder was preaching on authority when I went in. A Brother Peterson from Salt Lake City at meeting and roomed with me. He is selling a cutting and fitting apparatus for men's and women's clothes. Met Charley Johnson in Union Depot. Just taking train for Salt Lake.

## *April 22, 1907, Monday, Train to Kansas City[14] [p. 3]*

Rose about 5:40 a.m. To depot with Brother Peterson, who left for Salt Lake City 7:00 a.m. Union Pacific found my grip had been checked to Pueblo, so ate apples for breakfast. At Mr. Wadleigh's office, and he selected the views[15] and paid me $17. I did not get through in time to get the 9:30 a.m. train.

In automobile, took fifteen-mile ride, 10:30 a.m. to 12:00 noon, seventy-five cents. Enjoyed it very

---

8. The Utah Fuel Company was incorporated in 1899 as a subsidiary of the Rio Grande Western Railway to help exploit coal deposits at Sunnyside, Carbon County, Utah.

9. A person's name appears at the bottom of the page for the 20 April diary entry. We cannot determine whether the handwriting is Anderson's. The name is Albert Je[.] and may be the name of the train conductor. At this point, Anderson may have begun his practice of collecting autographs of selected people he met during his 1907 journey.

10. The railway route required Anderson to go to Pueblo and Colorado Springs before arriving in Denver. On his trip from Denver to Kansas City, he backtracked through Colorado Springs and Pueblo before heading east.

11. County seat of El Paso County, located in central Colorado at the confluence of Monument and Fountain Creeks near the eastern base of Pike's Peak.

12. William Henry Bennet is identified as a metropolitan police officer in Denver, "Badge No. 423," in Anderson's "1907–1908 Address Book," George Edward Anderson Manuscript Collection, LDSCA.

13. Ida Alleman (1872–1965) was a schoolteacher at the Springville Central School, in Anderson's hometown, and had recently been released from the Colorado Mission (name was changed to Western States Mission on 1 April 1907) on 28 December 1906. In April 1907, she was serving another proselytizing mission in the Central States Mission. Anderson visited her in Nauvoo, Illinois. See 2 May 1907 diary entry.

14. At this point, Anderson makes the following entry: "6:00 a.m., 1:30 p.m., Denver, 5:45 p.m., 7:40 p.m., Pueblo."

15. Anderson usually refers to landscape scenery photographs as "views" to distinguish them from portrait photographs, which are of people.

much. Beautiful homes and park, no frame buildings, many apartment houses. [Walter S.] Cheesman owns the water supply.[16] Free boarding school, Shriner's Temple.

Capitol building,[17] elevator, and 93 steps gave an excellent view of the city and [p. 4] well worth the climb. Ouray Indian chief among the portraits.[18] Portrait—colored glass of noted men and women in tower of building—Ouray. We could have gone higher, but the view was good from this elevation.

A museum in basement of the capitol.[19] The lights not as good as desired. Kit Carson rifle;[20] twenty-seven brass tacks told the number of Indians he had killed with it; and seven others; the number a later owner had killed. Mummies, bones, skulls, pottery, cloth, straps. Feather cloth from cliff dwellers in Mancos Canyon was a leading feature.

The Grand Army of the Republic[21] had an interesting and instructive department.[22] Flags that had been in the smoke of battle, portraits, Confederate and other money. Several men and lady seemed to be on duty here.

A botanical department[23] required more time than I could spend. The wild animals of Colorado were preserved in very natural positions. I should have visited the Young Ladies'[24] and Young Men's Christian Association[25] buildings if time had permitted. Many automobiles on every street. Women as well as men driving and operating them.

Left Denver for Pueblo 1:30 p.m. Snow disap-

---

16. Along with several individuals, Cheesman incorporated the Denver City Water Company in 1870. Later, Cheesman and a partner incorporated the Citizen's Water Company. Through a series of complex stock transfers and corporate procedures, Cheesman was in complete control of Denver's waterworks and pumping stations by 1894. The new company became known as the Denver Union Water Company.

17. Located at the corner of Broadway and Colfax is the gold-domed Colorado State Capitol Building. The cornerstone was laid in 1886. The building was not occupied until 1894 when the state legislature moved into the uncompleted building, which was not finished until a year after Anderson visited it. An opulent building of the period, it contains the world's entire supply of rose onyx in its interior.

18. The only colored-glass window of a Native American in the Colorado Capitol Building is of Chief Ouray (d. 1880), who was an important leader of the Taviwach band of the Utes, known as the *Uncompahgre* after 1876 when they were forced onto a reservation located on the Uncompahgre River in Colorado. Later, they moved to Utah and settled on a new reservation, now known as the Uintah and Ouray Indian Reservation.

19. The museum was administered by the State Historical and Natural History Society and remained in the capitol building until 1915, when it was moved across the street to the Colorado State Museum. These collections were moved again in 1976 to a new facility at the Colorado History Museum, located at Thirteenth and Broadway.

20. Christopher "Kit" Carson (1809–1868), American frontiersman. His rifle was part of the "Wetherill Collection," which was the feature exhibit at the museum beginning in 1891.

21. Anderson used the abbreviation *GAR* here. The GAR was a patriotic organization founded in 1866 to serve Union Civil War veterans. Its membership reached four hundred thousand in 1890. It was dissolved in 1956.

22. Known as the "Colorado War Relics Collection," it numbered almost two thousand pieces and covered the period of the Civil War through the Spanish American War.

23. Originally part of the museum exhibit, it was eventually moved to the Denver Museum of Natural History in the 1920s when the administrative state agency was divided to form two separate entities—State Historical Society and State Natural History Society.

24. Anderson used the abbreviation *YL*, which undoubtedly refers to the Young Women's Christian Association, which was located at Eighteenth and Sherman Streets and which was completed in 1899 and had eighty-five separate rooms. The building was known as the Young Women's Home and was operated by the YWCA.

25. Located at 25 East Sixteenth Avenue, the YMCA Building was completed in 1906, shortly before Anderson arrived in Denver. The building was well known throughout the Rocky Mountain region because of its gymnasium, reading room, library, lounge, chapel, and two hundred residential rooms.

pearing as we near Pueblo. 6:30 p.m., Pueblo. Called on Mr. and Mrs. E. L. Thomas, 109 North Union Avenue. Supper with them. Mrs. Thomas was Jennie Branch of Price, [Utah]. **[p. 5]**

Called on President[26] Lamb, 620½ North Main over 620. Elder Chipman of American Fork and wife there; also elder from Canada. Wished me to stay and go to evening meeting, but time would not permit. I had a pleasant chat with Mrs. Thomas and husband. She is anxious to go back to Utah. Would be better satisfied if her husband did not gamble occasionally. Feels that he will do better. 7:40 p.m., aboard for Kansas [City]. 9:00 p.m., in chair car and some sleep.[27]

## April 23, 1907, Tuesday, Train to Kansas City, Kansas City, Independence [p. 5]

Awoke about 4:00 a.m. Bison, [Kansas], first station I noticed. Daylight soon after 4:00 a.m. Stone for fence posts in west end of Barton County, Kansas.[28] Farmer said cost about fifteen cents each at [blank]. Two men to handle. Was very easily worked and as cheap as hardwood. Almost all houses are frame. Windmills. Notice the wheat is three or four inches high; some just coming through. Farmer told me that stone was found in draws on the land; sometimes hauled ten and twelve miles. Many windmills looking for water, rain; need it to make the grain grow.

A long wait of nearly two hours at [blank] for trains brought us into Kansas [City][29] almost dark. Some time before I got my grips cared for. **[p. 6]**

I found President Samuel O. Bennion's[30] address and phone number and concluded to go out to Independence.[31] It was after 10:00 p.m. when I reached the mission headquarters, 302 South Pleasant Street, Independence, [Missouri].[32] President Bennion took me to Sister Leonora McCarthy's for a bed, as all full at mission house. Elder George V. Harris of Salem, Fremont County, Idaho, was there also. Sister McCarthy made me welcome. I was thankful to get out of the noise, bustle, dust, and smoke of Kansas City. A wash, foot bath; I felt refreshed.

Incidents on the way. A young lady on the train going to Memphis, [Tennessee], bought a Morton view book[33] in Utah. In looking for a room in Kansas [City], I knocked where I saw a sign out; and a colored lady informed [me] the house was for colored folks. A poor colored man asked me to allow him to carry my grip. I told I was not going any farther. Was hungry

---

26. Anderson uses the term *President* when referring to a mission president, a conference president, or a branch president. The president of the Western States Mission, headquartered in Denver, was Joseph McRae (1865–1958), who served from 1901 to 1907. Elder Brigham F. Lamb (1878–1962) was a conference president on several occasions during his mission.

27. This material is placed in its chronological order instead of the sequential order as it appears in the diary. Apparently, Anderson sometimes made a partial entry on a day without finishing the entry. On the next day, he then began a new entry without leaving space to complete his previous entry. Later, he finished an uncompleted entry on the next available page; therefore, some of his entries for a particular day are separated.

28. Barton County is located in central Kansas, east of Rush County, where the small town of Bison is located.

29. Located on the Missouri River, at the mouth of the Kansas (locally called the Kaw) River, originally called Westport Landing.

30. Samuel O. Bennion (1874–1945) arrived in Missouri in 1904 and was appointed president of the Central States Mission in 1906. He served as mission president until 1934.

31. County seat of Jackson County, located in western Missouri, immediately east of Kansas City.

32. The LDS Church mission headquarters had only recently moved from Kansas City to Independence in March 1907—just a few weeks before Anderson arrived. This event was significant because it represented the first established presence of the LDS Church in Independence since the 1833 expulsion of the Saints.

33. A large softcover photographic booklet, *Souvenir of Salt Lake: The City Beautiful*, was published by Smith and Morton sometime around 1901. Another Smith and Morton publication, *1902 Pocket Guide to Salt Lake and Vicinity* (Salt Lake City: Smith and Morton, 1902), was also available at the time.

and wished [**p. 7**] a nickel, which I gave him. I wrote to Mr. Blake, also my wife. Eva [Anderson][34] a card, and packed up a number of papers, memorandums, etc. that I wished to go home.

The eastern part of Kansas has more trees. Is more thickly populated. Hills and hollows.

### April 24, 1907, Wednesday, Independence, Kansas City [*p. 7*]

Rose about 5:30 a.m. Bathed my feet. Prayer with Elder Harris. He then took me on to the temple lot.[35] Also over the twenty-six acres purchased by the [LDS] Church[36] and lying southeast of the temple block.[37] I selected points that I thought would make good views and show the temple ground so that a person from the outside could see how it was situated. This is a beautiful place—quiet and pleasant. Agreeable to the eye. I feel it a privilege to be in this [**p. 8**] land which the Prophet of the Lord designated as the center stake of Zion and where the great temple of our God should be raised.[38] At mission headquarters at 7:30 a.m.

where they sang. Then Elder Richins spoke on temporal law and sustaining the authorities of the land.

The questions were asked as found in the Young Men's Mutual Improvement Association manual[39] and discussed, and I gave my ideas on several points that were raised. The class was continued about half an hour. Then prayer by all standing in a circle.

I arranged to make a picture of the mission house, when the instrument[40] was blown over and so damaged by the wind that I could not make the picture. While it was being repaired, I went to Kansas City and met Elder [**p. 9**] Thomas C. Lowe of Elsinore, Utah, and Wesley V. Duke of Heber City, Utah. They were 1404 Locust Street, Kansas [City]. I had dinner with them, an excellent meal at fifteen cents with a private family who made a business of furnishing meals. Elder Lowe said he would spend the afternoon while Elder Duke made visits.

Visited place where for one cent you could make your name on plate,[41] hear all the popular songs, see the different events in history, testing strength, three photos of self on postal [card] for twenty-five cents, etc.

---

34. Eva Anderson [Noyes] (1889–1984), Anderson's daughter. She married Lyman Wells Noyes in 1910 before Anderson returned home from his mission.

35. The temple "lot" is a 2-acre tract located on the high point of the temple property—a 63.27-acre tract of land purchased by Bishop Edward Partridge (1793–1840) on 19 December 1831. The temple property was dedicated on 3 August 1831. Ownership of the temple property was by 1907 divided among several groups, including the LDS Church.

36. In 1904, under the direction of LDS Church President Joseph F. Smith (1838–1918), James G. Duffin (1860–1921), president of the LDS mission that encompassed Missouri, purchased about twenty-six acres of land, part of which (ten to twelve acres) had belonged to the original temple property. The current LDS Independence Visitors Center is located at 937 West Walnut on a section of the temple property purchased in 1904.

37. Apparently, Anderson means temple *lot* when he uses the term *temple block* in this reference.

38. See Doctrine and Covenants 57:1–5.

39. Anderson uses the abbreviation *Y.M.M.I.A.* here. Founded in 1875, the organization was created to help young LDS men develop their gifts and talents. It underwent many changes in structure and format and, in 1901, was divided into junior and senior classes emphasizing development in social, cultural, and theological lessons. A preliminary program consisting of prayer, announcements, and singing was introduced in 1900. Lesson 12, "Temporal Laws," *Young Men's Mutual Improvement Association Manual, 1906–1907*, 10 (Salt Lake City: The General Board of Y.M.M.I.A., 1906): 88–91.

40. Throughout his diary, Anderson commonly used the words *instrument* or *instruments* to refer to one of the cameras he was using or to his cameras in general.

41. A small, blue, metal plate inscribed "G. Ed Anderson Utah" measuring four inches by one-half inch is located in the George Edward Anderson Manuscript Collection, LDSCA.

***The Liahona Office Building***, *Independence, Missouri, 25 April 1907, Anderson Collection, LDSCA.*
*The Liahona, published by the Central States Mission of the LDS Church, contained information about Church affairs in*
*the mission; answers to questions submitted by members, investigators, and others; discourses by Church leaders and missionaries;*
*and news from all the Church missions in North America. The Owens Building was located on the corner of West Lexington and Liberty.*
*The entrance to the Liahona office can be seen between the power pole and the streetcar pole at the left of the photograph.*
*The entrance to the photo studio of Evan V. Davis can be seen at the far right side. Note "E. V. Davis" on the awning.*

**The Examiner Printing Company Building**, *Independence, Missouri, 25 April 1907, Anderson Collection, LDSCA. Located just down the street from the* Liahona *office at 202 West Lexington, two local Independence, Missouri, newspapers—the weekly* Jackson Examiner *and the daily* Independent Examiner—*were published here. In 1907, the LDS Sunday School rented a hall in the building for Sunday services.*

***The Stone Church*** (**RLDS**), *Independence, Missouri, 25 April 1907, Anderson Collection, LDSCA.*
*Located just beyond the original temple property on Lexington Street is the stone church built by the RLDS Church in 1888.*
*The tower on the left was originally designed to be much taller and have a pointed steeple. Later, a 150-foot radio transmission tower*
*was erected here to facilitate communication between Independence and Lamoni, Iowa. The facility became KLDS, one of the earliest*
*religious broadcasting stations in the United States, and served the needs and interests of the RLDS Church from 1924 until 1937.*
*The radio station (now known as KMBZ) is operated by Bonneville International Corporation—owned by the LDS Church.*

Walked to depot. Found trunk. Went on bluffs so could see Missouri River,[42] location of depot, Kansas City, Kansas, and Kansas City, Missouri. Very windy all day, so could not make pictures. Bought bell of moulding [?] of William Volker & Company. Enjoyed visit with Elder Lowe, and he was pleased to meet me. Kansas City about 6:30 p.m. [**p. 10**] Supper at [mission] headquarters, and then to the *Liahona*[43] office and assisted in mail. They sent out twelve sacks today. Slept at Sister McCarthy's.

## April 25, 1907, Thursday, Kansas City [p. 10]

Dull and cloudy and some mist or haze. Rose before 6:00 a.m. At temple ground; then to class meeting. Civil and religious law continued by Elder Evans. I gave a sentiment with the others this morning and felt free to take part in the exercises. President Bennion asked me to be mouth in prayer. Made view of mission house, the temple lot (two views), also

Examiner office,[44] and *Liahona* office,[45] the Reorganized Stone Church.[46]

Developed these negatives (six or seven negatives) at Mr. Evan Davis's studio.[47] Very kind. [**p. 11**] Negatives all came out good considering the dull day. Assisted after supper with mailing the *Liahona*. A pleasant chat with Elder Evans. Also Brother B. F. Cummings.[48] At Sister McCarthy's and wrote up diary for two past days. I feel so impressed with the necessity of making the views. I can see what a blessing they would be to our people in arousing an interest in this land and the work that is before us as a people in building up the center stake of Zion.

## April 26, 1907, Friday, Independence [p. 11]

Rose soon after 5:00 a.m. Beautiful morning. Some frost. Made another negative[49] of temple property from the southeast corner. Also several grounds at mission headquarters. See list.[50]

---

42. Originating in the Rocky Mountains, various headstreams join to form the Missouri proper in southwest Montana. The longest river in the United States, it flows about 2,565 miles in a meandering course to the Mississippi River north of St. Louis, Missouri. Between 1830 and 1838, thousands of Latter-day Saints gathered in Mormon settlements in Missouri. They utilized the common modes of travel of that day: wagons, canal boats, stages, and steamboats. Or they simply walked to Zion on the National Road or on other trails. The Missouri River played a significant role, however, during this period as a means of transportation.

43. The official publication of all the North American missions of the LDS Church from 1907 to 1945. Published in Independence, the *Liahona* was first published by the Central States Mission on 6 April 1907, just a few weeks before Anderson arrived, but was shortly thereafter merged with the *Elders' Journal*, a publication of the Southern States Mission, thus becoming *Liahona The Elders' Journal*.

44. Located at the corner of Osage and Lexington Streets, a hall in the Examiner Printing Company Building was used by the Latter-day Saints, under a one-year lease beginning on 24 March 1907, for Sunday School services held at 10:00 a.m. and preaching services held at 7:30 p.m.

45. The *Liahona* office was located in the Owens Building at 202 West Lexington.

46. The Reorganized Church of Jesus Christ of Latter Day Saints (RLDS) Stone Church was built in 1888 and stands just outside the original temple-lot boundary at 1012 West Lexington.

47. The Evan V. Davis Studio was located in the same building (Owens Building) where the *Liahona* was published. His studio was located at 104½ North Liberty. The ½ designation indicates the studio was on the second level.

48. Benjamin Franklin Cummings (1855–1913) was the editor of the *Liahona* in 1907 and had just arrived in Independence on 5 March to assume his position with the new LDS Church periodical.

49. Anderson is apparently referring to "taking a photograph" or exposing film.

50. Several small booklets containing lists of negatives and photographs are found in the George Edward Anderson Manuscript Collection, LDSCA. However, no 1907 photographic register is among those in the collection.

**The Independence Temple Property**, *Independence, Missouri, 26 April 1907, Anderson Collection, LDSCA. For many Latter-day Saints at the turn of the century, the Independence temple property was one of the most important historical sites in Mormonism. Unlike many other historical sites, the Rocky Mountain Saints desired to return to this spot to build a temple. Anderson notes in his diary on 24 April 1907, "This is a beautiful place—quiet and pleasant. Agreeable to the eye. I feel it a privilege to be in this land which the Prophet of the Lord designated as the center stake of Zion and where the great temple of our God should be raised."*

NO.1A.

**South Pleasant Street**, *Independence, Missouri, 26 or 27 April 1907, Anderson Collection, LDSCA. A view of the street where the LDS Church mission home and headquarters were located. The Church moved the headquarters from Kansas City to Independence in March 1907, just weeks before Anderson arrived. The mission home and headquarters represented the first permanent LDS Church presence in Independence since the 1833 expulsion of the Mormons from Jackson County.*

*LDS Central States Mission Leaders and Bennion Family, Independence, Missouri, 26 April 1907, Anderson Collection, LDSCA. The mission leaders are standing in front of the mission home and headquarters. Mission President Samuel O. Bennion's family—Charlotte Towler Bennion, Burvidge David Bennion, and Samuel O. Bennion—are on the hill above the sidewalk.*

President Bennion and wife[51] left for conferences in the central states. At class, made proofs[52] **[p. 13]** of negatives[53] and showed to President Bennion before he left. He gave counsel to all he left and his blessing. Sister Bennion was very sick last night but was healed by administration.

Albert Thatcher,[54] 117 Bowen Avenue, Independence, Missouri, and janitor of the "Rock Church" Reorganized Church L.D.S., assisted me in getting ladders and to the top of two-story brick building—also to top of west tower of the Rock Church—and I secured some negatives of temple lot and Independence. Very difficult climb we had in the church tower.

Developed negatives at Evan Davis's studio. Very kind. It was after 6:00 p.m. when I got to mission house, but sisters gave me supper.

---

51. Charlotte Towler Bennion (1875–1964).

52. At this point in the diary, a rather large section of material stands independent of the diary entries. Most of the material is in the form of autographs, as follows: "Independence, Jackson County, Missouri: S. O. Bennion, Taylorsville, Utah; Osburn Richins, Mesa, Arizona; Wm. E. Evans, Lehi, Utah; Earl Whiteley, Lindon, Utah; Elmer Strong, Provo, Utah; Elder George V. Harris, Salem, Idaho; Fannie Burnham, Salt Lake City, Utah; Minnie Anderson, Salt Lake City; and B. F. Cummings, 295 Center Street, Salt Lake City."

53. Anderson made several temporary photographs from his negatives. These temporary photos are not the final print copies.

54. Albert Thatcher (1855–1944), removed to Independence RLDS branch on 7 November 1906 from Stewartville, Missouri.

**LDS Central States Mission Leaders and Staff**, *Independence, Missouri, 26 April 1907, Anderson Collection, LDSCA. Samuel O. Bennion, Burvidge David Bennion, and Charlotte Towler Bennion are in the first row on the left. B. F. Cummings, editor of the recently established LDS Church newspaper for the Central States Mission, is seated in the doorway on the back row.*

Elder William E. Evans went to St. Louis to organize Relief Society. I, with Elder Harris, went to depot to see him off. [p. 14]

I have felt all day that I should have more time to get views of the important points in Church history; so, at the suggestion of Elders Richins and Evans, telegraphed W. C. Spence,[55] "Have fine views. Need more time. Can steamer ticket be extended? Wire G. Ed. Anderson."

Bed about 10:30 p.m. Still cold. Weary tonight.

## April 27, 1907, Saturday, Independence [p. 14]

Rose soon after 5:00 a.m. Wrote the White Star Line[56] about extending ticket. See letter.[57] Number and registered negatives and made out list. Also copied plot of temple lot and vicinity from map loaned me by Bishop May[58] of Reorganized Church.

At Mr. Davis's studio before 6:00 a.m. and developed negatives made last evening. Feel very well satisfied with the record made of the temple lot, pictures,

---

55. William Charles Spence (1851–1927) became the transportation agent for the LDS Church in 1881.

56. The White Star Line, established in Liverpool in 1849, was one of the many Atlantic transportation companies providing service between Great Britain and North America.

57. Anderson kept copies of his correspondence; unfortunately, the location of these 1907–8 letters is unknown.

58. Roderick May (1850–1930), RLDS Independence Stake bishop (served the same function as RLDS presiding bishop except with local responsibilities).

**Temple Lot**, *Independence, Missouri, 26 April 1907, Anderson Collection, LDSCA. Taken from the southwest. The Stone Church (RLDS) is in the left corner of the photograph. Note Anderson's photographic identification No. 2 in the lower right-hand corner.*

**Temple Lot**, *Independence, Missouri, 26 April 1907, Anderson Collection, LDSCA. A slightly different view of the temple lot from the southwest. Note Anderson's photographic identification No. 2A in the lower right-hand corner. The 2A represents the fact that the photograph is slightly different from the photograph of the same view identified as 2.*

***Temple Lot***, *Independence, Missouri, 26 April 1907, Anderson Collection, LDSCA. A street-level view of the temple lot. The streetcar, a prominent feature of most urban centers at the turn of the century, is moving into the picture with its destination sign,* Independence, *on the front of the car. The two previous photographs were taken from a two-story brick building that is hidden by the frame building on the right.*

jumping [?]. This eve visited main business part of town.

## April 28, 1907, Sunday, Independence [p. 15]

Beautiful day. Wrote Ida Alleman a card. Also White Star Line, Boston. Andrew Himes, Almira A. Himes, Lucy M. Himes—had dinner with these Saints.[59] Elder Thomas C. Lowe, Elders Duke, Strong, and much information from Father [Andrew] Himes about Reorganized Church,[60] Hedrickite Church, prophecies, etc.

"Buckskin Joe," or Joe Lee,[61] prophesied that the first man of the Hedrickite Church[62] or any other church that raised a hand to build a temple would be stricken dead. The Hedrickites had employed about twenty-five stone masons and was going to start work when the prophecy was made. John Hedrick,[63] brother of Granville Hedrick, went for a load of logs to make derricks with—for the stone. As he was coming into town, fell off load and broke his neck; so work was stopped. How the Swope tract was obtained, $40,000, etc.[64]

At Sunday School at 11:00 a.m. Went to Reorganized Church and heard Elder [blank]. Text—put on the whole armor of Christ.

Met Elder Cardon, who has just come from Utah. Also met at Sunday School—Elder M. Steele. He wished me to go with [p. 16] to Kansas [City] and take the train there. He is a post-office inspector. I concluded to go to Brother Himes (see over this page) [page 15]. Enjoyed the conversation with Father Himes. It was suggested that [I] get a picture of the Saints on the temple lot, which I did at 4:30 p.m. I got

---

59. Andrew Himes (1836–1910) and his wife, Almira Amanda Himes (1839–1924), moved to the Independence area around 1889. They had eight children, including Almira Amanda (1866–1942) and Lucy Minerva (1879–1975). According to local LDS Church records, Andrew, Almira, and Lucy were baptized into the LDS Church in 1901. However, the name of a son, Joseph Hyrum (1872–1915), might indicate the family had some type of contact with the Restoration previous to 1901.

60. The "New Organization," later known as the Reorganized Church of Jesus Christ of Latter Day Saints, held its first conference on 12–13 June 1852. Eventually, Joseph Smith III (1832–1914), son of the martyred Prophet, accepted leadership control of the RLDS Church in 1860. The first RLDS members to return to Independence arrived in 1867. The RLDS Independence District was organized in 1878. The RLDS Independence Stake was organized in April 1891. President Joseph Smith III moved to Independence from Lamoni, Decatur County, Iowa, in 1906; and the RLDS Church formally moved its headquarters from Lamoni to Independence in 1918.

61. This may be a reference to Joseph Smith Lee (1839–1922), who was known in the Independence area as the "Mormon Preacher." He was baptized into the RLDS Church on 21 July 1866 in Salt Lake City. He was living in Stewartsville, Missouri, in 1869 and moved his family near Independence in 1871. Lee was a wandering "preacher" who lived in a tent, working a few days a week trying to support himself and his family but spending most of his time zealously proclaiming the RLDS faith. He was later expelled from the RLDS Church in 1873.

62. Following Joseph Smith's death in 1844, as many as thirty individuals or groups attempted to establish alternative organizations to the LDS Church, which had moved to the Rocky Mountains under the leadership of Brigham Young. Only six distinct groups remained by 1865. Some unaffiliated Mormons in and near Bloomington, Illinois, rallied around Granville Hedrick (1814–81). The group, known as the Church of Christ (Hedrickite), began to gather in the Independence area in 1867 and eventually obtained legal title to what has traditionally been identified as the "Temple Lot." It is enclosed by Lexington, River Blvd., Walnut, and Temple Court.

63. John H. Hedrick (1819–72) and his wife, Elizabeth A. Hedrick (1825–85), were among the first "Hedrickites" to move to western Missouri, arriving in February 1867. John and Elizabeth purchased several lots which were part of the "Temple Lot" on 24 September 1867 for $200. They deeded these lots to Granville Hedrick in 1871. John died on 11 May 1872 and was buried in the Hedricks cemetery in Independence.

64. Miss Maggie C. Swope sold nearly twenty-six acres to the LDS Church on 17 March 1904 for $25,000. We do not know why Anderson uses the $40,000 figure. See 24 April 1907 diary entry.

**The Church of Christ (Temple Lot),**
*Independence, Missouri, 26 April 1907,*
*Anderson Collection, LDSCA. The two-*
*story, white frame building was dedicated*
*on 6 April 1902; it replaced a smaller*
*one-story frame building built in 1887.*
*Also known as the Hedrickite Church, the*
*Church of Christ (Temple Lot) building*
*was located on the temple lot near the rise*
*of the temple property purchased in 1831*
*by Edward Partridge. This view is taken*
*from the tower of the Stone Church*
*(RLDS). The building in the photograph*
*was burned down by an arsonist in Janu-*
*ary 1990 and was replaced by a new*
*structure built through voluntary donations,*
*including those from community members*
*and organizations, one of which was the*
*LDS Church.*

***A Group of Latter-day Saints Gathered on the Temple Lot***,
*Independence, Missouri, 28 April 1907, Anderson Collection,*
*LDSCA. This view includes George Edward Anderson—standing in*
*the back row on the far left.*

a youth [?] to expose plate so I could be in the group, but did not get a very good one. Was nervous.

Evening at meeting. Elder Richins called on Sister Anne Anderson to speak. She bore her testimony. At his request, I spoke principally upon the Word of Wisdom [D&C 89], my feelings on being in this land where the prophet had dedicated a spot for a temple, my father-in-law and how he felt regarding my mission work. Related incidents of the observance of the laws of gospel and the blessings they brought. Elder Richins followed, endorsing what I had said and bore testimony of the gospel. Sister Schultz of St. Louis, [Missouri], spoke of the satisfaction she had in visiting and the meeting, etc. Said the incidents related had been a benefit. I went to Kansas [City] with Elders Lowe and Duke and found a bed on Locust Street a few doors from where they room. Bed about 11:30 p.m.

### *April 29, 1907, Monday, Kansas City [p. 17]*

Rose 5:45 a.m. Cold bath. Breakfast with Elder Lowe. Twenty-one meals for $3 and very good. Home like.

Visited several photo stock houses, bought some Azo paper[65] etc., and looked at several cameras. Independence, and [with] kindness of Mr. Davis, fixed trays[66] and developed about sixty-five prints on Azo. Numbered and spotted[67] negatives; printed by gaslight.[68] Elder Harris assisted me in washing[69] the

prints. It was after 12:00 midnight, nearly 1:00 a.m., when we got to bed. Raining most of the day.

### *April 30, 1907, Tuesday, Kansas City [p. 17]*

Rose 5:45 a.m. Mr. Evan Davis gave me key to the gallery, and I mounted[70] and finished the views and delivered all except a set I took with me. Came out very good. B. F. Cummings was very pleased to get the views he ordered. I took a number more orders.

So late I concluded not to go to Nauvoo, [Illinois], until tomorrow. Sister Anderson said was plenty of hot water for bath. I enjoyed it very much getting a change of clothes. I am pleased with the results I get with developing paper.[71] Class this morning—tithing and consecration.[72]

### *May 1, 1907, Wednesday, Independence, Kansas City, Nauvoo [p. 18]*

Rose before 6:00 a.m. Elder Strong assisted me to [street]car[73] with grips. Just caught the train at Kansas Union Depot at 9:00 a.m., not five minutes to spare. Lunch on the train—eggs, cookies, prunes, etc. I brought from house.

Wrote number of letters on the train, one to Elders Harris and T. C. Lowe. Changed [train] cars a number of times. Quincy,[74] [Illinois], at about 4:30

---

65. *Azo paper* was a commercially made contact paper used by photographers at this period of time.

66. Here, Anderson is probably correcting problems with the trays themselves.

67. Often, a photographer used a small paintbrush to "spot" the glass negative to cover its flaws.

68. Gaslight was utilized as a source of projection light in the process of developing and printing photographs.

69. Photographers used clean water to rinse all chemicals from the final photographic prints.

70. Photographers attached a print to cardboard or other support.

71. Anderson was apparently experimenting with some of the recently offered commercial developing-out paper as opposed to printing-out paper.

72. Lesson 6, "History of Tithing," *Young Men's Mutual Improvement Association Manual, 1907–1908* (Salt Lake City: The General Board of the Y.M.M.I.A., 1907): 34–40.

73. One of the major features of most cities at the turn of the century, including Independence, was the presence of numerous streetcars. Several of Anderson's Independence photographs show the streetcar tracks in the roads and, in one case, a streetcar moving into the picture. Throughout the diary, including references in Chicago and Cleveland, Anderson mentions taking a "car." These entries appear to refer to this type of public transportation. Anderson also uses the word *car* to refer to a railroad car. When appropriate, he uses the term *automobile* for autos.

74. County seat of Adams County, located in western Illinois, fifty miles southeast of Nauvoo. The citizens of Quincy welcomed the Latter-day Saints in 1839 following the Saints' expulsion from Missouri.

*Quincy*, *Adams County, Illinois, 1 May 1907, Anderson Collection, LDSCA. In the autumn of 1838, Missouri State Governor Lilburn W. Boggs issued several orders to the state militia that included a call to either drive the Mormons from the state or "exterminate" them. By December 1838, these executive orders were no longer in force. These "lapsed" orders were responded to with eagerness by local civilians who believed that the state government would not intervene to protect the Latter-day Saints. Tremendous sacrifices, including the loss of personal property and land holdings, were made as the Latter-day Saints evacuated their homes in north-central Missouri during the winter of 1838–39. Most of the Saints traveled two hundred miles east to Marion, Missouri, where a ferry service operated to transport the refugees to safety across the Mississippi River into Illinois. The people of western Illinois, especially the town of Quincy, greeted the Latter-day Saints with much-needed help and kindness. Other Saints found refuge in Iowa, making their homes in the abandoned barracks of old Fort Des Moines across the river from Commerce, Illinois (later known as Nauvoo).*

p.m. Made a view of Quincy while waiting for train. On east side of Mississippi,[75] on the bluffs, presents a striking appearance from the west side of the Mississippi. Fine depot the Burlington [Railroad] has here.

8:00 a.m., reached Montrose, [Iowa]. Skiff going to Nauvoo, so I went over with them. Dr. Fager and Mr. Oschner[76] on the boat. Off the train and on to the boat without a moment's delay. Reached other side about 8:30 p.m. A new experience for me. The [Mississippi] River is about one mile wide here and several islands,[77] and it seemed to me that we were on to them every few moments. I found it was the reflection in the water.

I tried to find Sister Ida Alleman, also Elder Christiansen, but was too late; so went to bed at hotel about one and one-half miles uptown.[78] The fireman (went up part way with me) of the ferry boat, Mr. Oschner, and Fager hauled up my grips—two—and I left other two at boathouse.

## May 2, 1907, Thursday, Nauvoo [p. 19]

Found Sister Ida Alleman and Sister Bennion soon after 6:45 a.m. this morning and, with them, visited the most interesting points—old homes of the Saints, the Prophet's home, temple ground. In the afternoon, made views of the most prominent places. Brother Pettman[79] rowed Ida Alleman, Sister Bennion across the river to Bluff Park,[80] Iowa side, and get a beautiful view of Nauvoo. Enjoyed the ride very much; and sight, which we wanted, was grand. We can now understand why Nauvoo is said to be located on the most beautiful spot of the river.[81] On the return, we passed between the islands higher up the river.

Made a group picture of the Saints and elders and sisters in front of the place they hold meetings in. Also showing where the *Times & Seasons* was printed.[82]

---

75. Rising in Lake Itasca in Minnesota, it flows almost due south across the continental interior, collecting waters of its major tributaries, the Missouri and the Ohio, approximately halfway along its journey to the Gulf of Mexico. It is the largest river of North America, draining with its major tributaries an area of approximately 1,244,000 square miles or about one-eighth of the entire continent. A major trade and travel route, the Mississippi River was an important waterway throughout the nineteenth and early twentieth centuries.

76. Anderson spells the name *Oxner*. He is probably phonetically spelling Joseph C. Oschner's name, a resident of Nauvoo. We have corrected his spelling throughout the manuscript.

77. These islands mentioned by Anderson have been underwater since the Mississippi River rose more than twenty-two feet after the construction of the Keokuk Dam below Nauvoo in 1913, making the river at Nauvoo more like a lake.

78. "Upper" Nauvoo, also referred to as the "hills," is located on the bluffs, nearly seventy feet above the Mississippi River in 1907. To the west, on the "flats," is the location of historic Nauvoo. Several hotels were operating in Nauvoo at the time, but in all likelihood, Anderson stayed at the Oriental Hotel (now known as Hotel Nauvoo), located on Mulholland Street. In Anderson's travel notes, he had written "Nauvoo, Mr. Reimbold at [Oriental] hotel can give information."

79. William Pettman had been baptized recently in Nauvoo by Elder Karl Madsen Jr. on 31 March 1907.

80. The Methodists held camp meetings south of the small village of Montrose in the 1880s. Eventually, this area on the bluff overlooking the town and the river became a recreation area with several summer cottages. Today, Bluff Park is a year-round residential area within the city limits of Montrose. In the 1840s, many Latter-day Saints lived near Montrose, which was part of the Zarahemla Stake.

81. The flat prairie of western Illinois drops suddenly over a series of bluffs from which a flood plain extends toward the Mississippi River. Historic Nauvoo is built on the mud-flat area that forms a giant horseshoe bend on the east side of the river, presenting a striking view for people coming upriver. Joseph Smith said *Nauvoo* meant "the city beautiful."

82. Located on the west side of Main between Munson and Kimball Streets is the building, known as the Printing Office, where the *Times and Seasons* was printed. It is really one structure that is part of a three-building complex: a two-story brick home (Ivins–Smith–Taylor home) and two commercial buildings (Post Office and Printing Office) flanking the home. The press offices were first located in a warehouse basement at Water and Bain Streets. Eventually, the operations of the newspaper moved to the new Printing Office here. Don Carlos Smith (1816–41), younger brother of Joseph Smith Jr., and Ebenezer Robinson (1816–91) were the first editors. Joseph Smith and LDS Church Apostles John Taylor (1808–87) and Wilford Woodruff (1807–98) also served as editors. The last issue was released on 15 February 1846, just before the Latter-day Saints abandoned Nauvoo on their exodus west.

*Nauvoo, Hancock County, Illinois, 2 May 1907, Anderson Collection, LDSCA. This view from across the Mississippi River at Bluff Park, Montrose, Iowa, shows the Nauvoo House at the foot of Main Street on the "flats," slightly to the right of the center of the photograph at the river's edge. St. Peter and St. Paul Catholic Church tower and spire, one hundred feet from ground level, may also be seen on the bluffs in "upper" Nauvoo. One can imagine how imposing the Nauvoo Temple, its tower, and spire were as the temple stood on the summit of the bluff overlooking the lower part of the city and the Mississippi River. Facing west, it was visible from a distance of twenty miles. The top of the tower stood 158 feet above ground level and was graced by a golden statue of an angel flying in a horizontal position. The angel was dressed in a flowing robe and wore a cap (doubtless inspired by the clothing of the Old and New Testaments' temple priests). The angel also held a trumpet to his mouth and a book in one hand, representing one of the angels mentioned in Revelation 14.*

**Printing Office, Ivins–Smith–Taylor Home, and Post Office**, *Nauvoo, Illinois, 2 May 1907, Anderson Collection, LDSCA. A group of local Latter-day Saints and missionaries is standing in front of a complex of three buildings dating from the LDS period. Apparently, the Latter-day Saints utilized one of these facilities in 1907 for their Sunday meetings. The building on the left, the Printing Office, was the heart of the Church communication efforts for members of the LDS Church in North America. The* Times and Seasons *and the* Nauvoo Neighbor *were among the periodicals published in this building in 1845–46. The building in the center, the Ivins–Smith–Taylor home, was built between 1842 and 1844 and was among the earliest brick structures in Nauvoo. The building on the right, the Post Office, was also used as a general merchandising store for books and stationery between 1843 and 1846. Notice the subordinate relationship of the Ivins–Smith–Taylor home with the flanking commercial buildings that form a courtyard.*

**Smith Family Cemetery**, *Nauvoo, Illinois, 2 May 1907, Anderson Collection, LDSCA. On the Smith homestead was the family cemetery where Joseph Smith Sr., Lucy Mack Smith, Don Carlos Smith, and Samuel Smith were buried in the 1840s and 1850s. Joseph and Hyrum were both secretly buried here in unmarked graves after the martyrdom. Emma Hale Smith Bidamon was interred here in 1879. The Prophet Joseph Smith's son, Joseph Smith III, buried his first wife, Emmeline Griswold Smith, and two of their children on "God's Acre" also. Emma's grave is seen in the foreground. The graves of Emmeline and her children are seen above Emma's to the right.*

Everybody we meet treats us so kindly. Mr. Goulty,[83] photographer, allowed me to change plates[84] and to develop negatives. It was near 11:00 p.m. when I got through.

Made a view of the graves of Emma Smith Bidamon, also Joseph Smith [III's][85] wife and children,[86] Nauvoo Mansion,[87] Nauvoo House,[88] and many things that brought to mind the condition of our people sixty years ago.

## May 3, 1907, Friday, Carthage, Nauvoo [p. 20]

Rose before 6:00 a.m. Decided to go to Carthage[89] with Elders Rassmussen and Ralphs. Brother Charles R. Pitt[90] took us over in surrey.[91] I telegraphed to the White Star Line.

Cloudy and cold. Reached Carthage about 1:00 p.m. Many fine homes and farms on the way. Visited the jail[92] where the Prophet [Joseph Smith] and Patriarch [Hyrum Smith] were killed. Saw the hole in the door made by the bullet, the window from which the Prophet jumped. The well has been filled up and is marked by some flowers put out in a circle. Have removed the old courthouse[93] and will erect a new one. Prohibition town;[94] some fine homes. Cement sidewalks are taking the place of the boards. A number of fine churches.

We called to see the only Saint in town, but not at home; so told a neighbor to kindly let her know that we had called. R. W. Batts, a breeder of shorthorn

---

83. Frank Goulty, local businessman and photographer, published "cabinet cards" of historic buildings of Nauvoo with site identifications printed on the photographs themselves. Many of these views were reproduced as postcards in the 1890s and early 1900s.

84. The process of taking exposed glass negatives from the plate holder and inserting new, unexposed glass negatives.

85. The diary here reads *Joseph Smith Jr.* Anderson is referring to Joseph Smith III, the son of the Prophet Joseph Smith (1805–44). During the Prophet's lifetime, he was known as Joseph Smith Jr. while his father, Joseph Smith Sr. (1771–1840), was alive. Following his father's death in 1840, Joseph Smith Jr. dropped the *Jr.* from his name, and it was apparently picked up by his son, Joseph Smith III.

86. Emmeline Griswold Smith (1838–69) and their two children, Evelyn Rebecca Smith (1859–59) and Joseph Arthur Smith (1865–66).

87. Located at the northeast corner of Main and Water Streets. The Smith family moved into the two-story frame home on 31 August 1843.

88. Located near the south end of Main Street. A revelation known as Doctrine and Covenants 124 (January 1841) commanded the Saints to build a hotel for visitors to the Saints' new city. The Nauvoo House, however, was never completed until after the Saints' exodus in 1846 when Lewis Bidamon (1800–79), second husband of Emma Smith, constructed the smaller "Riverside Mansion" on part of the original foundation of the Nauvoo House.

89. The county seat of Hancock County, located approximately twenty-three miles southeast of Nauvoo.

90. Charles R. Pitt (1867–1939) had been baptized recently in Nauvoo by Elder A. C. Christensen on 31 March 1907, although his family came to Nauvoo in 1841 as part of the LDS gathering from England. His father, John Pitt (1827–1913), remained in Illinois with his father and mother, Thomas and Charlotte Hill Pitt, following the Saints' exodus. He was rebaptized on 31 March 1907, even though he had been baptized earlier in England. See 30 May 1907 diary entry.

91. A four-wheeled carriage with two or four seats.

92. Located at the southwest corner of the intersection of Walnut and Marion Streets.

93. The earlier courthouse, designed by Moses Stephens, was built in 1839 and was razed in 1906.

94. The Anti-Saloon League, along with the Women's Christian Temperance Union, played a significant role in establishing laws against the manufacture and consumption of alcohol in many communities and counties, especially during a third wave of prohibition sentiment that swept the nation in 1907.

**Mansion House**, *Nauvoo, Illinois, 2 May 1907, Anderson Collection, LDSCA. Local Nauvoo Saints and missionaries stand in front of the Nauvoo Mansion House, where the Prophet lived during the last year of his life. Thousands of Saints passed through this building to see the lifeless bodies of the martyrs in June 1844.*

**Nauvoo House (Riverside Mansion)**, *Nauvoo, Illinois, 2 May 1907, Anderson Collection, LDSCA. The "Riverside Mansion" was built by Lewis Bidamon, the second husband of Emma Hale Smith, on the southwest corner of the uncompleted Nauvoo House. The lifeless bodies of Joseph and Hyrum Smith were briefly hidden in unmarked graves in the unfinished area inside the walls of the Nauvoo House before being moved across the street to the Smith homestead property near the family cemetery. At the end of Main Street was the Nauvoo House dock and steamboat landing.*

***Carthage Jail***, *Carthage, Illinois, 3 May 1907, Anderson Collection, LDSCA. The events of 27 June 1844 gave Carthage Jail national fame. Built during 1840–41 of yellow limestone, the walls are 2 1/2 feet thick at the first level and 2 feet thick at the second level. The interior originally consisted of seven separate rooms, including the living quarters for the jailer and his family and a debtor's cell on the first floor. On the second floor was a larger cell, known as the dungeon, and the jailer's bedroom where Joseph and Hyrum Smith, John Taylor, and Willard Richards were located when the mob entered the building on the humid afternoon of 27 June. Anderson notes he took this picture in a snowstorm.*

cattle,[95] rents the jail. We found many names from Utah and elsewhere (in the book kept in the upper room) of those who has visited the old jail. We find a railroad here, also at the little town of Ferris, west of here.

Such a cold, stormy day that we did not remain long. Made a negative of the old jail in a snowstorm. It was after 9:00 p.m when we reached Nauvoo and thankful we were to get shelter from the cold. Much of the time I had to hold an umbrella in front to keep the snow from our faces. Many beautiful farms and homes passed on the way. We kept our spirits[96] [**p. 21**] up by singing the songs of Zion. Elders Ralphs and Rassmussen at Kendalls' and I at Childresses'.[97]

## May 4, 1907, Saturday, Nauvoo [p. 21]

Rose before 6:30 a.m. Ice one-quarter inch thick. Turned out a beautiful day. Made a number of negatives. Met Elder Carl Madsen Jr., Riverton, Utah, and Elder J. C. Roberts, Kanosh, Utah, who have charge of this conference.[98] With these elders, Sisters Alleman and Bennion, and Elders Ralphs and Rassmussen, we spent a very pleasant day making views of historical places—house of Orson Pratt,[99] foundation where the Prophet's store[100] stood, temple lot,[101] Charles R. Pitt's home—gathered interesting data here. See list of negatives etc.

Elders Ralphs and Rassmussen bid us good-bye, feeling that they should get back to their field of labor. This was about 5:00 p.m.

View of the cornerstone[102] by the kindness of Mr. Joseph Oschner. Near his home and opposite the Lutheran North Church,[103] we make a view of casks, barrels, and wine cellar of Arthur Cambre, who left this property [to] Benedictine sisters, who had the wine emptied out, twenty thousand gallons running down hill. This wine cellar and property located on west of second block south of temple block.

Mr. Goulty, the photographer, tried to get me on

---

95. Any breed of beef or dairy cattle that originated in northern England, having short, curved horns or no horns and usually red, white, or roan in color.

96. The diary contains the names of two missionaries at this point: "Elder James A. Ralphs, Rockland, Idaho, and Elder John F. Rasmusson, Ephraim, Utah." The names appear to be in Anderson's handwriting.

97. In his diary, Anderson spells this name *Childres.* Anderson's "1907–1908 Address Book" states: "Mrs. *Childress,* Water Street."

98. LDS missions were divided into conferences—geographical boundaries similar to LDS stake divisions in the area of intermountain Utah at the time. After 1922, conferences were known as districts. The presiding officer was usually a missionary who was responsible for local members and missionaries in his area.

99. Orson Pratt (1811–81), an original member of the Quorum of the Twelve Apostles, chosen in 1835. Several historical sites in Nauvoo were misidentified between the time the Saints left in 1846 and when visitors returned. The home identified as Orson Pratt's, located on the north side of Water Street, is actually the home of Jonathan C. Wright (1805–?).

100. Located on the south side of Water near Granger Street, the store opened for business on 5 January 1842 and thereafter became the hub of civic and religious activities in the city until Joseph Smith's martyrdom. The building is significant because the Nauvoo Female Relief Society was organized there on 17 March 1842 and because the first temple endowments were given there on 4 May 1842.

101. The Nauvoo Temple was built on the east side of Wells between Mulholland and Knight Streets.

102. Anderson may be referring to the Nauvoo House cornerstone (of which a photograph is found in the BYU collection), even though the original glass negative identifies the photograph as the Nauvoo Temple cornerstone.

103. Located at Wells and Ripley Streets, Christ Lutheran Church was built in 1876 and was composed of two congregations—an English-speaking and a German-speaking.

**Water Street**, *Nauvoo, Illinois, 4 May 1907, Anderson Collection, LDSCA. This view of Water Street shows Jonathan Wright's home on the left. Until recently, the home of Aaron Johnson, in the center of the photograph, was often misidentified as belonging to Orson Hyde. This photograph shows the level of the Mississippi River before the river rose in 1913 following the construction of the Keokuk Dam below Nauvoo.*

**Corner of Water and Bain Streets**, *Nauvoo, Illinois, 4 May 1907, Anderson Collection, LDSCA.*

**Red Brick Store Foundation**, *Nauvoo, Illinois, 4 May 1907, Anderson Collection, LDSCA. The missionaries are sitting in front of the foundation of Joseph Smith's store, known as the Red Brick Store. The store opened for business on 5 January 1842, but Joseph Smith was unable to continue an active role in its management after 1842. The second story was used by a number of associations and organizations, including the Nauvoo Temple Committee, the Nauvoo House Committee, the Nauvoo City Council, the Nauvoo Legion, the Nauvoo Masonic Lodge, the Nauvoo Female Relief Society, and various LDS Church priesthood quorums. The room was also used for blessing meetings and school classes. The store was also the Church and city administrative office building in Nauvoo. The Relief Society was organized here on 17 March 1842, and the first temple "endowments" were given on 4 May 1842 in the second story of the building. The Smith homestead and "Riverside Mansion," or Nauvoo House, can be seen in the background. The Red Brick Store was recently reconstructed based on archaeological, photographic, and contemporary evidence.*

***Nauvoo Temple Block***, *Nauvoo, Illinois, 4 May 1907, Anderson Collection, LDSCA. The view shows the Nauvoo Temple lot along Wells Street. The two-story Icarian schoolhouse in the center of the picture was built of Nauvoo Temple stone by the French communitarian group before its socialist experiment failed. Wilford Wood, a resident of Bountiful, Utah, purchased most of the temple site between 1937 and 1961. The Icarian schoolhouse was used as the LDS visitors center thereafter until it was torn down. The St. Peter and St. Paul Catholic Church and spire can be seen at the left of the photograph.*

***Charles and Emma Davidson Pitt Home***, *Nauvoo, Illinois, 4 May 1907, Anderson Collection, LDSCA. John Pitt, as a young boy, arrived in Nauvoo in 1841 and remained in Illinois following the Saints' departure in 1846. He, along with his son and daughter-in-law (Charles and Emma Davidson Pitt), had been recently baptized by missionaries on 31 March 1907. John sits reading a paper; the young couple in the background may be Charles and Emma. The Nauvoo House "Riverside Mansion" is the prominent building near the river on the left.*

***Nauvoo House Cornerstone***, *Nauvoo, Illinois, 4 May 1907, Anderson Collection, BYU. The Nauvoo House cornerstone was placed in the southeast corner on 2 October 1841. In 1882, Lewis Bidamon uncovered it and found the original Book of Mormon manuscript. Anderson wrote on the glass-plate negative, "Nauvoo May 4 1907 corner stone of Nauvoo Temple," which is seen in reverse on the top and left-hand side of the negative. Apparently, Anderson was misinformed about the origin of this stone.*

*Wine Cellar*, *Nauvoo, Illinois, 4 May 1907, Anderson Collection, BYU. Located two blocks south of the temple block were a wine cellar and a lot with casks and barrels strewn around. Following the Saints' departure, German and French immigrants settled in the abandoned city and developed a significant wine industry. The photograph was taken from the corner of Wells and Ripley Streets. The spire of the St. Peter and St. Paul Catholic Church is barely discernible, indicating the temple block is between the church and this particular block.*

*Nauvoo, Hancock County, Illinois, 4 May 1907, Anderson Collection, LDSCA. A view of the temple block from the J. S. Oschner Building on Mulholland Street. In the upper right is the St. Mary's Building. The roof on the far left is the two-story Icarian schoolhouse made of Nauvoo Temple stone. In the foreground is an old Icarian apartment building, which housed the millinery shop of Rose Nickace in 1907 and which faced Bluff Street. The two-story frame building next to the Icarian apartment building is another Icarian building that, in 1907, was a boardinghouse operated by Charles Pitt.*

***Snow–Ashby Duplex***, *Nauvoo, Illinois, 4 May 1907, Anderson Collection, LDSCA. The home was commonly known as the Lorenzo Snow home at the turn of the century. George Edward Anderson's personal memorandums indicate: "Not Lorenzo Snow's but Erastus Snow's house. I have in Nauvoo. See Mr. Reimbold can give information, said Brother Junius Wells."*

***Cultural and Masonic Hall***, *Nauvoo, Illinois, May 1907, Anderson Collection, LDSCA. It was originally a three-story building. In another Anderson memo, he notes, "Inscription cut in lock near landing, front door: M.Helm.G.M.A.L.5843." The inscription relates to the cornerstone laying by Meredith Helm, grandmaster of the Masonic fraternity in Illinois: "M[eredith] Helm G[rand] M[aster] A[fter] L[ight] 5843 [1843]."*

*Wilford and Phoebe Carter Woodruff Home*, Nauvoo, Illinois, May 1907, Anderson Collection, BYU. This extant, two-story brick home is located at the southwest corner of Durphy (Highway 96) and Hotchkiss Streets. The Woodruff family commenced building this fine brick structure after Wilford returned from a mission to England in 1841. Woodruff recorded in his journal on 23 November 1843, "The bill of brick I had from Pullin was 14574 bricks which amounted to $88.65." Sometime in the summer of 1844, the family moved into this typical Federal-style home. Within two years, they abandoned the home and began the trek west to the Rocky Mountains.

*Nauvoo Expositor Building*, Nauvoo, Illinois, May 1907, Anderson Collection, BYU. The Nauvoo Expositor *newspaper was published 7 June 1844 by several prominent dissidents in the LDS Church. Apparently, the publishers hoped to create a division within the Church and increase non-Mormon opposition to Joseph Smith's leadership. Its destruction by Nauvoo City authorities led to Joseph Smith's arrest, which ended in his martyrdom in Carthage Jail.

***John D. and Agatha Woolsey Lee Home***, *Nauvoo, Illinois, May 1907, Anderson Collection, BYU. Built on the west side of Hyde Street between Hotchkiss and Munson Streets, it cost $8,000. Following the evacuation of the Latter-day Saints during the winter of 1845–46, the home was sold for $12.50.*

top of the Saint Mary's Academy Auditorium.[104] [Catholic] sisters very kind but could not find the key. Made a view of street from James Ferrin's home. Also from Joseph Oschner's[105] [p. 22] building, get a fine view of the town. Looking south, also west, from the Spaulding Institute,[106] building being finished for boys' school by the [Catholic] sisters.

I could not develop tonight, as Mr. Goulty had

many negatives to develop. Elders Madsen and Roberts assisted me in carrying instrument, plates, etc. While I made a number of views of old homes, 1:08 p.m., telegram came that said, "May 4, 1907 Presume you are member of Utah Salt Lake party. If cannot sail advise Mr. Spence. White Star Line."

At singing practice for a few songs. Retired about 10:30 p.m. Dull and cloudy in afternoon.

---

104. Established in 1874 by Catholic sisters as St. Scholastica's—a young women's educational boarding school. It was renamed St. Mary's Academy in 1879.

105. The Oschner Building was located on the southeast corner of Mulholland and Bluff Streets, directly across the street from the present Nauvoo State Bank.

106. Located on the southwest corner of Mulholland and Wells Streets, the Spaulding Institute Building was later known as Bennett's Hall. The Catholic sisters expanded their boarding school in 1907 to include facilities for young men in this building.

## May 5, 1907, Sunday, Nauvoo [p. 22]

Rose 6:30 a.m. At Mrs. Dundey's near ferry for clean shirt etc. Shave. 7:30 a.m., at Catholic church[107] to see and hear services for communicants[108]—about thirteen boys and fourteen girls. Mrs. Childress's boy, Alvin, was received. Father Reimbold, the priest, conducted the services and administered the communion or sacrament to the first-year communicants and second-year communicants and the relatives who partook of it in honor of the communicants. Twenty-seven lighted candles, thirteen on one side and fourteen on other side of altar. The priest lit a small lamp under image of Virgin Mary.[109] [Altar] boys dressed in robes of purple and white assisted them. Also headed the procession, lit the candles. Songs by young ladies [choir members]—black caps, white waist, and black skirts. They sang as they marched. Also in the choir. I could understand very little the priest said.[110] Services over shortly after 9:15 a.m. [p. 23]

Sunday School at 9:30 a.m. Cold and some rain when we came out of services. Sister Bennion, Superintendent Elder Roberts,[111] Primary and Theology Department.[112] Lesson: "Coming Forth of the Book of Mormon." I spoke to the school at request of Elder Roberts. Also took part in the lesson. Enjoyed the school very much.

Being fast day, remained at meeting house until 2:00 p.m. reading the [Deseret] News and talking of the services we had witnessed today. Was strengthened and blessed by the testimony of the brethren and sisters. At the request of Elder Madsen, I spoke, bearing testimony of what the gospel had done for me and my loved ones. Also spoke of Sister Ida Alleman and her work at home. Ask the elders and sisters to pray for me that I might know what to do about taking the boat.

After services, I went home with Charles Robert Pitt and had supper with them. Talking with Father [John] Pitt, Mother [Margaret Brown] Davidson, and her daughter, Mrs. C. R. Pitt.[113] Invited Mother Davidson to meeting, but she did not feel like going. "Afraid would convert me," she said.

7:45 p.m., evening services. Elder Roberts presided. I occupied most of the time, being followed by Sister Bennion. Spoke on the harmony of the

---

107. St. Peter and St. Paul Catholic Church, located in "upper" Nauvoo on Wells Street, one block north of the temple block. This building was dedicated in 1873.

108. Although policies varied from parish to parish, traditionally, a group of children ranging between the ages of seven and ten completed their catechism classes and participated in their first confession before attending the communion service mentioned by Anderson.

109. About this same time of the year, Catholics traditionally participated in the "May Procession," which paid special homage to Mary, the mother of Jesus. The lighting of the lamp by the priest may allude to this special period of celebration but does not indicate that Anderson is witnessing this procession, since it was a special and distinct celebration from the one described by Anderson.

110. The priest did not face the people during the services and, in addition, celebrated the liturgical services in Latin. These factors made it difficult for people to hear and understand what he was saying.

111. The Sunday School organization was presided over by a superintendent, who corresponds to the current calling of an LDS Sunday School president.

112. The Sunday School organization underwent a major transformation at this time when several "departments" were organized (Kindergarten, for children four to six years of age who studied the life of Jesus; Primary, for older children who studied Bible stories; Parents Department, which studied parenting skills; First and Second Intermediate Departments, which studied Book of Mormon and Old Testament; and Theological Department, which, in 1907, was studying *Jesus the Christ* by James E. Talmage). Apparently, the Nauvoo Sunday School was made up of only two departments—the Primary Department, taught by Sister Bennion, and the Theology Department, taught by Elder Roberts, who also acted as the Sunday School superintendent.

113. Emma Evlin Davidson Pitt (1870–?) had been recently baptized in Nauvoo on 31 March 1907 by Elder A. C. Christensen. Also baptized were her husband, Charles R. Pitt, and her father-in-law, John Pitt.

*Nauvoo*, Hancock County, Illinois, May 1907, Anderson Collection, LDSCA. View of the bluff from the flats. The three-story home in the center is that of David and Mary Ann Hoopes Yearsley, built before the Saints abandoned their temple city. St. Mary's Academy on the left can be seen facing the Catholic church toward the center of the photograph. The white buildings on the left were part of St. Mary's and reportedly incorporated the old Nauvoo Legion Arsenal Building. In the foreground is an early spring view of one of many grape vineyards that dominated Nauvoo's landscape during Anderson's visit. Following the Saints' departure, French and German immigrants settled in the abandoned city and developed a significant wine industry.

revelations of Joseph Smith with the scientific facts of today—Word of Wisdom and the results of living its laws. The Lord blessed me in speaking, as I felt that I appealed and touched the hearts of some of the young men present and think they will quit the use of tobacco etc. Sister Bennion endorsed what I said and encouraged those present to put in practice.

## May 6, 1907, Monday, Nauvoo [p. 24]

Rose before 6:00 a.m. Wrote to wife, John Alleman, and journal for several days past. Received a letter from the White Star Line and feel that I will remain longer and get the views I set out for. Mr. Goulty, the photographer, could not allow me to develop this morning. Very busy. Changed plates and made a few more negatives. Also one of the elders and sisters and myself, Mrs. E. S. Dundey.

With Brother Nelson, called on at Charles R. Pitts and had a chat with Mother Davidson. Does not believe in polygamy.

Took a number of orders for the pictures I have made from the elders and Saints.

Attended Mutual Improvement Association.[114] All local officers. They had a very good meeting—songs, recitations, readings, lecture from *Young Ladies Journal*,[115] "Love," by Sister Laura Bennion. Sister Lawson, who presided, ask me to offer the opening prayer; also to make the closing remarks. Fixed up cash account and bed about 11:00 p.m.

## May 7, 1907, Tuesday, Nauvoo, Keokuk [p. 24]

Mrs. E. S. Dundey's. Rose before 6:00 a.m. Wrote several memorandums. At Mrs. Dundey's; my grips there. Left Nauvoo on ferry at 7:30 a.m. Montrose, [Iowa],[116] 7:50 a.m.—button factory using clam shells. Fishing or gathering clams this a.m. as we crossed on boat. With Elders Madsen and [p. 25] Roberts, Keokuk,[117] and through kindness of Mr. Anschutz,[118] photographer, developed Nauvoo negatives. All good. While they were drying, I took dinner and ate it at the locks just above the bridge and on the west side of the river.[119] No vessel going through, but I saw the way it was worked.

While waiting for the negatives to dry, I visited Thomas Howells, 1407 Timea and Fourteenth Streets. Brother Howells not at home, but showed his wife the views. Elder Roberts came and helped me to the depot and assisted me in packing up negatives etc. Elders Roberts and Madsen came to the depot and stopped with me until after 10:00 p.m. 11:47 p.m., took train for St. Joseph, [Missouri], and reached there about [blank].

114. Anderson uses the abbreviation *MIA* here. A society for young men's mutual improvement was organized 20 April 1873, and the Young Men's Mutual Improvement Association work was made universal throughout all settlements of the LDS Church in 1875. A society for young women began as the Cooperative Retrenchment Association in 1869 and then went through a series of changes. The name was changed to Young Ladies Retrenchment Association (YL for short) in 1871. In 1877, the name was changed to Young Ladies National Mutual Improvement Association. The young men's and young women's groups were combined around 1900 to form the Mutual Improvement Association (MIA).

115. Anderson is probably referring to the *Young Women's Journal* published between 1889 and 1929, which served the young female members of the LDS Church. See footnote above for *YL* abbreviation usage.

116. Located on the western banks of the Mississippi River across from Nauvoo in Lee County, Iowa. The first Latter-day Saints arrived in the area in 1839, and it was here that "a day of God's power" was manifested on 22 July 1839 when Joseph Smith healed large numbers of ill Saints.

117. Located in Lee County, Iowa, at the foot of the lower rapids of the Mississippi River. In 1853, it was selected as an outfitting place for the Saints who were crossing the plains that year.

118. The Harmon M. Anschutz Photography Gallery was located at 19 North Fourth Street, Keokuk.

119. The Des Moines rapids were a serious obstacle in the navigation of the Mississippi River at this point. Various lock systems had been constructed to facilitate movement upriver toward Nauvoo. The current lock system was constructed in 1913.

*May 8, 1907, Wednesday, St. Joseph, Kansas City [p. 25]*

Found I could not get to any point that I desired as well as I could have done if I had went to Kansas [City]. So spent the day at St. Joseph[120] and visited some of the photo galleries and Uhlman's Supply Depot. Left at 2:00 p.m. for Kansas [City]. Reached there about 4:00 p.m. Great fire in the Pepper Building[121] blocked the cars, so I could not get to Independence. Went to Elder Thomas C. Lowe's room and met Elder Duke and telephoned Elder Richins and said would meet me at 11:00 a.m. tomorrow and arrange for ticket. No supper and to bed about 10:00 p.m. Good dinner at St. Joseph for 15 cents.

*May 9, 1907, Thursday, Kansas City [p. 26]*

Rose before 5:35 a.m. Bath. Breakfast with Elder Duke. Twenty-one meals for $3, and it is good food. Out about five miles east of Kansas [City] and made a view of the Big Blue.[122] The elders, Lowe and Duke, along. Made the negative near the Missouri Pacific Railroad and Burlington and Southwestern Railroads.[123] Three railroads cross the stream here. Very muddy and sluggish.

Centropolis, [Missouri], a suburb of Kansas [City], one-fourth mile north of where made the negative, met Elder Osburn Richins 11:15 a.m., who got me special rate to Richmond. With Elders Duke and Thomas C. Lowe, visited some friends—Mrs. Chipman and daughter, also Mrs. [blank]—and had dinner with them. Also at the Stockyards,[124] which is across the road. Elder Duke went with me to depot and assisted in getting things to depot. Left about 6:00 p.m. Lexington Junction, Richmond,[125] about 9:35 p.m. Bed at Mrs. Behunin's.[126]

*May 10, 1907, Friday, Richmond[127] [p. 36][128]*

I rose early and found the directions to Edwin Whitmer's,[129] son of John C. Whitmer,[130] who lives

---

120. County seat of Buchanan County, located twenty-eight miles north of Kansas City in northwestern Missouri on the Missouri River.

121. The 9 May 1907 issue of the *Kansas City Times* described this fire on its front page. The building was located on the northwest corner of Ninth and Locust Streets. Some five hundred people miraculously escaped the burning building, and only two people died in the inferno. The fire began in the basement where Montgomery Ward and Company stored a large supply of hemp binding-twine.

122. Several Mormon communities were established in Kaw Township, west of the Big Blue River. In November 1833, in the "Battle above the Blue," three people, including one Mormon, were killed during the expulsion of the Saints from Jackson County.

123. Anderson uses the abbreviation *M.P. & B.R.R.*

124. Located at Genessee between Fourteenth and Sixteenth Streets, the Stockyards consisted of a maze of pens and chutes that had been started in 1870 as Kansas City emerged as the mid-continental trading hub and central distribution point of livestock.

125. The county seat of Ray County, located twenty-seven miles southeast of Independence.

126. At this point in the diary, Anderson added this historical information: "South side see photo David Whitmer, died January 25, 1888, aged eighty-three years twenty days, Richmond, Ray County, Missouri, May 10, 1907." Actually, Whitmer was not quite eighty-three years and twenty days old, as he was born on 7 January 1805.

127. Anderson added this historical information at this point in his diary: "Monument of David Whitmer; west side has Bible and Book of Mormon on top; 'The Record of the Jews and the Record of the Nephites are one'; Truth is Eternal; Father and Mother Whitmer; north side, Julia A. Whitmer; died Feb 25 1889; aged seventy-four years, eighteen days."

128. Anderson made many notes on pages 27 through 39. Following his directives, we have chronologically rearranged his notes.

129. Edwin Franklin Whitmer (1858–1941), grandson of Jacob Whitmer.

130. John Christian Whitmer (1835–94), son of Jacob Whitmer (1800–56), one of the Eight Witnesses of the Book of Mormon.

***Big Blue River**, Jackson County, Missouri, 9 May 1907, Anderson Collection, LDSCA. Anderson posed two Central States missionaries, Elders Lowe and Duke, next to the river. Two LDS settlements in Kaw Township were situated on the Westport Road, which led from Independence to the Indian Territory. The closest community to Independence was the Blue River settlement, five miles west of Independence at the point where the road crossed the Blue River. Orin Rockwell and his son, Orrin Porter, operated a ferry at the LDS settlement on the Big Blue.*

about two miles east of town. Anxious to get through, so went without breakfast. Readily found the place.

Mr. Whitmer said could not give me information I desired. Some things he did not believe that were taught [by Whitmerite Church],[131] and so he had taken no interest in them—not that he had anything against the [Whitmerite] people, "for my father was one of the best men that ever lived. I don't think I went to services over two or three times in my life." Recommended me to Francis M. Miller, his neighbor who belonged to the [Whitmerite] Church, also Philander A. Page,[132] who he said were reliable and could no doubt tell me what I wished.

A coal mine on Edwin Whitmer's place, Whitmer Coal Company. Shaft forty feet down; vein twenty-four inches thick. Coal $2 per ton. Driving an entry so can come out on level. Use gasoline engine to get out water; hoist coal with horse. Opened a year ago, six men at work, readily dispose of all they mine. A number of mines in the neighborhood along the railroad track.[133] [p. 37]

Had a long chat with Francis M. Miller. See memorandum in book, *An Address to All Believers in Christ*, he gave me.[134] Mrs. Miller was popping corn and preparing to entertain some children in the evening.

From Father Miller's, went to Philander A. Page's (about one-half mile from Miller's), son of Hiram Page, one of [the] Eight Witnesses. See signature and notes on page 27. Father [Philander] Page is really the head of the Church of Christ, or first elder, sometimes called the Whitmerites. See notes in same book with Francis M. Miller. Dinner (which I enjoyed very much, no breakfast) with them and they went on horseback while I went on foot to cemeteries. See notes in this book and others. Miss Page took me out home in buggy, and I made negative of her and father and mother and home. And supper and bed at their request. Very kind. Spent the evening until near 11:00 p.m. talking with Mother [Sarah E. Farris] Page. See notes. [p. 27]

Philander A. Page,[135] elder who gave me the above signature, said was present at the deathbed of Oliver Cowdery;[136] and his father, Hiram Page, was nurse. Oliver conversed with the brethren and reaffirmed his testimony to the Book of Mormon and to be faithful to their testimony. He asked to be raised up to bid farewell to his wife and daughter and "now lay my head down and breathe my last on Jesus' breast."

Was also present at the deathbed of David Whitmer.[137] Three or four brethren present, Julia

---

131. William McLellin (1806–83), an original member of the Quorum of the Twelve Apostles, chosen in 1835, organized the Church of Christ in Kirtland in 1846–47. He eventually persuaded David Whitmer (1805–88), one of the Three Witnesses of the Book of Mormon and president of the Church in Missouri in the 1830s before leaving the LDS Church in 1838, to take the lead of McLellin's Church of Christ in the fall of 1847. Hiram Page, in behalf of David Whitmer, later repudiated the organization in June 1847. In 1875–76, David Whitmer attempted to organize a new church based on a simple interpretation of the Book of Mormon—"original Mormonism" of the early 1830s. The group apparently ceased to exist with the death of later generations of Whitmers and Pages.

132. Philander Alma Page (1832–1919) was a son of Hiram Page (1800–52), one of the Eight Witnesses of the Book of Mormon.

133. The coal-mining industry in Richmond employed about a thousand people in 1907.

134. David Whitmer, one of the Three Witnesses, published a pamphlet entitled *An Address to All Believers in Christ* (Richmond, Missouri: David Whitmer, 1887). The pamphlet contained his testimony and other historical information regarding the early Church.

135. Apparently, Philander A. Page signed his autograph at this point and is referred to by Anderson in the diary entry.

136. Oliver Cowdery (1806–50), one of the Three Witnesses and Second Elder of the Church, died on 3 March 1850 in Peter Whitmer's home in Richmond.

137. David Whitmer (1805–88) died on 25 January 1888 at his home in Richmond.

***Richmond***, *Ray County, Missouri, 10 May 1907, Anderson Collection, LDSCA. A general view of the city of Richmond, Missouri, where the Prophet Joseph Smith and other Church leaders were briefly incarcerated in 1838 before being sent to Liberty Jail. Later, members of the Peter and Mary Musselman Whitmer family settled in Richmond. Family members, particularly David Whitmer, entertained hundreds of visitors who inquired about and heard the witnesses' testimonies of the Book of Mormon.*

***Pioneer Cemetery***, *Richmond, Missouri, 10 May 1907, Anderson Collection, LDSCA. Following Oliver Cowdery's rebaptism into the LDS Church in 1848, he made his way to Richmond, where his wife's family (Whitmers) lived. Although Oliver planned to make the trek west to Utah, he died in March 1850 and was buried in the Pioneer Cemetery.*

**Jacob Whitmer's Tombstone**, *Pioneer Cemetery, Richmond, Missouri, 10 May 1907, Anderson Collection, LDSCA. More than just a photograph of tombstones, this view reveals the history of the Whitmer family and their relatives in Richmond. Note the tombstone of Jacob Whitmer with the Book of Mormon motif (second row, right). Jacob Whitmer was a shoe-maker and farmer. An early supporter of the Prophet Joseph Smith, he was one of the Eight Witnesses to the Book of Mormon. He settled in Jackson County, Missouri, and was subse-quently driven from his home along with many other Mormons in 1833. Jacob left the LDS Church in 1838 and settled near Richmond, where he remained until his death in 1856.*

**David Whitmer's Tombstone**, *Richmond City Cemetery, Richmond, Missouri, 10 May 1907, Anderson Collection, LDSCA. David Whitmer was born near Harrisburg, Dauphin County, Pennsylvania. He was introduced to the Prophet Joseph Smith during a business trip to Palmyra, New York, in 1828. David was an early convert to the Church when he was baptized in June 1829. He was one of the Three Witnesses to the Book of Mormon and was appointed president of the Church in Missouri in 1834. He left the LDS Church in 1838, eventually settling in Richmond, where he ran a liv-ery stable. Elected mayor of Richmond in 1867, he was a well-respected member of the community until his death in 1888.*

Schweich[138] and David Whitmer,[139] his children, and his wife, Julia Ann,[140] [were] present and granddaughter, Mrs. Josephine Van Cleave,[141] and grandson, George Schweich,[142] and his son,[143] now schoolteacher. Sent for Dr. [George W.] Buchanan and ask if he was of sound mind as he wish to reaffirm his testimony of the Book of Mormon. [p. 28] The doctor said he was perfectly rational. He reaffirmed his testimony to those present and counseled them to be faithful to their testimony of Book of Mormon and the cause of Christ and to the [Three] Witnesses' testimony of the Book of Mormon.

Brother Page was also present at the deathbed of the following Eight Witnesses: [blank]

With John Whitmer[144] during his last sickness, about a week. Was firm to his testimony of the Book of Mormon, and it was frequently referred to during his last illness.

John Whitmer sent for Brother Page and Elder John C. Whitmer and John Short;[145] he died at Far West, Caldwell County. See page 36. [p. 29]

Jacob Whitmer,[146] one of the Eight Witnesses, died at Richmond. Was firm to his testimony. See picture of monument in old cemetery.

Hiram Page[147] died about fifteen miles west of Richmond at a place near what is now known as Excelsior Springs.[148] Father of Philander A. Page (he [Hiram] died in 1851).[149] Never faltered in his testimony about the plates and the characters. Often related to Philander what they had seen and passed through.

Memories about David Whitmer, as related to me [by] Brother P. A. Page: "As he closed his eyes in death, he opened his eyes and smiled as though he met someone. This was repeated three times."

Made view of David Whitmer tombstone. See page 26. [p. 30] Made negative of Richmond, [Missouri], from hill northwest of town. Also of the tombstone of one of Eight Witnesses, Jacob Whitmer, in the old cemetery. "In this cemetery lies the remains of Oliver Cowdery and Peter Whitmer[150] and wife,[151] in whose house [Fayette, New York] the Church was organized, April 6, 1830."

I could not locate the graves of Oliver [Cowdery] or Peter Whitmer [Sr.]. Many of the stones were broken off by the cyclone which struck Richmond June 1, 1878. This cemetery is in the northeast corner of town and just east of the road, on a little rise.[152]

---

138. Julia Ann Whitmer Schweich (1835–1914), daughter of David Whitmer.

139. David John Whitmer (1833–95), son of David Whitmer.

140. Julia Ann Jolly Whitmer (1815–89), wife of David Whitmer.

141. Josephine Helen Schweich Van Cleave (1856–1937), granddaughter of David Whitmer.

142. George Schweich (1853–1926), grandson of David Whitmer.

143. Either Paul Schweich or Van Schweich, great-grandsons of David Whitmer.

144. John Whitmer (1802–78), one of the Eight Witnesses of the Book of Mormon.

145. A prominent elder in the Whitmerite movement.

146. Jacob Whitmer (1800–56), one of the Eight Witnesses of the Book of Mormon.

147. Hiram Page (1800–52), one of the Eight Witnesses of the Book of Mormon, married Catherine Whitmer, daughter of Peter Whitmer Sr. and Mary Musselman Whitmer.

148. Located twelve miles northeast of Kansas City in Clay County.

149. Page's death was in 1852.

150. Peter Whitmer Sr. (1773–1854), an early convert of the Church. He followed the Church to Ohio and Missouri.

151. Mary Musselman Whitmer (1775–1855), an early convert of the Church. She followed the Church to Ohio and Missouri.

152. Located on Highway 13 just north of the center of the city is Pioneer Cemetery, where several members of the Whitmer family are buried. The LDS Church placed a monument to the Book of Mormon, the Three Witnesses, and the Prophet Joseph Smith there in 1911. Anderson was present on the occasion and left a photographic record of this event.

*Alexander Doniphan Home*, *Richmond, Missouri, probably May 1907, Anderson Collection, LDSCA. Doniphan became a legendary hero to the Latter-day Saints for his fearlessness in refusing an order to execute Church leaders, including Joseph Smith, in 1838. A prominent lawyer and state legislator, Doniphan represented the Saints on several occasions. After service in the Mexican War, he settled in Richmond, where he died in 1887.*

*Peter and Mary Musselman Whitmer Home*, *Richmond, Missouri, probably May 1907, Anderson Collection, LDSCA. Mary Musselman Whitmer may have been born in Germany or in Pennsylvania. Peter Whitmer was born in Pennsylvania. Five of their children were witnesses to the Book of Mormon. Mary is reported to have seen the Golden Plates herself. Oliver Cowdery, their son-in-law, died here in 1850.*

**David and Julia Ann Whitmer Home**, *Richmond, Missouri, probably May 1907, Anderson Collection, LDSCA. As the "most-interviewed witness" to the Book of Mormon, David Whitmer entertained many visitors in this home.*

The new cemetery,[153] where lies the remains of David Whitmer, is on the south end of a very prominent ridge or hill that runs north [—] [—] of town. The street south side of courthouse square leads west one-fourth to south end of new cemetery. This is a beautiful place. Well kept. Many fine monuments—one of the largest being to ex-Governor King erected by the state.[154] Notice a number of stones to Whitmers and others whose names are familiar in early history.

## May 11, 1907, Saturday, Richmond[155] [p. 31]

[George W. Schweich] said the manuscript of the Book of Mormon, also the characters that were taken by Martin Harris to Professor Anthon, were at Lamoni, [Iowa],[156] in possession of Joseph Smith [III], president of the Reorganized Church of Jesus Christ of Latter Day Saints. Had put them in his care because he believed he was an honest man and would take care of them; and another reason he had let them go out of his hands he did not wish his (Schweich's) children to make merchandise out of them or sell them.[157]

## May 12, 1907, Sunday, Richmond [p. 32]

Mrs. Julia [Whitmer] Schweich says they promised her father [?], David Whitmer, a nice Book of Mormon. She would like to have it. "Considerable Thomas about me. I must see before I believe."

"Oh, he never deviated from what he told us at first. What he taught us that high [blank?]. No one could harm my father. I could knock down and drag out."

Reporter called. She would not admit him. Shut the door in his face. Wrote an article saying David Whitmer had died in his arms.

Jacob T. Hicks, Liberty, Missouri, Clay County, photographer, made picture when he, [David Whitmer], [was] eighty-two years old. "The day I am at my own table am eighty-two years old and can carve my own turkey." [p. 33]

Mrs. Josephine [Helen Schweich] Van Cleave lives in Springfield, Illinois. Josie,[158] her daughter, has the trunk the manuscript was kept in.[159] Mrs. Van Cleave's mother is a relative of Lew Wallace, who wrote *Ben Hur*.[160]

Parties came to purchase the manuscript and said it would help Father [David] Whitmer in his old age and his grandchildren and others. He said, "They could work for their living as had he. I have never wanted for bread."

"Name your price."

"Would I sell my soul?"

The characters that Martin Harris took to Professor Anthon of New York were with the manuscript.

Once, Father [David] Whitmer had not looked at

153. Located on Highway 10, three-fourths of a mile from the courthouse.

154. Austin A. King (1801–70) presided over Joseph Smith's hearing in Richmond, 12–28 November 1838. He demonstrated a distinctive prejudice against the Latter-day Saints. He later became governor of Missouri, serving 1848–52.

155. An autograph of George W. Schweich appears here: "George W. Schweich, Grandson of David Whitmer, Broker." Anderson added the following information after the autograph: "*The Founder of Mormonism*, I. Woodbridge Riley, Dodd Mead & Co., New York." He also added: "Charles Murray Twelves, Mrs. Ruby Twelves, Mr. [George] Schweich's daughter, Mrs. Twelves, lives at Spanish Fork. Husband manages the independent phone company there."

156. Located in south-central Iowa in Decatur County, RLDS Church headquarters in 1907. Originally, the RLDS Church was headquartered at Nauvoo, Illinois, until 1866. It was then moved to Plano, Illinois, and then to Lamoni in 1881, and finally to Independence, Missouri, in 1921.

157. Ironically, Schweich offered the manuscript to the LDS Church for $5,000. He then offered it to the RLDS Church, and a purchase agreement was consummated in 1903 for $2,400.

158. Helen Farwell Van Cleave Blankmeyer (1885–?), also known as Josie.

159. Mrs. Van Cleave transferred this trunk and several historical items from the Whitmer family to the RLDS Church in 1957.

160. An enormously popular historical novel written in 1880 by Lewis Wallace (1827–1905).

the manuscript for a long time, and when they opened the trunk, found it was moldy. But on examining the manuscript, it was not mold. Tied with the same yarn strings for years. **[p. 34]**

Mr. J[ohn] Encoe (photographer and jeweler) asked me to stay overnight with them and take supper with them last evening.[161] As I could not locate the Elders Berry or Hardee, I stopped.

I had a long chat with Mr. Encoe yesterday, while I was waiting for negatives to dry[162] and clear up, regarding the moral condition of the world. He believes in a man being pure and clean. His wife [Ollie B. Encoe] a fine lady, and done all she could to make it pleasant for me. Told me some of his experiences in the world with men and women—the diseased condition they get in through impure lives.

At the telephone, trying to locate the elders. Mrs. Frank Stiegall phoned that they left her home Saturday morning for Richmond. A few moments at the Methodist Sunday School. At services, Baptist Church. Minister's text: "Thy Kingdom Come." Afternoon at Mr. George Schweich's and his mother's, Mrs. Julia [Ann Whitmer] Schweich. See notes. Spent some time looking at things in the home of David Whitmer, where Mrs. Schweich lives.[163]

## May 13, 1907, Monday, Richmond [p. 35]

Rose about 5:45 a.m. Wrote some in journal. Tried again to find Elders Hardee or Berry. Called at

post office, telephone, and boarding houses, which I have done the past two days. Also on Mrs. Carter's. Found there would be no train to Lawson, [Ray County], until 8:23 p.m.

J. Encoe and wife have been very kind to me. Asked to eat with them, and I have slept there two nights, Saturday and Sunday. Mrs. Encoe said had extra bed and would be pleased to have me stop. She also asked me to ask the blessing at a number of meals.

Made negatives of place where old jail stood that Parley P. Pratt[164] and Morris Phelps[165] were confined in this a.m.[166] Powell brothers have a blacksmith shop on part of the ground. Showed me the ashes (wood) from the fireplace. Also the bricks etc. of foundation. One of brothers has a key that belonged to the jail, which was demolished by the cyclone which struck Richmond June 1, 1878. One of the brothers is now mayor of Richmond. The old jail was on the street north of David Whitmer's. In the Whitmer lot when I made negative.

Mrs. [Julia Ann] Schweich, David Whitmer's daughter, (see page 39) **[p. 39]** was putting out washing. Seventy-two years old.

Developed negatives at Mr. Encoe's. He did not charge for the developing I done. No charge for meals or lodging and wished me success on my journey. Mrs. Encoe said believed the Lord would bless me and I would get along all right—that providence helped those who were trying to do good. A boy, Gerald, and Silvia, the girl [blank].

161. The residence and business of John Encoe may have been located at 305 North College and North Main Street. The family consisted of John (54 years), Ollie B. (37 years), Gerald (7 years), and Sylvia (5 years).

162. The process of developing negatives required the use of water. As part of the finishing process, the negatives had to be completely free of water.

163. Located on East Main Street near Richmond's city center, the frame home was built or rebuilt after a cyclone hit Richmond in 1878.

164. Parley Parker Pratt (1807–57), a member of the original Quorum of the Twelve Apostles, chosen in 1835.

165. Morris Phelps (1805–76), a member of the LDS Church in Missouri.

166. The location of the jail is between Shaw and Thornton Streets, one block north of the David Whitmer home. Several LDS Church leaders, including Parley P. Pratt and Morris Phelps, were arrested on various charges ranging from murder to treason, following the capitulation of Far West to the Missouri State Militia on 31 October 1838. Later, Pratt and Phelps, along with Luman Gibbs (1785–1860), Darwin Chase (1816–63), Norman Shearer (1821–?), and King Follett (1788–1844), were placed in the Richmond Jail. They were eventually moved to Columbia, Missouri, after Chase and Shearer were released.

Very warm during the day. The negatives I developed almost frilled.[167] Just before I got to the depot, commenced to rain; and it just poured down. I like to have got wet through in going one-fourth block. Train left for Lawson, about 8:30 p.m. Still storming when we got to Lawson. A colored porter helped me to shelter and to the hotel across the street. Too late and stormy to hunt a cheaper place. Wrote, cash account, etc.

## May 14, 1907, Tuesday, Lawson, Elmira [p. 39]

Rose about 6:00 a.m. Still cloudy and cold. Seventy-five cents for bed and breakfast. Train for Elmira, [Ray County], 11:27 a.m. Walked out to David Bisbee's[168] about two and one-half or three miles southeast of Elmira. There about 1:15 p.m. Through the fields part of the way so I would not get so muddy. The blue grass and brush wet. [—] soon had a good dinner, which I enjoyed. [p. 40]

Found I was not far from Crooked River Battleground.[169] Mr. Bisbee gave me all the information he could and said the Thompson boys would help me out. They live close to the ford. He phoned them I was coming.

Mrs. Trout, Mr. Bisbee's daughter, has a boy, Clyde, between three and four who reminds me more of Lowry[170] than any child I have seen since I left.

Delivered the good wishes of Philander A. Page to Father Bisbee and family and [—] [—] the Thompson brothers. Gentleman overtook me in buggy and drove me right to their place. Remember very distinctly the visit of Elders Andrew Jenson, [Edward] Stevenson, and [Joseph] Black,[171] and said they had promised to send them a [—] [—], so they would know what they were doing in this country. Had not received it.

I rode back to Elmira with Jim Green, the gentleman driving the buggy, and led the horse, which the Thompson brothers let me have. By the time I got back with the instrument, it was too late to make the picture; so I went to James F. Thompson's, who had said could keep me overnight. His wife soon had a good supper for me, and I was getting dry and comfortable. Edgar White and wife, neighbors, came over, and I showed them the views and answered their questions about the Mormons [p. 41] and how and why they were driven out of the state. Read to them letters from the infancy of the Church. Told Virgil Thompson, seven years old, son of James F. Thompson, the story of Abdel Caleb, which was listened to with marked attention by the older ones as well.[172] Near 11:00 p.m. when we retired.

---

167. The emulsion on the negatives began to separate from the substraight (glass or cellulose nitrate).

168. Possibly Jacob Whitmer's grandson, David P. Bisbee, born in 1848, son of Mariann Whitmer Bisbee.

169. LDS apostle and Far West Militia captain David Wyman Patten (1799–1838), along with James Durphey (1793–1884) and Charles C. Rich (1809–83), led a group to Crooked River and clashed with a Missouri militia unit at dawn on 25 October 1838. Three members of the Far West Militia, including David W. Patten, and one Missourian were killed. Exaggerated reports of the incident led Missouri Governor Lilburn W. Boggs (1792–1861), who served from 1836–40, to issue several executive orders including his extermination order of 27 October 1838, authorizing the state militia to drive all the Mormons from Missouri or to exterminate them. Although the state militia did force the evacuation of Mormon settlers from Daviess County by 1 December 1838, the final Mormon exodus from the state, which took place from December to April 1839, was accomplished through non-Mormon civilian pressure.

170. George Lowry Anderson (1903–90), Anderson's son, was three years of age when Anderson left Springville, Utah, in April 1907.

171. These three Utah Latter-day Saints left Salt Lake City on 6 September 1888 to visit Church historical sites. Andrew Jenson (1850–1941) worked in the LDS Church Historian's Office and was an avid compiler of historical sketches, manuscript histories, and chronologies. He was sustained as assistant Church historian in 1898. Edward Stevenson (1830–97) was an early convert to the Church and a member of the Church's First Council of the Seventy. Joseph S. Black (1836–1910) was an LDS bishop at the time.

172. We have not been able to determine what the Abdel Caleb story is about, but we think it may relate to Anderson's role as a water master in Springville. He apparently was well known for his stories about children who were miraculously saved from drowning in irrigation ditches. The Abdel Caleb story may be related to one of these incidents.

***Crooked River Battleground Site***, *Ray County, Missouri, 15 May 1907, Anderson Collection, LDSCA. Far West Militia captain David W. Patten, an LDS Church apostle, arrived with a small detachment of militia on the upper right ridge above Crooked River at dawn on 25 October 1838. Patten divided the group into three companies before descending upon the renegade band of Missouri militia under the command of Samuel Bogart, who had taken several Mormon hostages. The Mormon group routed the Missouri militiamen from their camp on the eastern side of the river. As the Mormons continued in pursuit, Patten was mortally wounded north of the river crossing near where the two men are standing just above the ford.*

## May 15, 1907, Wednesday, Elmira, Mirabile [p. 41]

At James F. Thompson's, two and three-fourths miles southeast of Elmira. Rose before 5:00 a.m. Cold and cloudy. Breakfast soon after 6:00 a.m., and then over to J. L. Thompson's.

The brothers had a team hitched up and soon had us on Crooked River Battleground, or Bogart's Battleground.[173] It is about one-half mile north of their, the Thompson brothers', homes. These same two brothers took Brothers Andrew Jenson, [Edward] Stevenson, and [Joseph] Black onto the ground in 1888. Edgar White went with us, and a brother of James F. Thompson came while we were at work and is in one of the pictures. Secured an excellent place to make the picture on the west side of Crooked River, showing the ford, also the battleground, which has been cleared and is now farmed. We are looking north and in the clearing which the road on the other sides of ford leads [p. 42] to the battleground, which lies just east of the river. And it was on this bank where Bogart and men were camped. To the right of the center of the picture can be seen the hill down which Colonel Page[174] charged, and it was behind the trees on this hill where the old field house was and where Colonel Page divided his men. Tried to get some point that would show the river in several places and the battleground, but no elevation suitable. Banks too high and too many trees, which prevent us from seeing the stream any great distance. It is true to name.

Returned to James F. Thompson's. Made a negative of him, wife, and boy. Boy frightened, and it was a long time before we could get him to get before the instrument. Mrs. Thompson wished me to stop for dinner, but I thought better. Made Elmira in time to go to Mirabile, [Caldwell County], with mail. Mr. Thompson volunteered to help me, and we went through the fields and woods almost straight west to Elmira. Mr. Albert McCordboug, [?] who we hailed near the "muddy ford," passed us on the other side one at a time in a single buggy. [p. 43]

We made good time, Mr. Thompson carrying the instrument part of the time. Reached Elmira about 11:45 a.m. and bade Mr. Thompson good-bye and thanked him for his kindness; also his wife. Did not make any charge, so I told him I would send him picture of the battleground—also one of his family. I must send one of battleground to J. L. Thompson, as they made no charge.

The sun out a little while. I made negative of battleground. Mr. J. L. Thompson knew a Mr. Orem, schoolteacher, who he understood had gone to Utah and was mining. I think manager Utah Apex [?].

12:30 p.m., left Elmira with mail. Mr. Ray McCollough is name of the boy. I talked with him about smoking. Only seventeen years old and has an old pipe between his lips often.

Cold and cloudy and some rain. Six or seven cemeteries between Elmira and Mirabile. Some fine homes and farms. Plenty of wood—elm, oak, etc. Roads very heavy in places. Mud would pile up on the wheels. Mirabile about 2:45 p.m. Made view of post office.

Sent my instruments to Far West, [Caldwell County], with Mr. Ruben Sloan. Took my instruments and satchel etc. to J. D. Whitmer,[175] Far West, Kingston, R.F.D. No. 2, Caldwell County, Missouri. [p. 44] Mr. Bell Clevenger was kind enough to take me part of the way, and I walked the balance; and by

---

173. Samuel Bogart, Ray County Militia, captured several Latter-day Saints and was camped near the Crooked River crossing when Patten's men arrived to free the prisoners. The site was commonly known as "Bogart's Battleground" by local inhabitants after the battle in 1838 and as "Crooked River Battleground" by Latter-day Saints.

174. In all likelihood, Anderson means David W. Patten, commander of the Far West Militia.

175. Jacob David Jefferson Whitmer (1844–?), son of John Whitmer (1802–78).

**Crooked River Battleground Site**, *Ray County, Missouri, 15 May 1907, Anderson Collection, LDSCA. As he made preparations to take this picture, Anderson notes in his diary that Crooked River "is true to [its] name."*

keeping on the grass, got along very well. Found my instruments—[they had] reached Mr. Whitmer's just a few moments before I did.

Passed some places with fat stock, mules, sheep that had just been shorn, hogs, goats. Mr. Whitmer and wife and son made it very pleasant. Showed them the views I had along and talked about Utah, [1893] World's Fair, Chicago, our Church, the Reorganized Church. Mrs. [Celia Ann Tattarshull] Whitmer said that "when Joseph Smith [III] spoke when the church was dedicated here that he said that his father never had more than one wife and did not teach plurality of wives. Did not impress him as telling the truth. Invited other officials home to dinner but did not want Joseph Smith [III]."[176]

## May 16, 1907, Thursday, Far West [p. 45]

John Whitmer's hotel just south of the temple. See old barn. Wamsley Hotel east of John Whitmer's hotel. Joseph Smith home southwest of temple sixty rods. "Cellar kitchen [blank]." Just southwest and across the street from temple block is the Reorganized Church, dedicated November 18, 1906. Joseph Smith [III] spoke and said his father (the Prophet) never taught polygamy or more wives than one. Did not impress his hearers as true. [RLDS] Bishops Kelley[177] and White[178] spoke. Frederick Smith spoke.[179]

Public hall was just across the street, south from the temple lot. Old apple tree marks the spot. J. D. Whitmer saw it tore down because afraid would fall on the stock. Ten rods southwest across the street from the temple block was the "Committee Store." Two hundred houses in Far West. Hundreds of foundations when the Mormons left. [p. 46]

John Chamberlain told Mr. [John David] Whitmer that the old cottonwood tree which stands on the temple site was just a riding stick when he came here in 1866. Lived in house I made the picture from for twenty years.

The Reorganized Church, through Bishop Kelley, bought 160 acres southwest of temple, and their church stands in the northeast corner.

Old Mormon cemetery is one mile [north]west of the temple block.

Elmer Entrakin, his wife Bertha, allowed me to develop plates. Jacob D. Whitmer, wife Celia Ann, and son Harry[180] could find original plat of Far West. Piece of wood from Joseph Smith's house.

Ray McCollough of Mirabile told me there was mention of the temple lot etc. in their civil government.

J. D. Whitmer felt that Joseph Smith [III] did not speak as he knew, and Mrs. Whitmer of same opinion. Invited Bishop Kelley and another one home, but not Joseph Smith [III].[181] [p. 50]

---

176. Anderson records the following historical details at this point: *"History of Caldwell and Livingston Counties*, published by St. Louis Natural Historical Co., 1886, page 99. 'First schools were taught by Mormons in the vicinity of Kingston. The first school was taught by a young Mormon lady, Mrs. Mary Ann Duty, in an abandoned cabin on Long [Log] Creek. This was in the summer of 1838.'"

177. Edmund Levi Kelley (1844–1930) was appointed RLDS Church Presiding Bishop in 1891. Anderson spells the name of RLDS Bishop Kelley and his brother, RLDS Apostle Kelley, inconsistently (*Kelly* and *Kelley*). We have corrected Anderson's spelling. See 6 August 1907 diary entry.

178. Anderson may be referring to I. N. White (1841–1925), called to the Council of Twelve Apostles, RLDS Church, in 1897.

179. Frederick Madison Smith (1874–1946), Joseph Smith III's son and at the time a member of the RLDS Church's First Presidency. He later became president of the RLDS Church in 1914 at the death of his father.

180. Harry Elmore Whitmer, born in 1880.

181. At this point, Anderson included several rough quotations from a book he was reading and wrote the following: *"An Illustrated Historical Atlas of Caldwell County, Missouri*, compiled, drawn, and published from personal examinations and surveys by Edward Brothers of Missouri, 1876, General Office, 204 South Fifth Street Philadelphia, Pennsylvania." Anderson's notes at this point are contained in Appendix One. We have copyedited Anderson's notes, but we have made no attempt to compare the accuracy of the resulting notes with the original source.

***Far West Temple Site****, Caldwell County, Missouri, 16 May 1907, Anderson Collection, LDSCA. Caldwell County was created in December 1836, principally as a "Mormon county." Far West quickly became the commercial and ecclesiastical center for the LDS Church, as well as the county seat. By 1838, Far West had 150 permanent homes, four dry-goods stores, three family groceries, two hotels, several blacksmith shops, a printing shop, and a schoolhouse that doubled as a courthouse and church. Joseph Smith designated this spot for a temple.*

***Far West Temple Site****, Caldwell County, Missouri, 16 May 1907, Anderson Collection, LDSCA. On 8 July 1838, a revelation called the Quorum of the Twelve Apostles "to go over the great waters" to preach the gospel. The revelation specified a date (26 April 1839) and a place (the Far West Temple site) for their departure to the British Isles. Before the appointed time, however, an expulsion party in several counties forced the Saints from their homes and farms in Missouri. Enemies of the LDS Church taunted that this particular revelation could never be fulfilled and threatened those who might attempt to return to Missouri. Nevertheless, before dawn on the appointed day, Brigham Young, Heber C. Kimball, Orson Pratt, John E. Page, John Taylor, Wilford Woodruff, and George A. Smith gathered at the temple site to begin their mission to England. At least fourteen other men and four women met in Far West for the brief but impressive religious service. Alpheus Cutler laid the southeast cornerstone, and Wilford Woodruff and George A. Smith were ordained apostles before the group was dismissed.*

I had dinner with Elmer Entrakin while negatives were washing. Very kind. Mrs. Entrakin suffering with headache. Would not make a charge. Said [I] was welcome and to call again.

It was near 11:00 p.m. when I went to bed last night. Reading *History of Caldwell County*. Several pages devoted to the Mormons.[182]

Question with Mr. [John David] Whitmer if George Schweich had a right to sell [?] the manuscript of the Book of Mormon. He thought they might belong to the original church and that could be settled by court.

Never paid much attention to his father's testimony of the Book of Mormon until he was dead. Then, he thought more of it in one year than he had in twenty years before. Said George Schweich mortgaged the manuscript for $1,800. Then had to raise the money.

## May 17, 1907, Friday, Far West [p. 51]

In conversation with Mrs. Sarah [Whitmer] Kerr,[183] she said would like to have a picture of Martin Harris. Has in her possession oil paintings[184] of Oliver Cowdery and his wife, Elizabeth Whitmer[185] and Oliver Cowdery's father. Think it was Lyman.[186]

Elizabeth Whitmer Cowdery, Oliver Cowdery's wife, died and buried at South West City, McDonald County, Missouri, about fifteen years ago. Her daughter, Mrs. Maria L. Cowdery[187] Johnson (she was married to Dr. C[harles] Johnson). Mrs. Johnson died forty-eight hours after her mother [i.e.,] Elizabeth Whitmer Cowdery. Oliver Cowdery's wife was John Whitmer's sister and Mrs. Sarah [Whitmer] Kerr's aunt. Dr. Johnson, Maria L. Cowdery's husband, survived his wife twenty years.

Made negatives of the paintings, and Mrs. Kerr wished me to stop to dinner. Near 11:30 a.m., so I had dinner and then to Whitmers and left my instrument, coat, etc. And across the country to Ray's southeast but could get no horse or conveyance, so walked on towards Kingston.[188] Stopped for a rest and drink [p. 52] at the poor farm,[189] in charge of John Batson. Frame, two-story house. Well painted, good barns and grounds. Mr. Batson's son told me the place was about self-supporting. Had nine inmates at present. About 4:30 p.m. or 5:00 p.m., Kingston seven miles southeast of Far West or Kerr.[190] Supper and bed at Mr. Andrew Jackson A. J. Seeley's.[191] His wife was [blank] Smith. Belongs to Reorganized [Church]. I visited cemetery and found the tombstone of John Whitmer.[192]

---

182. See Appendix One for the quotations from *An Illustrated Historical Atlas of Caldwell County, Missouri* that Anderson included in his diary. In the middle of these quotations, Anderson made the following entry: "See *History of Caldwell County*, page 103. How was going to make a 'Mormon County.' Mormon Occupation, page 106. Early History of Mormonism, 'Joe Smith,' Witnesses of Book of Mormon, etc."

183. Sarah Elizabeth Whitmer (1837–?), John Whitmer's daughter, married James Edward Johnson in 1856 and Christopher Kerr in 1882.

184. These paintings were eventually purchased by the RLDS Church from Sarah Whitmer Kerr's daughter, Ella Johnson, in 1930.

185. Elizabeth Ann Whitmer Cowdery (1815–92), daughter of Peter Whitmer Sr. and Mary Musselman Whitmer.

186. Lyman Cowdery (1802–81) was Oliver's brother, not his father, whose name was William Cowdery (1765–1847).

187. Maria Louise Cowdery (1835–92). Anderson spelled the name *Mira;* we have corrected it throughout.

188. County seat of Caldwell County, located seven miles southeast of Far West.

189. A farm that houses, supports, and employs the poor at public expense. A county institution, the poor farms in Missouri were later known as *county houses* or *county farms*.

190. Here, *Kerr* probably refers to the Kerr farm near Far West.

191. Andrew Jackson Seeley was apparently known as *A. J.*

192. The Kingston Cemetery is located just northeast of the courthouse square.

**Site of Joseph and Emma Hale Smith Home**, *Far West, Missouri, 16 May 1907, Anderson Collection, LDSCA. Anderson notes in his diary that he had obtained a "piece of wood from Joseph Smith's house."*

*Elizabeth Ann Whitmer Cowdery Painting*, Kerr Home, Caldwell County, Missouri, 17 May 1907, Anderson Collection, LDSCA. The view is a photograph of a painting of Elizabeth Whitmer Cowdery that belonged to her niece, Sarah Whitmer Kerr. The painting, along with several others, may have hung in the Kirtland Temple.

North and South Methodist Churches, divided since the Civil War.[193] Mrs. Seeley says that the war brought freedom not only to the Negro but [also] the whites. "Before the war, you must not be known as North Methodist or L.D.S. if you wished to get away with your life." Christian Church, North and South Methodist, Reorganized, Colored Methodist, used to be a North and South Colored Methodist but the United Presbyterians [blank].

David and Oliver Seeley went from Connecticut to New York and from there, and A. J. Seeley's grandfather married Eunice Stewart.

---

193. Several American denominations, including the Methodists, divided into a north and a south group during the years preceding the Civil War. The Southern Methodists disagreed with the antislavery attitudes and activities of their northern counterparts and organized a separate denomination in 1844.

*May 18, 1907, Saturday, Kingston, Kerr House [p. 53]*

Wrote to my wife. Wrote to Elder Osburn Richins about ticket. See No. 18. Wrote to Elder J. C. Roberts at Nauvoo, also Keokuk, [Iowa], J. S. Anderson, Rexburg, [Idaho], on Independence postcard. Swope tract, John Alleman, 149 South Paulina Street, Chicago.

Rose soon after 5:00 a.m. Feel rested. Breakfast with Father Seeley. Made out lists for Nauvoo and Independence orders. Spent the forenoon and until 4:00 p.m. writing. See above.

Mail carrier did not bring my camera etc. At 7:00 p.m., started for Far West on foot. Liveryman wished $1.50 for rig. It was dark or almost when I reached the poor farm. Mrs. Batson said could give me bed and asked me to have supper. I told her had supper with Father Seeley. When they lived between Hamilton and Kingston, Elders Allgood and Rieser had stopped with them. I thanked them for kindness and said would leave early in morning. Wished me to stay for breakfast.

*May 19, 1907, Sunday, Far West, Kingston, Kerr Farm [p. 54]*

Rose about 5:00 a.m. or little before. Mr. Batson's son fast asleep. Soon on the road to Kerr [house]. After crossing Shoal Creek, found gentleman in the fields who said I was going the wrong way to Whitmers. Turned round. Very lucky to find anyone around so early in the morning. I remembered crossing the bridge when I went to Kingston and that I came out of timber to left of bridge.

Soon at Kerr [house]. Found them separating milk. Invited me to go to house and have breakfast, which I enjoyed very much after the walk. [blank] Mrs. Kerr's son, Mr. Johnson, asked me many ques-

tions about Utah crops. I showed him the views. Found Mr. [Christopher] Kerr a pleasant old gentleman; not much to say. Mr. and Mrs. Whitmer made me welcome. Shaved and at the Reorganized Sunday School. A Mr. Friend acting as superintendent. Mr. Swenson invited me to join a class. Four classes and must have been about forty present. See picture.

I suggested that a picture be made, and all grouped on the north side of the building after school.

Worship at 11:00 a.m. Two visiting elders present, Hedrick and Charles P. Faul of Stewartsville, Missouri. Mr. Hedrick the speaker. [**p. 55**]

Dinner at Whitmers'. Mr. Johnson and William Alonzie Troupe took me to Kingston. Five pair of grey mules. Stopped at poor farm and made a view. Kingston—negative of John Whitmer's tombstone. After talking to Father Seeley, decided to go back to Far West and from there to Cameron, [Clinton County], and then on to Gallatin,[194] [Daviess County], and reached Haun's Mill via Chillicothe, [Livingston County], and Breckenridge, [Caldwell County]. So back to Far West. Supper at Mr. Kerr's. Spent some time showing them views and talking about Utah.

Attended services at Reorganized Church. Charles P. Faul (bishop, agent) spoke. Subject: "Man." Made arrangements with him after meeting to take my instruments etc. to Cameron. Bed about 11:00 p.m.

*May 20, 1907, Monday, Far West, Cameron [p. 55]*

Rose soon after 5:00 a.m. Bid good-bye to Whitmers, folks, and ask the Lord to bless them. At Swensons and found William A. Troupe ready to start.

Mr. Swenson ask me to take breakfast. I did. Told him that Mrs. Whitmer wished me to eat there. Stopped at Mr. Swenson's and put the instrument in

---

194. County seat of Daviess County, located near the Grand River southeast of Adam-ondi-Ahman. The 1838 Missouri conflict began at the "Election-day Fight" that erupted at Gallatin when the Latter-day Saints attempted to exercise their voting privilege on 6 August. Along with the Battle of Crooked River in October, the "Election-day Fight" stimulated Missouri Governor Boggs to issue the "Extermination Order" on 27 October 1838.

**RLDS Sunday School Group**, *Far West, Missouri, 19 May 1907, Anderson Collection, LDSCA. Members of the group gathered for the photograph on the north side of their recently dedicated building.*

**John Whitmer's Tombstone**, *Kingston City Cemetery, Kingston, Missouri, 19 May 1907, Anderson Collection, LDSCA. John Whitmer was among the earliest converts to Mormonism and was one of the Eight Witnesses to the Book of Mormon. He served as one of Joseph Smith's scribes and was appointed Church historian in 1831. His Church history record was entitled "The Book of John Whitmer," covering the years 1831–38. He also edited the Church newspaper,* Messenger and Advocate, *from 1835 through 1836. He left the LDS Church in 1838 and remained in Far West, Missouri, until his death in 1878.*

**"Poor Farm,"** *Kingston, Missouri, 19 May 1907, Anderson Collection, LDSCA. Two days before he took the photograph, Anderson said the farm consisted of a "frame, two-story house. Well painted, good barns and grounds."*

*T. B. Buzzard Home*, near Adam-ondi-Ahman, Daviess County, Missouri, 20 May 1907, Anderson Collection, LDSCA. Anderson notes in his diary, *"About one-half mile west of town, met Mr. T. B. Buzzard, who wished view of home and took me to Diahman in buggy."*

buggy; and soon after 6:30 a.m., we were again on the road to Cameron. Mr. Troupe a good, sociable companion, and I talked with him about smoking. Also about good companions. He is very anxious to go to Utah. I gave him several addresses.

Cameron about 9:00 a.m. Ten miles. Had to wait a little while until instruments etc. came. Found them at Bert's Store; and, with assistance of Mr. Troupe, soon at depot. [p. 56] Cameron a neat, thriving town. Largest I have seen since Richmond. 11:57 a.m., left for Gallatin. Fare, sixty-four cents. Reached soon after 1:00 p.m. Tried to find someone going to Adam-ondi-Ahman.[195] Livery wished $1.50, so concluded to walk

and carry instrument. About one-half mile west of town, met Mr. T. B. Buzzard, who wished view of home and took me to Diahman[196] in buggy. When we reached McDonald Ford, about four miles northwest of town, had trouble to get mare into Grand River.[197] Mule colt along. Mare never in water before. I got out and led her to water and petted her, and she soon went across. I called to leave my camera, as I could see the water had gone into buggy. Soon got me across and was very pleased to find that water had not reached plates, package of five-by-seven films.

Made negatives of Lyman Wight's house.[198] Also the old site of Adam-ondi-Ahman. Nothing

195. Located in Daviess County on the Grand River about twenty-five miles north of Far West. Originally settled by Latter-day Saints in 1838.

196. *Diahman* was a popular name for the Mormon settlement at Adam-ondi-Ahman during the late 1830s. Anderson is inconsistent in the spelling of *Diahman*. We have corrected his spelling throughout.

197. River rising near Creston, Union County, in south-central Iowa, flowing in a southerly direction into Missouri. The river merges with the Thompson River and Shoal, Medicine, and Locust Creeks near Chillicothe, Missouri, before joining the Missouri River.

198. One of the few buildings surviving in 1907 from the early Mormon period. Lyman Wight's (1796–1858) second cabin was located halfway down "Tower Hill."

***Lyman and Harriet Benton Wight Home***, *Daviess County, Missouri, 20 May 1907, Anderson Collection, LDSCA.*
*Anderson's photographs provide information on buildings that are no longer extant, thus freezing in time important Church history sites for future scholars to study and interpret. Now known as "Lyman Wight's Second Cabin," it was one of the few Mormon-period structures still standing in 1907. Meetings were held here during the last few weeks that the Saints lived in Adam-ondi-Ahman, although the home had not been completed at the time. Whether the Wights actually lived here is not known.*

***Lyman and Harriet Benton Wight Home**, Daviess County, Missouri, 20 May 1907, Anderson Collection, LDSCA. This is the second "cabin" built by Lyman Wight at Adam-ondi-Ahman. A Campbellite in Kirtland, Ohio, Lyman Wight quickly converted to Mormonism in 1830. He was among the Saints driven from Jackson County, Missouri, in 1833. He was called as a member of the high council in Clay County, Missouri, in 1834. Later, he was imprisoned with Joseph Smith at Liberty, Missouri, in 1838–39. Lyman was called as a member of the Council of the Twelve Apostles in 1841. Following Joseph Smith's death, Lyman moved to Texas and eventually left the LDS Church in 1848.*

now left to mark the place but excavations and foundations. Here Mr. Cravens[199] had a son killed by lightning.

The town was on the western slope of a ridge that lies northwest of Lyman Wight's home and Adam's altar.[200] At the end of this ridge stands the fine house of Charles Ferat and his corrals, feed pens, etc. Quite a hole has been dug under a large tree in the hill east of Lyman Wight's house, and the people of Gallatin and vicinity say it is Adam's grave[201] [as reported in] the *Democrat*, published at Gallatin, in their Christmas edition of 1905.

---

199. Anderson inconsistently spells this name *Craven* and *Cravens*. We have used *Cravens* throughout.

200. Tradition indicated that an altar made by Adam could still be seen on the top of "Tower Hill."

201. Reflecting this local non-Mormon tradition, the Missouri State Historical Society and the Highway Commission placed a marker at the county courthouse square in Gallatin in 1953 that reads in part, "At this place, also known as 'Adam's grave,' [Joseph] Smith announced the discovery of the altar, on a nearby hill, where he said, 'These ancients worshipped.'"

**The Valley of Adam-ondi-Ahman**, *Adam-ondi-Ahman, Daviess County, Missouri, 20 May 1907, Anderson Collection, LDSCA. The view is from "Tower Hill." Daviess County was organized in 1836 with Gallatin designated as the county seat in 1837. Only a few Latter-day Saints lived in the county in 1836, but a large number of Mormons settled in the area during the next two years. In February 1838, Lyman Wight built a cabin in what would shortly become Adam-ondi-Ahman. Diahman, as it was popularly called, grew to four hundred people with another six hundred Latter-day Saints scattered throughout Daviess County. Most of the Saints settled on land under "preemption rights," which meant that the government had not yet made the land available for purchase. The mobs who drove the Mormons from their lands in October and early November 1838 knew that within days the U. S. government would offer the land for sale. With the Latter-day Saints gone, local mob members and other non-Mormons purchased the improved lands and reaped the benefits of the labor of the Saints.*

*May 21, 1907, Tuesday, Gallatin [p. 59]*

Cold this morning. I rose about 5:30 a.m. Foot bath. Went direct to depot but could not get my camera etc. until about 7:00 a.m. when agent came. Then, I went direct to Mr. Cravens's and got information, as on pages 57 and 58 and 59. I intended to go across river and get another view, but dull and cloudy and no eight-by-ten [p. 60] plates. Returned to town carrying instrument. Mr. Schultz, photographer, allowed me to change plates in his darkroom. Also sold me some eight-by-ten plates. [p. 57]

E. Holmes Cravens was born in Diahman, and the house he was born in was moved and set in the west of the Lyman Wight house.

The old Lyman Wight house and land was deeded

to Sarah A. McDonald and children by her father, John Cravens.[202] He came to Adam-ondi-Ahman in 1837.

Charles Ferat married Julia McDonald, daughter of Sarah A. McDonald.[203] Has a nice farm home, about eight or nine rooms, but has moved to Jameson, [Daviess County], for better school facilities. Is fattening stock and hogs there. Has about 192 or 200. John Cravens has about one hundred acres, and his son, John, lives there in a new frame house north of the Wight house. [**p. 58**]

Dr. John Cravens had a store there in 1838 and 1840, in Diahman. Also, Benjamin Kimball Clendersen was last man to run store in Diahman. He thought this was best location for the county seat. The center of the county was near here; and [because of] the lay of the country, less bridges, roads, etc., would have to be built. Geographically, this was where the county seat should be. And so he contended for years—but lost in favor of Gallatin.

North and South Methodists divided in 1844. Bishop had many slaves and wished him to free them. He said he did not own a slave. They belonged to his wife; and she could do as she pleased about it.

Mr. E. Holmes Cravens was for 1840 too young to know what caused the trouble between the Mormons and other settlers but understood from the talk that it was because the Mormons did not treat [**p. 59**] their neighbors fair and wished to have this country for themselves.

Mr. Cravens has six children. Lives just a little northwest of Gallatin.

Upland is selling for $75 per acre. Bottomland worth $100 per acre.

A neighbor (old lady) of Mrs. Cravens, when she heard I was from Utah, said that the Mormons when here would steal cows and horses etc. and that is what caused trouble. A Mormon went to one of his Gentile[204] neighbors and told him he had revelation from the Lord that the cow belonged to him. The neighbor said he had seen the Lord since and He told him the cow belonged to him and to keep the old [—].

At 11:00 a.m., the cornerstone of the courthouse was laid by ex-Governor Dockery.[205] I made several pictures of building on northeast corner of it. Crowd and procession. Hundreds of buggies and people came in from the surrounding towns. The railroads brought many. [**p. 60**]

Two Gallatin men assisted me in carrying goods to Wabash Depot. Left there about 5:00 p.m. for Chillicothe. There about 6:00 p.m. Tried to find place to change plates. Three photographers, but all closed. Watton, Haufman, names of two. Found supper and bed at Mr. Myers's, two or three blocks north of depot.

Breakfast this morning: two glasses buttermilk. Dinner: bowl soup and crackers and piece of pie. A good supper at Myers. Wrote some in journal and to bed before 9:00 p.m.

---

202. John Cravens purchased most of the central area of Adam-ondi-Ahman and renamed it Cravensville. The renamed town existed for thirty-two years and had enough residents to vie with Gallatin for the county seat of Daviess County, but the land was eventually returned to farming and grazing after 1872.

203. Sarah A. McDonald may be the daughter of Absalom McDonald, who had escorted Stevenson, Jenson, and Black to various sites in 1888.

204. Usually referring to a person of a non-Jewish nation or non-Jewish faith, but in this context, a *Gentile* is a non-Mormon.

205. Alexander M. Dockery (1845–1926), a resident of Daviess County, served as Missouri's governor from 1900 to 1904.

***Daviess County Courthouse Cornerstone-Laying Ceremony***, *Gallatin, Missouri, 21 May 1907, Anderson Collection, LDSCA. Gallatin is the county seat of Daviess County. This view is an example of Anderson's efforts to help finance his mission by taking photographs of places or events that might interest non-Mormons who he hoped would buy his photographs.*

***Cornerstone of Daviess County's New Courthouse***, *Gallatin, Missouri, 21 May 1907, Anderson Collection, LDSCA.*

## May 22, 1907, Wednesday, Chillicothe, Breckenridge [p. 61][206]

I rose soon after 5:00 a.m. and at the depot. Left for Breckenridge at 6:50 a.m. Arrived there before 8:00 a.m. By inquiry, soon found Mr. All Guffy (who had brought a number of hogs to the stockyards). I rode with him to point one-half mile from Marshall's Mill and the county bridge, or Craig's Bridge. Haun's Mill,[207] or site of old "Mormontown," is about one-half mile west of bridge. [p. 63]

Craig's Bridge is two and one-fourth [miles] west and six miles south of Breckenridge, and Braymer, [Caldwell County], is eight miles, little south of east of the bridge. Milwaukee and St. Paul Railroad runs through Braymer.

Albert Kromeich said, "John Wells went to blacksmith shop to get work. Could not do it because had no coal. Would do it in the morning, and when he got there, had coal in sack and water was dripping from the sack."

Also, "Mitchell Gray said that one of the Mormons stood up on a big post near the mill and said they could not kill him with powder and lead. And one of men said, 'I'll show him whether powder and lead can reach him,' and he picked him off."

[Albert Kromeich] said, "The report when he came here was that the Mormons would not work but would go to their neighbors' cribs and take the corn etc., and that's what caused the trouble. Gudgill moved and took possession of one of the old Mormon houses, and it was set on fire and left a bad scar on leg of one of the men. Burnt and woke them up in the night, and they thought the Mormons had come back and set the fire."

I suggested [p. 64] that it was a long way for a Mormon to come back and do the job and that the experience of a few weeks past would make them hesitate about visiting Haun's Mill even if it was in the night.

Aunt Mary McLallen: "A lady came to visit the place. Mrs. Alice McRae went with her. The lady knew where the well was and was parting the brush and thick undergrowth to get to the well when Mrs. McRae said, 'That's where those hateful Mormons are buried.' The lady said, 'Yes, that's where my poor boy is laid.' Mrs. McRae told her friends or neighbors then she felt so hurt the way she had spoke and would not have said it for anything if she had known.[208] This lady came here every year for awhile to see the well. Think her name was Alice M. Smith.[209] She finally quit coming, and do not know what became of her."[210] [p. 62]

John B. White's folks used to own the site. Laf B. White is the one who sold it. Sold to Gascanue. Forty acres in this piece. The Whites removed the locust trees, the millstone, etc. Ike White's forty—Elmer Parker bought from the Whites and still owns and paid north of the forty that Haun's Mill was on.

George M. McLallen, Route 6, Braymer, Caldwell County, and wife and mother, Nancy Jane McLallen. Dinner and many interesting notes.

---

206. Anderson made his entry for 22 May on several pages—but not in sequential order. We have attempted to sequence the material in chronological order as suggested by Anderson.

207. Originally founded by Jacob Haun in 1834, the Mormon settlement of Haun's Mill on Shoal Creek, located on the eastern edge of Caldwell County, bordering Livingston County, about sixteen miles east of Far West. Haun's Mill was attacked by a renegade Missouri militia unit on 30 October 1838, which killed eighteen and wounded another thirteen.

208. We have moved two separate Anderson entries to place them in proper chronological order.

209. Mrs. McRae is probably referring to Amanda Barnes Smith (1809–86), who lost her ten-year-old son, Sardius Washington Smith (1828–38), as well as her husband, Warren Smith (1794–1838), during the massacre. These are the only two people with the name of Smith who were killed. Mrs. McRae probably inaccurately recalls that Mrs. Smith returned every year for a period of time. More than likely, she came back several times before the Latter-day Saint exodus in 1838–39.

210. The material in this paragraph is a merger of two paragraphs that Anderson wrote on page 64. He crossed out most of the material in one paragraph, but some of the crossed-out material seems necessary for the reader to understand the story here.

**John B. McLallen**, *Breckenridge, Missouri, 22 May 1907, Anderson Collection, BYU. McLallen's home was a favorite stopping place for LDS missionaries. Identification of this photograph was discovered through the writing on the back of the original glass negative. In addition to McLallen's name, "Breckenridge RFD #1" was included (see p. xix). In all likelihood, Anderson intended to make a print from his negative at a later date and send a copy to McLallen to thank him for his hospitality.*

After hiving a swarm of bees, George McLallen accompanied me to the site of Haun's Mill. There only three pieces of or logs of the old dam in the creek. Made a negative of this showing the location of dam by two boys at each side of the stream. Can get a fair view of location of the mill, blacksmith shop, etc. from a bare hill on the south of creek and west of the mill. The exact location of the well cannot be made, as the ground has been plowed and farmed. Two of the McLallen boys agree on [blank]. [**p. 60**]

Mrs. George B. McLallen assisted me all afternoon, and we found location for view of the site of mill, dam, creek, etc.; but too late to make it, and we need an axe to cut away the trees, brush, etc.

He took me to his uncle's, John B. McLallen and Mary B. McLallen. They made me welcome and invited me to stay. Said all the Mormons stayed with them, and they were welcome at any time. George B. McLallen telephoned to Braymer for some eight by ten plates, and the photographer said would send over in the morning. George said to use [**p. 61**] my own pleasure; I could stay here or go with him. I concluded to stop at Uncle "John's."

Supper with their son, James E. McLallen. Found a number of the elders had stopped here. John Aylett[211] and Sylvester H. Cox put up the room [in which] we ate supper. Names of others who assisted: Elders Jensen and Bert Egbert and Thomas Chambers. They cut the timber. Mr. McLallen hauled logs to mill. Done about seventy-two hours work. Eight have had lunch at one time. "Long Mike" name given one of elders by Uncle John.

Told me of times the elders had helped in the hay, clearing brush, etc. "They were not afraid of work. Never found one that would not work. Many hours in the evening was spent in singing. They was the best songs I ever heard." [**p. 64**]

Elders Lyons, Ingrams, Pace, Jessie, Moses, "Long Mike's" name was Matheson, Elder Nalder, Elder Howard, Elder Duffin. Picked cherries, berries, etc.

## May 23, 1907, Thursday, Haun's Mill [p. 68]

Rose about 5:00 a.m. Not feeling very well. Breakfast with Aunt Mary B. McLallen. At Parker's and White's to get permission to cut out trees etc. that would obstruct view. Also at Mr. Lane's. All over the ground on south side of creek but could not find better place for view than selected yesterday. Took George M. McLallen along [**p. 69**] the south side creek. Mail carrier brought plates: sixty cents, plates, ten cents for mailman. Dinner at George M. McLallen's.

After dinner, started for Haun's Mill. Bowels troubling me. Very warm, and it was an effort for me to work. James E. McLallen, Ed, met me and with axe he brought soon cleared off the trees that obstructed the view of mill, creek, etc. This view we made from the south side of the creek and looking northeast [blank]. Crossed the creek and located one of the old millstones, which we worked out of the ground and down to the edge of the creek and made two or three negatives of it, putting an inscription on one side.[212] Mr. H. Elmer Parker [and] Levi Nichols furnished paint and brush. The other stone have not been able to find. Was used for a step at one of the houses for a number of years. Changed plates in Mr. H. E. Parker's cellar. Also invited me to eat with them.

Made a general view of site of Haun's Mill site [**p. 70**] from the north looking southwest, showing bluffs and timbers on south side of creek, and it was from this direction and likely at this point when the mob came out of the timber. When they attacked the settlement, a heavy growth of timber was here. Also the road out of the south [?] I am told. The company (mob militia) came from a place call Mooresville, [Livingston County], east of Breckenridge.

---

211. John Argent Aylett (1868–1947) served in the Northern States Mission 1888–1900, laboring primarily in Missouri. Apparently, Anderson is reflecting about missionaries who had been there several years earlier.

212. Anderson made at least three separate negatives of this particular millstone. They are numbered 49, 49A, and 49B. Images 49 and 49A are slightly different views of the stone, with the painted side facing Anderson. The final image, 49B, appears to be the same stone except it has been turned around to the reverse side.

**Haun's Mill Site**, *Caldwell County, Missouri, 23 May 1907, Anderson Collection, LDSCA. Anderson notes in his diary, "Made a general view of site of Haun's Mill site from the north looking southwest, showing bluffs and timbers on south side of creek." For two weeks, a company of militia troops from Livingston County had harassed the Mormons located on Shoal Creek, driving off their livestock and demanding that the Saints leave their homes. Two hundred to 250 troops from Livingston, Daviess, and Carroll Counties eventually attacked the settlement on Tuesday afternoon, 30 October 1838.*

*Millstone at Haun's Mill*, *Caldwell County, Missouri, 23 May 1907, Anderson Collection, LDSCA. Anderson painted an inscription on one side of the stone. Note Anderson's identification number, 49, in the left-hand corner. His diary mentions that he took several images. Nos. 49A and 49B have also been identified. The picture shows a good example of the reverse writing on the negative: "#1 Haun's Mill, May 23, 1907, 2¼ miles west, 6 miles south of Breckenridge and [—] Braymer 8 miles."*

*Millstone at Haun's Mill*, *Caldwell County, Missouri, 23 May 1907, Anderson Collection, LDSCA. This view of the millstone is identified by Anderson as 49B. Apparently, the stone has been turned around to show the reverse side without the writing.*

After getting this view, went to Uncle John B. McLallen's, but I felt so poorly I found it quite an effort. Ate a bite but felt worse and so miserable I could not take any part in the conversation. Several called. Weak under the knees, back, and chilled at times; then hot and feverish—good deal like a person feels who is coming down with the grippe.[213] It was an effort for me to do anything this afternoon.

## May 24, 1907, Friday, Haun's Mill [p. 67]

I spent a miserable night tossing and rolling about—fever and wild dreams. Up a number of times. I did not eat breakfast or dinner. A few blackberries for supper, hot water. Bowels kept me moving often during the day. Slept a good deal of the time. Did not think it wise to try to go, for I felt weak.

In the afternoon, had chat with J. R. (Dick) Lane.[214] [p. 65] J. R. Lane has been here since nine days after the battle [1838]. [p. 63] J. R. Lane says the well was a little farther south and east than the location given. Said it could not be given exactly. [p. 65]

What he told George E. Anderson: "Jacob Gudgill run the mill. Bought it, was my understanding. After Jacob Gudgill died, it fell into his son's hands, John T. Gudgill. Then it went into Spencer Gregory's. It remained in his hands until it went down and did not amount to anything."

Charles R. Ross[215] never owned the mill but just leased it. Spencer Gregory was a rich man; also Gudgill.

One of those killed was not put in the well. His name was Lewis.[216] He was on the fence and thought he was out of reach away on the side hill. Rockholt had a long-range rifle and said he could make him get off that fence. He shot him through the shoulder, and he died the same night and was buried on his brother's farm (David Lewis)[217] on the south side of the creek and about twenty steps from where Frank White now lives. Later, his bones, at the suggestion of the county court, was removed to the cemetery. When the bones were taken up, there was a hole in the shoulder blade that you could put your thumb through. Was buried with clothes on for we found bull[.]. Been there two years when father took him up. [p. 66]

The well where the bodies was put in was from fifteen to eighteen feet. Just digging. It was never walled up. There was about three feet of dirt on the bodies. The next spring, there was a bad smell came from the well, and the neighbors filled the well full. In time, it settled and you could plainly see where the well was.

One woman wounded in the battle. She was hid behind a saw log, and her hand showed, and someone put a bullet through it.[218]

This place is for sale cheap. James L. McLallen owned it; then J. C. McRae; then to Spencer Gregory; then John B. McLallen; and from him to Laf B. White. White to [blank].

John Schooler, his wife's uncle, said he was in this battle; and the first forty acres of land he owned he bought with the money the state paid him for services. Told Mr. Lane this: "The Mormons would gather in

213. Anderson used the word *grip*, which we assume means *grippe*—an acute febrile contagious virus disease identical to or resembling influenza.

214. The material that follows has been rearranged, according to Anderson's instructions, to place it in chronological order.

215. Ross was a member of the company that attacked Haun's Mill. In February 1839, he moved into a house that occupied the property where the bodies had been placed in the well following the massacre. Ross is the one who filled in the well because of the offensive smell.

216. This entry is probably referring to Benjamin Lewis (1803–38), who was among the casualties. Lewis was married and was the father of six children. His brother, Tarlton Lewis (1805–90), was also wounded in the attack and was responsible for burying his brother in a shallow grave.

217. David Lewis (1814–55).

218. This entry is probably referring to Mary Stedwell, who was shot through the hand while trying to escape.

***Haun's Mill****, Caldwell County, Missouri, 23 May 1907, Anderson Collection, LDSCA. Seventeen Latter-day Saints and one friendly non-Mormon were killed at Haun's Mill during the attack on 30 October 1838. Another thirteen Mormons were wounded, including one woman and a seven-year-old boy. No Missouri militiamen were killed, though three were wounded. Among those brutally murdered was seventy-eight-year-old Thomas McBride, who surrendered his musket to militiaman Jacob Rogers, who shot him and then hacked his body with a corn cutter. William Reynolds, another militiaman, found ten-year-old Sardius Smith trembling with fear under the bellows in the blacksmith shop. Reynolds summarily executed him and bragged afterward, "Nits will make lice, and if he had lived he would have become a Mormon." Because the attack was unprovoked in a time of truce between the local Latter-day Saint community of Haun's Mill and their Missouri neighbors, had no specific authorization, and was made by a vastly superior force with unusual brutality, the attack has come to be known as the "Haun's Mill Massacre" in Latter-day Saint history.*

***H. Elmer Parker Home,***
*Caldwell County,
Missouri, 25 May
1907, Anderson
Collection, LDSCA.
Anderson notes in his
diary, "Made a view at
H. Elmer Parker's. Took
them some time to decide."*

bodies of twelve or fifteen, and if a neighbor had a fine horse, cow, or something they wished, they would go and say the Lord told them to take it."

"John B. Woodbury run under the bank of the creek and got away. Just as he dropped under the bank, the bullets whistled around. Lived here thirty or forty years." [p. 67]

"Uncle Dick Lane was about six years old (born in 1832). His father, C. R. Ross, with his father-in-law, four teams in all, came in nine days after the battle—from Tennessee. Has been constable for forty years and justice of peace four years. You can ask my neighbors as to my standing regarding truth."

Took hot water, also a bath, and felt some better. The sleep and rest done me good. A heavy rain in the afternoon and evening. Dr. John F. Mackey [p. 68] (his father's name is James G. Mackey[219] and has always been a friend to the Mormons).

The doctor called to see Uncle John B. McLallen and examined him. Said he had heart and liver trouble and that is what caused dropsy.[220] That he could help him. Uncle John is pretty sick man. Could see that the night I came. Reminds me of the trouble Father had.[221] In the evening, I told boy and girls the story of Abdel Caleb. Bed about 10:00 p.m. I can tell I am some better.

---

219. James G. Mackey escorted Edward Stevenson, Andrew Jenson, and Joseph S. Black in 1888 to the Haun's Mill site. During this visit, the four men found the old millstone that had been placed there the previous year by Mr. Fuller, a son of Josiah Fuller, one of the men killed in the massacre. Fuller had been assisted by Charles R. Ross, who knew the approximate location of the well because he added fill dirt to it after moving to the site in February 1839. Prior to Fuller and Ross moving the stone to the well site, it had been lying near the actual mill site.

220. Edema, an abnormal, excess accumulation of serous fluid in connective tissue or in a serous cavity.

221. George Anderson (1837–1906), Anderson's father, had died on 9 April 1906.

## May 25, 1907, Saturday, Haun's Mill [p. 71]

Rose before 5:00 a.m. Feel some better. The tablet I took acting. Do not pass much, but distress is very keen. Can see that it would not done for me to try to go to Breckenridge yesterday. I would not have got there.

An egg and some rice tasted very good this morning. Spent until about 9:30 a.m. writing up diary.

Will be glad when I can get where I can get a change of clothes. These are sour. Very much kindness has been shown to me by these people.

Hot water, milk and sugar, and some peaches and rice—all I felt I could eat at noon.

Blessed Brother McLallen at his request. He said would like me to bless him before I left. I also told him he should be baptized. Had been baptized into Baptist Church. Did not think it was necessary for him to be baptized again. I said it was most assuredly that he should receive that ordinance from someone holding authority. He was an old man. Had heard the gospel and should not neglect to have this done before he was called to the other side. John Aylett had told him he would be baptized for his father who was dead and would be baptized for him when he died.[222] I told him no. He had a chance to receive the gospel here and should do so.

Bid them all good-bye, and Ed McLallen helped me to next neighbor, H. E. Parker. [p. 72]

Made a view at H. Elmer Parker's. Took them some time to decide. Change of plates in their cellar. On to Marshall's Mill. Tried to find a shot to get a view of mill and bridge and creek, but could not find one. George McLallen assisted me. About 5:15 p.m., left and went to Mr. Blair's on the road to Breckenridge. Concluded not to leave Breckenridge tonight as could do nothing there until I get in to post office.

I rode with Mr. Odell as far as Mr. Willard F. Blair's, who had left word that he wished me to stop at Braymer, and I waited until he came. Also visited his neighbor, Chapman, but he did not have time to look at the pictures. Daughters of Mr. Blair invited me to supper, which I enjoyed. Found me a bed with the hired boy. Mrs. Blair thought I would have to sleep in a chair. I would have readily done it or gone on if I had felt well.

## May 26, 1907, Sunday, Haun's Mill [p. 72]

Rose before 5:00 a.m. Slept very well—much better than the previous nights. Still troubled with my bowels. Only passed a bloody fluid, and pain at rectum almost constantly.

A [blank] Willard F. Blair. A beautiful view of Haun's Mill country from here. Mr. Blair's and Chapman's home on a rise which extends more or less rolling to Breckenridge. From Blair's and Chapman's, a level tract or bottom to Shoal Creek about one and one-half miles or two miles. Then, on the south side, the bluffs or hill rise mostly covered with timber here and there. Shots cleared and [p. 73] left Mr. Willard F. Blair about 7:00 a.m. A breakfast: graham bread, eggs and oatmeal, and prunes. Satisfied. Ever I come this way again, stop, give the country a good name, and could always find something to eat and lodging with him.

Carried the instrument about mile when Mr. Gooley overtook me and a ride of two miles on a surrey was very acceptable, for when on my feet, I am in distress. Mr. Gooley had visited Utah and the West. Went into Breckenridge the same way I came out and had a look for my knife. Could not find it, but found a gentleman who said the other millstone was at Mar-

222. Latter-day Saints believe that baptism, together with the laying on of hands for the gift of the Holy Ghost, is essential to salvation, but that these ordinances must be performed by the proper priesthood authority. Salvation of family members and friends who have died without an opportunity to accept the restored gospel or be baptized by someone holding the priesthood can benefit from an ordinance called baptism for the dead. Joseph Smith revealed the doctrine of "baptism for the dead" in August 1840. At first, LDS Church members began to perform proxy baptisms in the Mississippi River at Nauvoo, Illinois. When the Nauvoo Temple was partially finished, this ordinance was performed in a wooden baptismal font (later it was replaced by a stone font) in the basement of the building. In 1907 the ordinance was performed in LDS temples in Utah (St. George, Logan, Manti, and Salt Lake City).

**Potter's Slough**, *near Montrose, Lee County, Iowa, 29 May 1907, Anderson Collection, LDSCA. To find this location, Anderson consulted with local residents and also "had an atlas, which gave me some ideas as to location." The man in the skiff may be Fred B. Horton, who took Anderson to the site.*

**Potter's Slough**, *near Montrose, Lee County, Iowa, 29 May 1907, Anderson Collection, LDSCA. Anderson gave his guide a photograph "for his labor." Potter's Slough is the traditional site of the "miracle of the quail," which helped sustain about 640 destitute Latter-day Saints who camped near the Mississippi River in October 1846 after they had been forced from their homes in Nauvoo.*

shall's Mill. He also had me make a view of gristmill.

Depot 10:21 a.m. and at Chillicothe 10:51 a.m. Found mail and permit and left at 11:59 a.m. Changing cars at Palmyra Junction, 2:55 p.m. Quincy, [Illinois], 3:30 p.m., where we remained until 6:20 p.m. Fine waiting room. I took advantage of the rocking chair, for I was in distress when I moved about. No spitting allowed upon the floors, sidewalks, halls, etc.

Turned cold. Reached Montrose, [Iowa], about 8:00 p.m. No skiff from Nauvoo, so I was soon hunting a room. Feel much better when I sit. Found a room at restaurant, one [block] south, one [block] west of depot. Returned soon after 9:00 p.m.

## May 27, 1907, Monday, Montrose [p. 74]

Rested much better than the previous nights. Rose about 4:30 a.m. Better with my bowels. Distress not so severe and lingering [?]. Cold. Fixed up negatives, plates, etc. and went to Keokuk. Did not take breakfast. Separated clothes for washing. A long talk with Mr. Ineles about water filters, also shaft holders. Peculiar man. Said could sell his patents to moneyed men but would not do it. If I could get him a good man in Utah to handle his filter or shaft holder, would see that I did not lose anything. Gave me $1 to write and push the matter.

Keokuk before 2:00 p.m. Mr. Anschutz arranged for me to develop about 5:00 p.m. Developed all the negatives and washed, by 6:45 p.m., thirty; last two eight-by-ten.

Started a letter to Eva today. Received one from Olive. Lowry broke his arm. Bed about 9:15 p.m. Bed at house one-half [block] east, first [block] north of depot.

## May 28, 1907, Tuesday, Keokuk [p. 75]

Rose about 5:00 a.m. Rested very well. My bowels are improving. Small movement, first since Saturday. Not so much distress. Two boiled eggs and bread and butter for breakfast.

Named negatives. Some not dry. Packed so could be shipped if necessary. Mr. H. M. Anschutz very kind. Offered to loan me his telescope lens.[223] Reading up Mormon history last night in *Encyclopedia Britannica.*[224] Young lady belonging to the Reorganized Church he found working at his home. H. M. Anschutz, 19 North Fourth Street, phone—studio, 209, residence, 284.

Negatives ready by 2:00 p.m., but Mr. Anschutz not back from dinner, so will not get to Montrose until evening. Lunch on cookies and fruit cake that I once [?] put up. Also prunes.

Out to see Thomas Howell, 1407 Timea Street. A few moments chat with him. He had not heard of the elders. All the hands at Mr. Anschutz's interested, ladies and all. I left a *Deseret News* with them. Mr. Anschutz made no charge for developing and furnished me six eight-by-ten plates, one five-by-seven. Wishes me to [**p. 76**] make him a view of Nauvoo. Left Keokuk for Montrose, 7:40 p.m. Could not find elders there but found ticket to Chicago. Bed about 9:30 p.m. A talk with Mr. Noles.

## May 29, 1907, Wednesday, Montrose, Nauvoo, Potter's Slough [p. 76]

Rose soon after 5:00 a.m. Very pleased to find my bowels act natural. A chat with the restaurant man.

---

223. Most cameras had a normal focal lens that replicated "human vision." A longer focal length had a magnifying quality similar to that of a telescope.

224. Anderson may have been reading the *Encyclopedia Britannica: A Dictionary of Arts, Sciences and General Literature* (New York: Charles Scribner's Sons, 1904), 16:825–28. The article describes Joseph Smith's parents as "a poor, ignorant, thriftless, and not too honest couple." It also asserts that the Book of Mormon "in reality was written in 1812 as a historical romance by one Solomon Spaulding, a crack-brained preacher."

**Brigham and Mary Ann Angell Young Home**, *Nauvoo, Illinois, May 1907, Anderson Collection, LDSCA. A recently identified Anderson photograph shows the Young home as it appeared in 1907 after a second story had been added to the west wing. Following the death of Joseph Smith in June 1844, President Young's residence became the center of Church activity and business. Whether the enormous investment of human and financial resources needed to complete the Nauvoo Temple with the probability of its eventual abandonment by the Saints was necessary was one of the major issues facing Church leaders. Brigham Young noted in his holograph diary under Friday, 24 January 1845, that Heber C. Kimball and Bishop Newel K. Whitney came to his house and participated in sacred ceremonies they had been taught by Joseph Smith. "We washed, anointed, and prayed. Had a good time. I inquired of the Lord whether we should stay here and finish the Templ[e]. The answer was we should."*

Will get out early and make a view of Potter's Slough.225

Breakfast: two boiled eggs, small dish oatmeal, bread and butter, and potatoes. Finished letter to Eva.

Fred B. Horton, who I found has been in Salt Lake, working on steam shovel—boiling, cooking clam shells just north of town. Said digging for clams could make about $2 per day. He thought he could gather a ton a week if he worked at it steady as at any other work. They get $19 a ton for the shells at the button factory and sometimes find a pearl which will bring them a good price. One found that brought $71 this spring. Cooking opens up the shell, and they examine the [—] [—] clam (before they throw it into the river) for pearl. Also for slugs or little pearls, which they get $2 an ounce for. Some of the diggers get as [.]as as $30 and $40 per month extra money for this besides the money for shells. [p. 77]

Clams look just like oysters side by side. It takes an expert to tell which is the oyster. The clams are

225. A *slough* is an inlet on a river, a place of deep mire or mud.

tough and cannot chew them. A number here who follow the business of digging clams out every day, windy or sunshine. Slow between here and islands.

Fishing brings good returns at present, as buffalo fish are six cents per pound, carp four cents. Three men landed about four this p.m. who (went out this morning) with three barrels of buffalo fish. Two hundred pounds fish to the barrel. That would mean $36 for the day's work. They put them on the train at once. Caught with seine.[226] They had a small skiff, which was propelled by gasoline engine,[227] and they towed along a small, flat-bottom boat. Heard them say they had been as far down the river as Keokuk. Astonished to see the speed at which the boats go propelled by these gas motors.

Four men putting new bottom in old boat or raft, which they propose to use to take wheat, corn, wood, etc. to market. That would hold about twelve cords wood, cotton, batten, asphalting paint, [—], tar, rope. [p. 78]

Carried my instrument to Mr. Hitchcock's between two and three miles northwest of Montrose, and from the upper window of his barn got a better idea of the location of the slough. Also had an atlas, which gave me some ideas as to location. At the suggestion of Mr. Bishop, stepson [?] of Mr. Hitchcock, I rode back to town with him; and Fred B. Horton got a skiff and took me to Potter's Slough, and I made two negatives. The west bank has been clear off to within about 150 yards of the mouth on the west side. Much the best way to go with a skiff. Quicker and can get around much faster.

If it had been a bright, sunshiny day, in one view you can see both banks, the mouth, the [blank], the place where the Saints camped,[228] the island in river (which has been formed since the Saints crossed in 1846, about one mile long, one-half wide, heavily timbered [—] a sandbar), and the cannery at Montrose. I think we may see it anyway. I also made a view looking the other way. We got back in time to catch the boat for Nauvoo, and he will take a view for his labor. Quails [blank]. Ford on to the islands. Two teams came across while we were working.

Left my instrument at Mrs. Gundy's and called at Mrs. Maud Ross's, who lives with her father, John Kendall. At Charles R. Pitt's and with them took supper at William Guilliman's and spent the evening. I told the story of Abdel Caleb. Their daughter Minnie played [p. 79] several selections on piano. Thirteen years old. Boy, Willie, ten years old. Mrs. Guilliman asked me if I had lodgings. Could stay with them. Sister Pitt said I better stay with them, so I did, as my satchel was there. We sang a number of Sunday School songs. I led in prayer, and we retired about 10:45 p.m.

## May 30, 1907, Thursday, Nauvoo [p. 79]

Rose about 5:00 a.m. Feel much better. Wrote up diary for yesterday. The [Deseret] Semiweekly News for May 27 was eagerly looked over. Told Father Pitt and son [Charles R. Pitt] and wife [Emma Evlin Davidson Pitt] of my experiences at Haun's Mill, the massacre, etc. Glanced over the *Liahona* for May 25. A beautiful view of the flat, river, Montrose Bluff Park, etc. is had from this home.

Wrote to my wife while I was waiting for my

---

226. A *seine* is a large net with sinkers on one edge and floats on the other. The seine hangs vertically in the water and is used to enclose fish when the seine's ends are pulled together or drawn ashore.

227. Experimental electric and internal-combustion engines were being tested and built on a limited basis. Apparently, Anderson is describing one of these early outboard motors. His "1907–1908 Address Book" indicates: "Wm. Galloway Co., Waterloo, Iowa, engines gasoline, etc., see catalog Farmers' supply." Ole Evinrude of Milwaukee, Wisconsin, who is recognized as one of the early developers of the outboard motor, produced his first gasoline-powered outboard engine in 1907. Evinrude would start to manufacture them commercially in 1909 under the Evinrude Motor Company name.

228. Following the final exodus from Nauvoo in September 1846, the Latter-day Saints on the Iowa shore were critically short of adequate supplies and shelter. As many as seven hundred were camped there when, on 9 October 1846, a flock of exhausted quail landed in camp. The Saints felt God had intervened to save their lives.

shoes to be mended. Wrote All Guffy at Marshall's Mill about knife. Sprinkling most of the afternoon. Nineteen years ago today, was married in the Manti Temple.[229] [p. 80]

John Pitt came to Nauvoo in November 1841. Boat came as far as Warsaw.[230] Could not get above rapids. Mother, Charlotte, and brother, James Pitt (carpenter), and grandmother, Mrs. Robert Pitt,[231] ninety-two years, came to see cornerstone laid.[232] Also his uncle, William Pitt[233] (who lived in Salt Lake), and others in spring of 1841.

When John reached here in November, the temple was up to the first round windows. In the spring of 1842, he was baptized for his health[234] in the font of the temple, which rested on the backs of twelve wooden oxen with brass horns, six on each side.[235] The walls was not very high.

Was baptized in England by Thomas Kington,[236] his uncle, when thirteen years old.

Wooden oxen was removed later and stone ones put in. [p. 82]

Neighbor boy, who was breaking up land with oxen, wished to go to Crooked Creek for grist, and John got his father's horses and went along. [p. 80] When the Prophet [Joseph Smith] and Patriarch [Hyrum Smith] were killed [27 June 1844], was at Brown's Mill on Crooked Creek north of Carthage for a grist. Was fishing at dam while waiting for grist when a man on white horse with long white hair, no hat on, rode swiftly by, his hair flying, crying, "The Mormons will be on you and kill every one of you. Joe Smith and his brother Hyrum have been killed in Carthage Jail." Was going to bring home hog with them but got scared and [p. 81] only brought the grist.

---

229. George and Olive were the second couple married or "sealed" in the recently dedicated LDS temple located in Manti, Sanpete County, Utah, in May 1888.

230. Located about fifteen miles south of Nauvoo. It was an important river community in the 1840s. The Anti-Mormon party in Hancock County was founded there by Thomas Sharp, the editor of the *Warsaw Signal*, in 1841. Men from the community were among those involved in the murder of Joseph and Hyrum Smith in 1844.

231. Hannah Hill Pitt, wife of Robert Pitt.

232. The Nauvoo Temple cornerstone was laid on 6 April 1841.

233. William Pitt (1813–73) started a brass band in Nauvoo and eventually immigrated to Utah.

234. Rebaptism was a common nineteenth-century practice among the Latter-day Saints. They were rebaptized for such reasons as to show rededication to the Church, to help with health problems, to prepare for a mission, or to join a united order. Also, Saints were sometimes rebaptized just before going into the temple to be married.

235. One of the main features of the Nauvoo Temple was a large white limestone laver resting on the backs and shoulders of twelve life-sized stone oxen in the basement of the structure. Water was supplied from a thirty-foot well located nearby in the temple basement. A temporary wooden structure built of pine timber was dedicated by Brigham Young on 8 November 1841. It rested on the backs of twelve wooden oxen, copied from a five-year-old steer. Later, it was replaced by the stone baptismal font before the Saints abandoned their temple and homes in 1846. While the font was used for several types of baptismal ordinances, the principal use of the baptismal font in the Nauvoo temple, however, was for the ordinance of baptism for the dead—a proxy baptism in behalf of dead friends and relatives who had not been baptized by Mormon priesthood authority.

236. Thomas Kington (1794–1874), husband of Hannah Pitt (1794–?), was the superintendent of a United Brethren circuit in Herefordshire, England, before being baptized into the LDS Church by Wilford Woodruff on 21 March 1840. This was the beginning of what is probably the most remarkable missionary success in the history of the LDS Church. By September nearly one thousand members lived in the area. Kington had established a branch of the Church in Dymock, his hometown, with fifty members, including members of the Pitt family.

***Chauncey and Eliza Jane Churchill Webb and Joseph and Jane Bicknell Young Homes**, Nauvoo, Illinois, May 1907, Anderson Collection, BYU. On the "flats" in Nauvoo, Illinois, these homes stood on the west side of Granger between Kimball and Parley Streets. The Webb home still stands today in Nauvoo.*

James Pitt, carpenter (brother of John), assisted in putting up the Prophet's store [Red Brick Store]. Reuben Hedlock[237] was the man he worked under. The house where Charles lives now was built by Mormons.

His father, Thomas Pitt, was a carpenter. Stayed and worked at his trade for some settlers who came in as the Mormons left. "Called themselves new citizens." They interceded for him with the mob. John still owns the old homestead of his father. Home still standing.

After the Saints were driven from Nauvoo, John went to McDonough County,[238] the town of McComb, county seat, and split rails at $1 a hundred. Only thing he could get cash for. Found some Mormons there by the name of Miller.

His brother, James, put some papers in the cornerstone of the temple. His mother told him of this. [p. 82] John Pitt was born in Dymock, Gloucestershire,[239] England, December 30, 1827.

---

237. Anderson spelled the name *Ruben Hadlock*. Reuben Hedlock (1801–?) was a carpenter and builder. He was appointed president of the elders quorum in Kirtland, Ohio, in 1837. He served a mission in England in 1840–41. In Nauvoo he prepared the engravings for the facsimiles in the Book of Abraham in 1842 and assisted in the construction of the Red Brick Store. He returned to England, where he presided over the LDS Church mission from 1843 to 1845.

238. McDonough County, Illinois, borders Hancock County on the east.

239. Anderson's diary reads "Dimock, Herefordshire," here. We have corrected the entry to read "Dymock, Gloucestershire." A village and parish in Newent District, Gloucestershire, Dymock stands on the Leadon River and is on the Hereford and Gloucester canal. Early Mormon missionary efforts in the Dymock area were very successful when Wilford Woodruff arrived in the region in the spring of 1840. Mary Pitt, possibly a relative of John Pitt, had been confined to her bed for six years and had not walked without crutches for eleven. She was healed by the administration of Brigham Young, Wilford Woodruff, and Willard Richards on 18 May 1841. Several people in the area were baptized during the day and a large group of Saints enjoyed a feast together.

***Heber Chase and Vilate Murray Kimball Home***, *Nauvoo, Illinois, May 1907, Anderson Collection, LDSCA. Restored by Dr. James LeRoy Kimball, a grandson of Heber C. and Vilate Murray Kimball, the building was dedicated on 3 July 1960 as the first of many restoration projects in "Old Mormon Nauvoo." In 1962, Dr. Kimball became the first president of Nauvoo Restoration, Inc. (NRI) and was charged with the mission "to acquire, restore, protect, and preserve, for the education and benefit of its members and the public, all or a part of the old city of Nauvoo." Since then, NRI has restored thirty-one structures. NRI and Restoration Trails Foundation (RLDS) have made Nauvoo one of the finest restorations of a mid-nineteenth-century town in America.*

Never belonged to any other church. Was baptized by Elder Carl Madsen of Riverton, Salt Lake County, Utah, Mississippi River, March 30, 1907.[240] Also, his son, Charles Robert Pitt, and wife, Emma E., baptized same date by Elder Christiansen.

Sang a number of songs. Ask me to lead in prayer. Retired about 10:15 p.m. I have felt much better all day. Think it was well that I rested.

## May 31, 1907, Friday, Nauvoo [p. 82]

Rose 5:00 a.m. and finished letter to my wife, All Guffy, Uncle John B. McLallen. [p. 83] Wrote to Lowry. Uptown with Father [John] Pitt and saw his property. Some fine homes.

Developed negatives of Potter's Slough and made negative of rocks of Nauvoo Temple.[241] Have been chipped up considerable by relic hunters. Found Elders Roberts and Madsen, and they were anxious to learn of my experiences in Missouri. Found my clean clothes. Bath at Kendall's. Gasoline on fire. Elder Roberts discovered it just in time. Would have been too late in few moments.

Dinner at Brother Nelson's. Holds the priesthood. Came from Canada. No children. Talked of going to South America with people who would form a "country of pure-minded people" that such a result had been talked off.

Elders Roberts and Madsen told me of visiting daughter of Phineas Young,[242] who was acquainted with the Prophet, Hyrum, Brigham Young. What she said of them.

Book of Mormon class at Sister Grimes's conducted by Elder Roberts. Young and old seem interested, and they had me tell of my experiences in Missouri.

Found Martha Marshall grubbing locust shoots on the lot where Emma Smith is buried. I cleaned some off, and Charles Pitt will put in part of the lot.

James Pitt assisted in putting in cornerstone,[243] also some papers in stone box.[244]

## June 1, 1907, Saturday, Nauvoo [p. 84]

Bed last night at Charles Pitt's about 10:30 p.m. Rose 5:00 a.m. Still cloudy, cold, and windy. Pitts put up a stove. Breakfast about 6:40 a.m.

John Pitt had an uncle, William Pitt, in Salt Lake City. Had two sons that worked in Oregon [.]ine. Visited them. See R. C. Pitt.[245]

Eliza Parsons, sister in England, has seven daughters, one son, Postern Cottage, St. Owens Street, Hereford. Daughters all married and families. Son, carpenter, also joined the army. Worked and bought his discharge and leave home, but went away again and never heard from him. See this sister and tell about Joseph Smith [?].

Edwin Olson,[246] 2707 Clark Street, Milwaukee—wrote postcard today. Elder John Alleman—wrote postal card. John Lowry Sr.—wrote to about shaft supporter, also about water filter. Also wrote to Olive.

---

240. The dates in the official Church record (31 March), the *Liahona* (29 March), and Anderson's diary (30 March) contradict each another.

241. Following the Saints' exodus in 1846, the Nauvoo Temple was gutted by an arsonist fire on 9 October 1848. Several walls were razed by a tornado on 27 May 1850. The wall was purposely leveled in 1865 to prevent an accident. Stones from the temple were used by people in the area as building material. A few symbolic stones (star, moon, and sun stones) survived.

242. Phineas Young (1799–1879), a brother of Brigham Young. He married Clarissa Hamilton and Lucy Cowdery. We cannot determine which daughter Anderson is referring to in his diary.

243. The Nauvoo Temple cornerstones were placed in position with impressive ceremonies during a Church general conference on 6 April 1841.

244. This sentence seems out of place but reflects the information Anderson gives on 30 May about the Pitt family's arrival in Nauvoo.

245. Robert Calvin Pitt (1849–1938), William Pitt's son.

246. Edwin Orlando Olson (1867–1928) was married to Dora Lowry (1869–1960), Olive Lowry Anderson's sister. Olson worked at George Edward Anderson's studio in Springville, Utah, and was at the time serving as a missionary in the Northern States Mission. Anderson visited him in Watertown, Wisconsin. See 8 July 1907 entry.

I intended to go to Chicago today but could not make picture of the City of Nauvoo. Assisted Charles Pitt to fix doubletrees,[247] swing, etc. Called on William Guilliman. Pitts' folks had two lady visitors come from Fort Madison, [Iowa], so I went and stayed with Elders Madsen and Roberts. Bed about 10:00 p.m. Before retiring, had quite a chat with elders about experiences in Missouri.

## June 2, 1907, Sunday, Nauvoo [p. 85]

Rose about 5:30 a.m. Fast day. Cold but clear. Suggested to the brethren that we take a walk and get warm. Walked to the boat landing on the north side of Nauvoo, then on to the hills. Beautiful view, fresh and green. Wild roses in bloom. Nauvoo is certainly a beautiful creation. Meadow, vineyards, blackberries, etc. Farmhouses to the water's edge. The Kimball property looks like an ideal farm.[248]

Sunday School at 8:15 a.m. Text after opening exercise was Mark 1:5, "And there went out to him all the land of Judea and they of Jerusalem and were all baptized of him in Jordan, confessing their sins." Lesson: "Events Preceding the Second Coming of the Savior."[249] I took part in the lesson, answering some questions. Elder Roberts asked me to tell a story. Told about Wasel Darrow having her eyes opened.

Home with Brother James Nelson after school. Fast meeting at request of Elder Madsen. Spoke to the Saints. Broke fast at Brother Grimes' about 4:00 p.m. Had a very good dinner—potatoes, corn, lettuce, bread, fruit, and cakes. [p. 86]

Evening service at 8:00 p.m. Elder Roberts ask me to speak on my experiences in Missouri and Book of Mormon. A good turnout and listened to with marked attention. Retired about 10:30 p.m. Bid most of the folks good-bye.

## June 3, 1907, Monday, Nauvoo, Chicago [p. 86]

Rose before 6:00 a.m. Breakfast at Kendalls with Elders Madsen and Roberts. Wrote to sister and mother, Mrs. M. A. Anderson,[250] No. 2 Oxford Flats [?], West North Temple.

Visited the block where the grove was located that the Prophet and Brigham Young gave some powerful discourses—fourth block east of the temple block.[251]

Dull and cloudy and could not get the view I wished of Nauvoo, so I sent lens telephoto with Elder Madsen.

Dinner at Mrs. Maud Ross's with the elders. Bid them good-bye, and Elder Madsen went across to Montrose and assisted me on the train, which I took at 2:27 p.m. We can see Nauvoo for some distance as we go up the river. Train late at Burlington, [Iowa], about forty minutes. A gentle rain commenced soon after [p. 87] we left Burlington. Car was beautifully lighted with electric lights. Reached Chicago[252] about 9:35 a.m. Madison Street car going west and was put off two blocks from 149 South Paulina Street. Elder Curtis up, and he called Elder John Alleman. A hearty handshake, as only given by elders and loved ones. Reading of mail, and found bed across the street at Mrs. Ware's. Retired about 11:00 p.m.

---

247. A crossbar over the tongue of a wagon to which two pivoted, horizontal crossbars, known as whiffletrees, are attached for harnessing two draft animals abreast.

248. In all likelihood, Anderson is referring to the Phineas Kimball (1780–?) and sons' family farm property, not the property of Heber C. Kimball (1801–68), an original member of the Quorum of the Twelve Apostles, chosen in 1835. Hiram M. Kimball (1806–63), the resident agent of the family, maintained property for his father, Phineas, and his brother Ethan. Eventually, Hiram joined the LDS Church and immigrated to Utah, but descendants of Phineas remained in Nauvoo until the 1960s.

249. Lesson 36, "Jesus the Christ to Return," *Sunday School Outlines, Theological Department First Year* (Salt Lake City: Deseret Sunday School Union, 1907), 42.

250. Mary Ann Thorn Anderson (1835–1928), Anderson's widowed mother.

251. The east grove was on the east side of Robinson Street between Mulholland and Knight Streets. Later identified as the Old Public Green.

252. County seat of Cook County, located in northeastern Illinois, on the southwestern tip of Lake Michigan.

## *June 4, 1907, Tuesday, Chicago [p. 87]*

Rose before 6:00 a.m. Bath. At mission house met Sister Ellsworth,253 president's wife, Sister Alleman, Ida and Laura Bennion, Sister Russell, Sister [blank], Danish sister, Brother Gustave Ed. Anderson, who left for Utah tonight. Brother [blank] Ramsey and wife and babe called during the day.

Unpacked trunk, valise, etc. today. Took the bottle of preserves to Sister Ellsworth, as I thought bottle was broke. It was not. [**p. 88**] Dinner at mission house at invitation of Sister Ellsworth. Also told me to make myself at home. Gave me the freedom of the place to finish pictures etc.

Haircut, depot for valise, etc. Walked down Madison Street. Ate for breakfast: graham loaf, bananas, and figs. Raining this morning. Found the brethren and sisters interested in the views and history of same. Evening at mission house looking up history around New York. Bed about 12:00 p.m.

## *June 5, 1907, Wednesday, Chicago [p. 88]*

Rose 6:15 a.m. Sun shining, beautiful day. Cars, drays,254 vehicles going night and day. Made a view of church this morning about 8:15 a.m. So much traffic that had to keep on the watch to get a clear view. Tried to show the street and mission house. Received letters from my wife, Stanley, also Brother John McLallen.

Wrote Olive this a.m. Naming and numbering [**p. 89**] negatives. Sorted them at mission house and spotting them out at Paltridge's, Madison Street, west of Paulina. Dinner at mission house, also breakfast.

Negative of elders who are laboring in Chicago and stopping in basement of church. Also Sister Ellsworth and elders and sisters who are at mission headquarters, which joins the church on the south. (President Ellsworth255 gone east with Apostle George A. Smith.)

**Group of LDS Central States Missionaries**, *Chicago, Illinois, probably 5 June 1907, Anderson Collection, LDSCA. The view shows a group of Chicago missionaries. Mission President German Ellsworth was successful in his efforts to strengthen the LDS Church's presence in Chicago and present a positive image of the Church. The publication of the Book of Mormon and an unofficial Church hymnal are some of the positive impacts of his tireless efforts.*

Church faces north on corner of [blank] and Paulina Streets.256 Mission headquarters fronts on Paulina Street. Elder John Alleman showed me through church. Excellent rooms for class within basement— several of which are occupied by elders who are laboring in Chicago. Fine pipe organ in auditorium proper. Seats all arranged in semicircle towards pulpit and slant towards the speaker, gallery. Dimensions [blank].

Called to see Sister Sorensen, but not at home.

253. Mary Rachel Smith Ellsworth (1876–1953).

254. A low, heavy cart without sides, used for haulage.

255. German Edgar Ellsworth (1871–1961) served as president of the Northern States Mission from 1904 to 1919.

256. The church, a building purchased from an evangelical Protestant group, was located at Paulina and West Monroe Streets.

Theater, five cents, moving pictures, [**p. 90**] songs etc. Lunch, ten cents. Walked back from Sister Sorensen's. I waited there about hour for her to return home. Sister Sorensen, 219 West Erie Street, third floor in the rear.

## June 6, 1907, Thursday, Chicago [p. 90]

Rose about 6:15 a.m. Bath, breakfast at mission house, spotting out and numbering negatives. Also developed two or three negatives. Quit about 4:00 p.m. and looked up the Photo Jewelry Company.

Found Sister Sorensen Hyldall's. Supper with her and a very pleasant chat. "I am so thankful that the Lord opened my eyes so I could see where I was." I enjoyed very much the lunch she prepared for me: eggs boiled in cream, bread and butter, strawberries, and an orange good enough for King Edward.[257] She told me of the success of her daughter who has been in laundry business. Her son in the City Hall. Other two sons making success of the commission [?] business. Rise during busy season at 3:00 a.m. At barns at 3:30

a.m., store 4:00 a.m. and 4:30 a.m. Quit at 10:00 p.m. Lost one son last winter. Granddaughter. Elders wrote name today. See page [blank].

## June 7, 1907, Friday, Chicago [p. 91]

Rose after 6:00 a.m. Bath. Raining most of the day. Cool. Wrote Photo Jewelry Company about paper. Received letter from dated June 4. All well. Answered it. Called on Mr. W. D. Ordway of Aldrich and McAuley, Home Insurance Building,[258] and received order for views of Uintah Railway[259] and Rio Grande Western.[260] [**p. 90**] Mr. Ordway interested in looking at views and talking about Utah and Colorado etc. [**p. 91**]

What a sight it is to get in town among those great skyscrapers.[261] I thought there would not be much of a chance for a fellow if there was an earthquake.

Retouched and cleaned negatives[262] until near 4:00 p.m. Sister Ellsworth told me when to come to meals. I was late tonight, but gave me supper. Spent the evening writing to my wife. Mr. Deardoff interested in looking at views. He fixes cameras, 64 Wabash Avenue, sixth floor.[263]

---

257. Prince Albert Edward (1841–1910) was the eldest son of Queen Victoria and became king of Great Britain in 1901.

258. A nonextant, nine-story building located on the northwest corner of LaSalle and Adams Streets. It was the first steel-frame skyscraper built in the world and was completed in 1885.

259. By October 1904, the Uintah Railway completed a line from Mack, Colorado, on the mainline Rio Grande Western to Dragon, Utah. Essentially a one-commodity railroad, the Uintah hauled loads of gilsonite from the mines in Uintah County, Utah, and Mesa, Garfield, and Rio Blanco Counties in Colorado.

260. Anderson uses the abbreviation *R.G.W.*

261. Called the most radical transformation in the structural art since the development of the Gothic system of construction in the twelfth century. Chicago arose from the ashes of the Great Fire in 1871 to develop the skyscraper as well as many other innovations of modern architecture.

262. This entry probably implies that Anderson is involved in more than simply "spotting" the negatives.

263. On pages 92–95 of his diary, Anderson had the missionaries sign their autographs as follows: [**p. 92**] "Elder G. N. Curtis, Logan, Utah; Sister Hope Russell, Salt Lake City, Utah; Elder J. M. Anderson, Morgan City, Utah (sweet singer; sang in priesthood meeting, "I Know That My Redeemer Lives," Saturday, June 15); [**p. 93**] Wiley M. Cragun, View, Weber County, Utah; Elder D. G. Edmunds, Wales, Sanpete County, Utah; Laura Bennion, Taylorsville, Utah; Elder Ira J. McKell, Spanish Fork, Utah; Elder James Rasmusson, Ephraim, Sanpete County, Utah; D. H. Fowles, Hooper, Utah; [**p. 94**] Elder H. S. Vance, 568 East Sixth North Street, Provo City, Utah; Elder John E. Peterson, Union, Oregon; Joseph Peterson, Kanesville, Utah (going to Des Moines, Iowa, to teach in the Drake University); James Petersen, Riverton (neighbor of Elder Carl Madsen at Nauvoo); P. P. Peterson, Kanesville, Utah; Elder Lorenzo Harris, Woodruff, Idaho; [**p. 95**] Elder M. M. Dahle, Rigby, Idaho." The following names are probably in Anderson's handwriting: "John Frankland, Robb Jones."

At the conclusion of the autographs, Anderson made the following notes on page 95: "N. Johnston, Chicago, 90 Ashland Boulevard, 57 North Ashland Avenue. See card. Wishes to be remembered to Brother Morten [?] at Liverpool. Also Sister Matilda Peterson of Ogden, who is attending summer school, Chicago."

## June 8, 1907, Saturday, Chicago [p. 96]

I spent most of the day at the gallery of Mr. Martin on Madison spotting out negatives, reducing, intensifying,264 etc. Also some time writing up a history or notes of Kirtland, Palmyra, etc.

In the evening, gave Elder Curtis a lesson on his Kodak.265 I would have printed some negatives today, but Mr. Martin did not think it best, as he was busy.

## June 9, 1907, Sunday, Chicago [p. 96]

I did not retire until twelve last night, so did not get up this morning until near 7:00 a.m. Bath, shoes shined, etc. At office and spent until 9:30 a.m. writing up notes of Kirtland. See back of book.266 Sunday School: Brother Sears, superintendent, requested me to speak. Told story of Wasel Darrow. [p. 97] Lesson was 56th, 57th, 58th chapters of Alma.267

Surprised and pleased to meet Sister Joel Ricks,268 Hotel De Prado 215, here with Brother Ricks's sister,

Mrs. Nibley,269 who has come to go home with her son, Brother Nibley,270 who is attending school here.

Met Brother Peterson and wife, who visited Springville four years ago the eighteenth of this month. Myron Crandall gave them wedding reception. They invited myself and Elder Curtis home with them, and met Sister Peterson's mother, Sister Post, and her daughter, Pearl, and had dinner and lunch with them. Brother Peterson and wife have three babies, the youngest not ten weeks old. We take the Logan Park271 car and walk to the Albany district.272 Spent a very enjoyable afternoon. Learned how Sister Post received the gospel.

Evening meeting, 7:30 p.m. Elder James Rasmusson of Ephraim spoke in Norwegian. I followed. Related my experiences [p. 98] in Richmond with the posterity of the witnesses of the Book of Mormon, the morning at the [1893?] World's Fair, etc. Followed along the same line by Elder Edmunds. I spoke about twenty minutes.

Made a negative of the Sunday School this morn-

---

264. When a photograph was overexposed, Anderson could, with the use of a compound, bleach away the silver. The density of an underexposed negative could be increased to achieve an opposite result.

265. In 1888, photography made a dramatic shift when George Eastman introduced his famous "Kodak" camera—the first camera that was simple and portable enough to be used by a large number of amateur photographers. The camera received its name from the *ko-dak* sound the string-cock, cylindrical shutter made when the button was depressed during exposure. This camera drastically affected all professional photographers, including Anderson.

266. See Appendix Two.

267. Lesson 48, "Helaman's Army of 2,000 Young Men," *Sunday School Outlines, Second Intermediate Department, First Year Book of Mormon, 1907–1908* (Salt Lake City: Deseret Sunday School Union Bookstore, 1907), 27.

268. Susette Cardon Ricks (1861–1919), wife of Joel Ricks (1858–1944).

269. Ellen June Ricks Nibley (1856–1935).

270. Preston Nibley (1884–1966) was studying journalism at the University of Chicago at the time. He had returned from an LDS Church mission in Germany in 1905 before coming to Chicago to pursue his academic studies. Nibley was appointed as an assistant Church historian for the LDS Church in 1957.

271. Chicago is known for its incredible park system. The city's motto is *urbs in horto*—city in a garden. Chicago was reminiscent of London, a city known for its park system, more than any other American city at the turn of the century. Park laws passed in 1869 established three park districts as municipal corporations—the West, the South, and the Lincoln Park systems. The South Park Commission spent $24 million to develop a two-thousand-acre system of parks and thirty-five miles of boulevards for the 1893 World's Columbian Exposition. Logan Park is one of the small neighborhoods later developed around a park that was part of the urbanization of Chicago during the last quarter of the nineteenth century.

272. Located north of the Logan Square neighborhood on the northwest side of Chicago, Albany Park was named after the hometown (Albany, New York) of a local real estate developer.

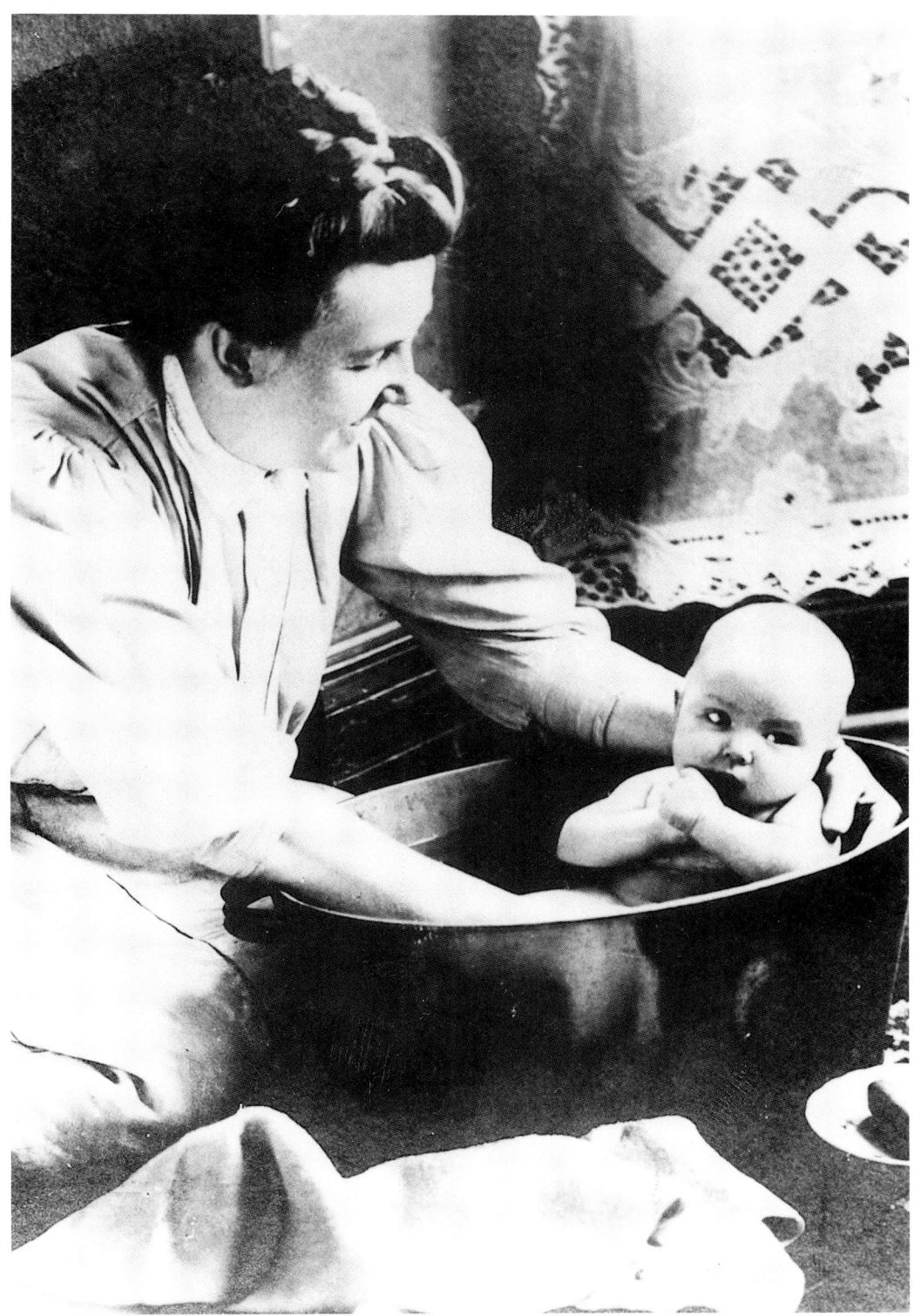

*Rachel Smith Ellsworth and Daughter*, *Chicago, Illinois, 11 June 1907, Lehi [Utah] Library Historical Archives. The view is of President Ellsworth's wife, Mary Rachel Smith Ellsworth, and their daughter, Ruth Ellsworth [Knudson]. Ruth Ellsworth Knudson recalled that her mother told her George Edward Anderson happened to walk into the mission home where he saw Sister Ellsworth giving her three-month-old baby a bath. Anderson said the scene would make a great photograph and asked permission to take it. Later, a soap manufacturer offered Sister Ellsworth $100 if she would allow the company to use this photograph in a billboard advertising campaign in Chicago. She declined this lucrative offer, feeling it was not "seemly for a mission president's wife to be seen on a billboard."*

ing. Invite Elder James Peterson of Riverton, [Utah], to sleep with me. He has just come from Utah on a mission. Labor in Chicago. Herbert Robinson here studying music.

Met John F. A. Howard, D.C., Office, 203–204 South Wiler [?], Second and Brady, Davenport, Iowa. Used to live two blocks from us. Wishes to hear from Add and to be remembered to him. Attended morning services at 11:30 a.m.

## June 10, 1907, Monday, Chicago [p. 99]

Rose about 6:00 a.m. Breakfast at the mission. Developed negatives made yesterday. One was light streak; other good.

Sent *Knight of Twentieth Century*[273] to Elder Carl Madsen, Nauvoo. *History of Mormons*[274] by Roberts to H. M. Anschutz, Keokuk. *Illustrated Book of Chicago*[275] to Edda.[276] Wrote to Rob Jones. Also to wife and card—boy with bubble soap—to Lowry.

Could not develop prints at Mr. Martin's, so will buy material and develop myself. Went to town and made some purchases so I could finish the pictures. Did not get back until after 7:00 p.m. Revolving stairways—see people going up and down. It was a strange sensation.[277] Brother Page here and took twelve of brothers and sisters to the theater tonight. **[p. 100]** I stayed home and watched the office.

## June 11, 1907, Tuesday, Chicago [p. 100]

I did not rise as early as usual. Elder Peterson rooming with me.

I out looking for pans[278] etc. for finishing pictures. It is a chore. Into the ten-cent stores, and it is wonderful—the extent and variety of goods we can find. I called on Mr. Curver of the Photo Jewelry Company, and he gave me an order for $9 worth of paper to replace some that was not good.

I spent the afternoon and until 8:00 p.m. in the evening looking up material for printing. Did not get out to the Photo Materials Company. Made negative of Sister Ellsworth's baby in bath.[279] Wrote to Brother Ellsworth about views. Also ask him let see Brother George A. Smith see letter and give me instructions about where, **[p. 101]** when to make views etc.

The evening: developed negatives, also films. It was near 12:00 p.m. when I went to bed. Raining tonight and this evening. Ate bananas, pie, and candy for lunch.

## June 12, 1907, Wednesday, Chicago [p. 101]

Rose about 6:30 a.m. Had breakfast about 7:30 a.m. Finished batch of about thirty prints. Elder McKell assisted me in mounting. Elders Curtis and Alleman watched and helped occasionally. Wrote to

---

273. H. C. Hensel, *Knight of the Twentieth Century* (Chicago: H. C. Hensel, n.d.).

274. In all likelihood, Anderson is referring to *The Latter-day Saints' Tour from Palmyra, New York, to Salt Lake City Through the Stereoscope: A History of the Church of Jesus Christ of Latter-day Saints* (Salt Lake City: The Deseret News, 1904); (Ottawa, Kansas: Underwood and Underwood, 1905).

275. Apparently, no book titled exactly as Anderson noted in his diary has been published, but two books with similar titles are *Illustrated Chicago of Today* (Chicago: Knight Leonard and Company, 1891) and *Chicago Illustrated* (Chicago: R. F. Griffis, 1892).

276. Edda Anderson [Brandley] (1892–1974), Anderson's daughter, later married Louis Orson Brandley in 1919.

277. Jesse W. Reno produced the first "escalator" in 1891. It was, however, at the Paris Exposition of 1900 that his incline belt, which provided transportation for passengers riding on cleats attached to a belt, received the name *escalator*. Otis Elevator had the proprietary rights to produce the escalator at the time.

278. Because Anderson had decided to set up his own temporary developing room, he had to purchase chemicals and trays (or pans) to hold the solutions used in the developing process.

279. The child mentioned here is Ruth Ellsworth [Knudson], born on 11 March 1907. She currently lives in Arlington, Virginia, and helped locate and identify the photograph mentioned by Anderson.

President Ellsworth and ask or posted the letter that I wrote yesterday. A farewell party was given to Sister Ida Alleman at the mission house by Sister Ellsworth. Had a very pleasant time. Games, refreshments. Bed about twelve.

## *June 13, 1907, Thursday, Chicago [p. 102]*

I was out and made some purchases for finishing pictures. Develop some. Over fifty, ten by twelve prints. Wrote to Junius F. Wells,[280] also President McQuarrie,[281] in relation to monument[282] and other views in the East.

Elder Ira McKell assisted me with the prints—washing and changing. Had to make up fresh hypo and refix the prints.[283] It was near 10:00 p.m. when I got through. Elder McKell helping finishing in the back rooms of the church. Bed about 11:00 p.m. Address of B. H. Roberts was a very fine answer to the ministers of Salt Lake and neighborhood.[284]

## *June 14, 1907, Friday, Chicago [p. 103]*

Rose soon after 5:00 a.m. Bath. Over to the church and, by 7:30 a.m, had most of pictures spotted. Out to Sixty-First [Street] between Wentworth and LaSalle Streets to get the paper ordered by (Mr. Curver) of the Photo Jewelry Company. Met Mr. Chamberlain, and he readily gave me the paper.

Dinner while we were waiting for paper to be prepared, cut. Brother James Peterson went with me. We then visited the stockyards.[285] Through Armour Packing Company[286] place and saw the way they kill the pigs, stocks, etc. Do not wish to see it again. Will be glad when man does not have to satisfy his appetite on meat. Government inspector examined each animal after it was slaughtered. Also the entrails. Fifteen hundred an hour capacity of [p. 104] hogs, thirty-five hundred head of stock per day. Five hundred thousand the capacity of the meat and lean and lard pail factory per day. Putting up pork in glasses. Also

280. Junius Free Wells (1854–1930) was responsible for identifying and purchasing, for the LDS Church, the Mack farm property in Sharon, Vermont, and erecting a memorial to the memory of Joseph Smith there in 1905. He was the organizer of the YMMIA (1875) and the *Contributor* magazine (1879), which served both the young men and young women groups of the LDS Church. Sustained as an assistant Church historian in 1921, Wells was instrumental in purchasing Anderson's glass-plate negative collection for the LDS Church shortly after Anderson's death in 1928.

281. John G. McQuarrie (1867–1962) served as the president of the Eastern States Mission, headquartered in New York City, from 1901 to 1908.

282. Refers to the Joseph Smith Memorial Monument in Sharon, Vermont, which had been dedicated on the one-hundredth anniversary of the Prophet's birth in December 1905. The monument is thirty-eight feet high—one foot for every year of the Prophet's life.

283. Obviously, Anderson was experiencing some difficulty in stabilizing ("fixing") the prints and was forced to do the procedure over again. *Fixing* involved the process of removing the silver salts from a negative. Sodium hyposulphite was generally employed for this purpose. Throughout the diary, Anderson usually abbreviates sodium hyposulphite with the word *hypo*.

284. The LDS Church First Presidency had issued an "Address to the World" at the recent general conference in Salt Lake City, published in the *Improvement Era*, 10 (May 1907): 481–95. The Ministerial Association of Salt Lake City, an evangelical Protestant group, responded in a "Review" that was critical of the Church, published in the 4 June 1907 *Salt Lake Tribune*. Elder B. H. Roberts countered in a meeting held in the Tabernacle on 9 June 1907. A written report of this talk was published in various newspapers, including the 10 June 1907 *Deseret News*, which Anderson may have been reading at the time.

285. The Union Stock Yards and Transit Company opened on Christmas Day 1865 and eventually closed in 1971. This facility was the center of the nation's meat-packing industry. Interestingly, the original 320 acres of the stockyards were purchased from John Wentworth (for whom Joseph Smith wrote the famous document containing the Articles of Faith).

286. Founded in 1868 by Philip Armour, Armour and Company originated a number of slaughtering techniques, the use of waste products, and the sale of canned meat. The company also greatly expanded the use of refrigeration for shipping meats all over the United States.

chipped beef in barrels for Japan. Refrigerators' capacity of ten thousand. Were well filled. Saw the Jewish quarters for beef.[287] It is surely a wonderful system they have worked up for handling the hogs etc.

It was 5:00 p.m. when we returned home. Separated the pictures and packed them for parties. At the invitation of Elder McKell, I spoke at street meeting on the corner of Paulina and Grand. My first experience, and it was difficult. Sister Bennion, Elder Anderson also spoke. A fair crowd. Brother McKell opened the meeting. I was able to speak, they thought, about fifteen minutes. Held conversation with Mrs. Volker after meeting.

## June 15, 1907, Saturday, Chicago [p. 105]

Rose about 6:00 a.m. Mixed chemicals. Made several changes in negatives. Concluded to attend priesthood meeting held in basement of church at 10:00 a.m. Elder Ira J. McKell presiding. Two sisters present. All bore testimony and explained how they conducted the work. I enjoyed the testimonies very much. I spoke about ten minutes at the close of the meeting at suggestion of Elder McKell.

Run through a batch of pictures. It was after 10:30 p.m. when I went to bed. Elder McKell assisted me with the work. Painted the trays.[288] John Alleman also assisted me. Found I am making headway with the developing paper.[289] Very tired tonight when I got through. Finished about sixty prints: fifty-three, ten by eight; five to seven, five by seven.

## June 16, 1907, Sunday, Chicago [p. 106]

Rose about 6:00 a.m. Bath, shave, and at church and fixed the pictures and cleaned up for Sunday. Putting all the pictures away. Sunday School, 58th, 59th, and 60th chapters of Alma.[290] Good sacrament meeting, and enjoyed the talks of Elder Peterson and Dr. [blank] very much.

With Elders McKell and Rasmusson, went out to Mr. Smith's for dinner and had a very pleasant time. Showed the pictures and talked the gospel to Mr. Smith. Enjoyed the ride, and that part of the country is more like home. Trees and grass along the street.

Evening meeting at 8:00 p.m., which I opened by prayer. Talked with the elders after meeting about prayer etc.

## June 17, 1907, Monday, Chicago [p. 107]

Rose 6:00 a.m. Wrote L. T. Briggs. See Letter No. 5. Fixed up cash.

Sent views of Chicago to my nieces, Mern and Lilly Anderson, Provo. Also Ellwood. Sent temple rock, Nauvoo, wood from Haun's Mill, and shells from button factory, Nauvoo. Three pictures from great painting, "Golgotha," one for James Rasmusson, one for George E. Anderson, one for Ira J. McKell, who will take them home with him.

Received letter from my wife. Started letter to her and Lowry.

Wrote Photo Products Company about paper.

---

287. Jewish dietary laws required that animals be slaughtered by the ritual method of *shehitah*. The specially trained slaughterer (*shohet*) recites a prayer and, with a special knife that is razor sharp, cuts the animal's throat by moving the knife in a single, swift, uninterrupted sweep. The cutting severs the main arteries, rendering the animal unconscious and allowing the blood to drain from the body.

288. The developing trays or pans were typically made of metal and were susceptible to rusting. They were, therefore, "painted" to prevent rust, which is a strong detriment to any chemical process.

289. The commercial developing paper was often much faster than Anderson may have been used to using. Many experienced photographers were frustrated by the precision required by the new paper. Anderson was apparently experiencing similar feelings.

290. Lesson 49, "The Last Days of the War," *Sunday School Outlines, Second Intermediate Department, First Year Book of Mormon, 1907–1908* (Salt Lake City: Deseret Sunday School Union Bookstore, 1907), 28.

**Union Park**, *Chicago, Illinois, 17 June 1907, Anderson Collection, LDSCA. The view shows Elder J. Morgan Anderson at Union Park.*

Made negatives of Elders Anderson also James Rasmusson and Ira McKell at Union Park.[291] Beautiful place. Made negative of Miss Ware's place. [p. 108]

Ida Alleman went home today with Ira J. McKell of Spanish Fork, [Utah]. Tears of joy she shed when she found she was going to have a companion.

Developed negatives tonight in basement of mission house. Bed about 12:00 midnight. Read *Independents*[292] before retiring.

The leaving of Sister Alleman and Elder McKell caused quite a stir today. Glad to be going home, but feelings of sorrow at parting with the friends etc. Brother Peterson, who has been rooming with me, will be Brother James Rasmusson's companion. Met Dr. E. G. Hughes of Spanish Fork today. Is on his way home with wife and family.

---

291. Established in 1854 because residents petitioned the city to prevent developers from parceling out the land. The original thirteen acres were bought for $18,000. The park is now bounded by Lake Street and Washington, Ashland, and Ogden Boulevards.

292. Anderson may be referring to the Springville, Utah, paper, *Independent*, or the Nauvoo, Illinois, paper, *Independent*.

## June 18, 1907, Tuesday, Chicago [p. 109]

Rose before 6:00 a.m. Bath. Wrote or finished letter to wife and Lowry. Breakfast at mission house. Dinner with Elder James Rasmusson in church and told Sister Ellsworth I would eat with him, as Elder McKell had left and he wished a companion. Warm.

Developed, toned[293] a batch of views. They did not come out good. Flawed and blistered.[294]

Finished my letter to my wife and Lowry this morning. Supper: blackberries sent by a sister. Bed about 11:00 p.m. A long sleep in the church waiting for elders to return.

## June 19, 1907, Wednesday, Chicago [p. 109]

Rose about 6:00 a.m. Shave. Wrote Ira J. McKell's father and mother. Wrote Photo Products Company about developing paper.

Tried to sing[295] with Elder Rasmusson, "Sowing," "Now Let Us Rejoice,"[296] and "Come Ye Elders." I

may learn. Prayer and then breakfast with Elder Rasmusson. Spent the day in the stores of Chicago and learned a good [p. 110] many things that will be beneficial to me about mounting different kinds of paper etc.

Talked with Sister Ellsworth about her baby. She gave it a pill yesterday, and it was very sick.

Lunch in town. Back about 6:00 p.m. in the elevated.[297] Fixed up cash, and it was 12:25 a.m. before I got to bed.

## June 20, 1907, Thursday, Chicago [p. 110]

Rose about 6:30 a.m. Breakfast: eggs boiled in milk, boiled tomatoes, and macaroni. Washed up dishes with help of Brother Rasmusson.[298]

Made masks[299] for eight by ten negatives. Prepared rice and pie plant for dinner. Printing and developing this afternoon and evening. Near 8:30 p.m. when I got through. Tried to assist in singing this morning. Bed soon after 10:00 p.m. Warm.

---

293. Anderson used gold chloride, not sepia, to tone (color) his photographs. He could achieve a variety of colors in the final print. His choice was based on preference.

294. Anderson is probably referring to a "marring" of the emulsion on the surface of the print, which, when wet, was very soft and fragile.

295. Apparently, Anderson is trying to improve his singing abilities during his stay in Chicago when he participates in proselytizing activities. Anderson repeatedly alludes to experiences in singing with the missionaries, members, and non-Latter-day Saint members in his diary. Evidently, the Northern States Mission emphasized music as part of the proselytizing approach. The *Liahona* reported in the 20 May 1907 issue the comments of a Northern States missionary: "There is something in our songs that appeals to most people, and it seems they would never tire of hearing them sung." Obviously, in Chicago, Latter-day Saint missionaries would have naturally been associated with the Mormon Tabernacle Choir's second-prize award at the National Choir Invitational held in conjunction with the 1893 Columbian Exposition. The *Latter-day Saint Psalmody*, first published in 1886, was a popular LDS hymnal with several printings and editions and was likely used by missionaries during this period. However, in 1908, German Ellsworth, president of the Northern States Mission, published *Songs of Zion*, an unofficial hymnbook with several editions and printings, which he evidently felt suited the missionaries' needs better than the official LDS Church publication.

296. An LDS hymn written by William W. Phelps (1792–1872).

297. Anderson is referring to the elevated trains that operated in Chicago at the time. They had been recently built to avoid the large number of accidental deaths at crossings in the city. Downtown Chicago has been known as the "Loop" since 1897 when these elevated lines joined into an overhead loop of tracks encircling an area that covers thirty-five blocks.

298. At this point, Anderson gives the following information, which is probably related to letters he wrote on June 20: "Ed Olson, Fort Atkinson, Jefferson County, Wisconsin, on back of view of footman, Nauvoo. Good Health Publishing Company, Battle Creek, Michigan (see Letter 13). W. P. Buchanan, Philadelphia, 1226 Circle Street. Vegetarian Company, 78–84 Madison Street, Chicago."

299. The masking process allowed the photographer to control the contrast.

## June 21, 1907, Friday, Chicago [p. 111]

Rose 5:30 a.m. Bath. Wrote Elder Osburn Richins, see No. 12; Elder E. A. Richards, Morgan City, [Utah]; and James A. Anderson; John D. Whitmer, Far West, Caldwell County, Missouri; James P. Thompson,[300] Elmira, Ray County, Missouri; Charles P. Faul, Stewartsville, Clinton County, Missouri; Mrs. John E. Batson, Kingston, Caldwell County, Missouri.

Finished a batch of photos and mailed them: John D. Whitmer and James P. Thompson.

Very warm. Let my room go to an elder and family who was on road home. Downtown and made some purchases of fruit, strawberries, etc. Made a strawberry shortcake with cornflakes and berries.

Had better success with the paper today. Found out the cause of yellow prints. Done some cooking today. Bed about 10:30 p.m.

## June 22, 1907, Saturday, Chicago [p. 112]

Developed pictures a good part of the day and had very good success. At 3:00 p.m., made several negatives of the laying of cornerstone of the Salvation Army—new building on Madison Street, about three [blocks] east of Paulina.[301] The experience I am having with developing paper etc. is very valuable to me.

Received a letter from Elder Ed Olson tonight. He is well and enjoying his labors.

This forenoon, packed up pictures for Nauvoo and wrote Elders Roberts and Madsen. Evening, developed negatives, mopped up oil cloths, reduced negatives, and waited for Elder Rasmusson to come. But he did not get here until after 11:00 p.m., so I made my bed on bench in church. Let Elder Iverson have my room. Rain about 7:30 p.m. Very tired.

## June 23, 1907, Sunday, Chicago [p. 112]

Rose about 6:00 a.m. Bath over to the room. Shave and Sunday School. Elder Mills gave the lesson and was very good [p. 113] meeting. Asael Woodruff and Elder Iverson the speakers. Three new elders came today—Elders Campbell of Providence, Utah; Flake of Snowflake, Arizona; and Wanless, Lehi, [Utah]. Elder Campbell ate dinner with me.

I was too weary to go out to see Sister Sorensen today. Lost so much sleep. Afternoon listening to Elders Mortensen and Fowler relate their experiences. They left for Independence, Missouri, 5:30 p.m.

A gentleman, in talking about social economics and how the Mormons stood on the trial of Orchard,[302]—we told him the people could use their own pleasure about joining a union. But the advice was not to join secret unions or bind themselves—but be free to act as their judgment suggested was best.

Evening meeting: Dr. Hardin and Elder Iverson the speakers. Very warm. Rain. Will go to bed early tonight.

## June 24, 1907, Monday, Chicago [p. 113]

Rose before 6:00 a.m. and fixed up for printing, which I did in afternoon. Arranged the prints, negatives, etc. so could get at them readily. Having better

---

300. Earlier, Anderson identifies a James F. Thompson. See 15 May 1907 diary entry.

301. Located at 1512 West Madison, the Chicago Temple Corps Building was eventually dedicated on 5 April 1908. The auditorium could hold eight hundred people. Along with several other apartments and halls, it was a significant addition to the Chicago philanthropic community's efforts to reach out to the urban poor.

302. National attention had been focused on what would become the most famous trial in Idaho state history when Idaho officials, with the consent of Colorado authorities, kidnapped three officials of the Western Federation of Miners (WFM) in Denver and secretly brought them to Boise, Idaho, to stand trial for the murder of former Idaho Governor Frank Steunenberg. Steunenberg was murdered on 30 December 1905 by Harry Orchard, who had turned state's witness against the leaders of the WFM, claiming they planned and paid for the assassination because of Steunenberg's role in the labor-related violence six years earlier. Virtually daily reports in the *Chicago Tribune* appeared detailing the trial being held in Idaho. Of special interest was the fact that Chicago labor attorney Clarence S. Darrow was one of the defense attorneys for the WFM leaders, who were eventually acquitted.

success with the paper now. Understand how to work it. [p. 114]

Made a strawberry shortcake, cookies, pie plant today. Brother Rasmusson and Brother Iverson and the new elders went out to the stockyards today.

Elders Rasmusson, Campbell, Peterson, Sister Russell, and I held a meeting on the corner of Madison and Troop. Commenced soon after 7:45 p.m. A fair crowd. Brother Rasmusson presided, and we spoke as follows: Elder Peterson, myself. Elder Campbell and Elder Rasmusson sang "O My Father."[303] Sister Russell dismissed. A very fair crowd and interested. They said would come to our meeting. Sister Russell and myself and Elder Peterson held conversation until near 11:00 p.m., people asking questions. All bore a strong testimony of the Book of Mormon. Wrote R. J. Briggs.

## June 25, 1907, Tuesday, Chicago [p. 114]

Rose 5:30 a.m. Straightened up in the eating room and then morning devotions. Elder Rasmusson suggested that I take charge this week. Read a chapter in Galatians. Song and prayer.

Spent some time this morning relating to new elders my experiences in Missouri getting the views. Out and sold two views of Salvation Army laying cornerstone. In the evening, left five with Captain Anderson.[304] Developed a good many prints this forenoon. Also afternoon. Better success; understand it better as each day I try.

Elders Vance and Peterson took dinner with us: bread and butter, pie plant, onions. [p. 115] Did not cook because I was washing prints. At Aberdeen Bakery, get from four to five loaves of bread for ten cents—graham.

Evening, shave and went onto Madison Street to find our elders holding street meeting, but did not find them. Thirteen [?] young men, one older with lady in wagon bearing inscription "Moody Bible Institute,"[305] sang number of songs and prayer and speaking between. Burden of their talk was to acknowledge Christ. Also that they were saved. A young man in charge seemed earnest and sincere. One young man related how reckless he was. Had a praying mother, and he found Jesus. How mother felt. Distributed a tract, "Are You an Honest Seeker?" See [blank].

Farther west about two blocks, Volunteers of America[306] were holding a meeting. A fair crowd. American flag. Big drums, guitars, mandolins were in audience and used to accompany them in the songs. Whitehead gentleman talking when I came up. Entertaining speaker. Told of company that were selling the elixir of life. How people poured in the money. Arrested. It was water. Gospel compared. While he was talking, some would shout "Amen," "Glory to God," etc.

A lady then stepped forth and said they were short in their offering and urged the crowd to make up the money needed, and sister passed around the crowd and got eleven cents. While she was doing this, a good-looking young lady sang "Where Is My

---

303. LDS hymn written by Eliza Roxcy Snow (1804–87) in 1843 and considered one of the greatest of all LDS hymns. The third stanza articulates the Mormon belief in both a Father and a Mother in Heaven.

304. The Salvation Army began working in England but spread to North America in earnest in 1880. Its work was an effort to launch a great crusade in American cities in a battle to win souls for Christ. Salvationists wore military-style uniforms, and members were assigned ranks—such as captain, lieutenant, or cadet.

305. Dwight Lyman Moody (1837–99), a well-known revivalist, founded one of the nondenominational church programs in Chicago in 1858. He established the Chicago Bible Institute (1886), later known as the Moody Bible Institute, to help those without a college education to prepare themselves for foreign or home missionary labors. By the turn of the century, it was the largest denomination in Chicago.

306. Ballington Booth (1857–1940), son of Salvation Army founder William Booth (1829–1912), and Ballington's wife, Maud Elizabeth Charlesworth Booth (1865–1948), established the rival Volunteers of America in 1896 after resigning from the Salvationists organization. The Chicago post was involved in religious as well as welfare work. Apparently, the Volunteers of America started the Santa Claus program when workers, garbed in St. Nick costumes, posted themselves along the streets and asked for donations for their welfare work.

Wandering Boy Tonight?" and the others joined in chorus. The first sister passed around the basket and got a few cents. Still short, so the leader [p. 116] made a strong appeal for thirty cents to make up the offering, which was soon made up; and all were invited to their services in hall close by next Sunday. Fielding would administer the Lord's supper.

A block or two farther down, three men and boy were holding meeting. An elderly man without coat on was talking in excited manner up and down the street. A song was then sung, and a small man in broken tongue urged people not to be afraid of prayer.

I next went to Salvation Army quarters to see if could dispose of pictures. Holding a meeting that was new to me. Stout man speaking and crying. Others shouting, "Glory to God," "Hallelujah," "Amen." One man seemed to be just converted, for he was praying all the time, on his knees in part of the hall, then in the other, and face upturned and hands stretched out as though he was pleading for mercy. Sometimes, he would bow his head, and I could not hear what he said.

All knelt, some prayed, some sang, and others shouted as above. One man beat the chair with his hand. Another hit the drum. The lady danced for a second or two, stood on a chair, read from the Bible. They spoke of it as a Pentecost,[307] and all seemed to enjoy it. I never saw such a meeting. [p. 117]

It was near 10:30 p.m. when they dismissed. As they passed out, shook my hand. Said was pleased to see me here. Shook each other by the hand, and the "Good night" and "God bless you" was very earnest, and some would say "Glory to God," "Amen."

Left pictures—five—with [Salvation Army Captain] L. Anderson. It was after 11:00 p.m. when we had prayers and got to bed. Some rain today.

## June 26, 1907, Wednesday, Chicago [p. 117]

Rose about 6:30 a.m. Song, prayer, breakfast. Washed dishes, which we did not do last night as wished to go in the street. Wrote up journal for yesterday. Now 9:15 a.m. Will finish up pictures.

Spotted and packed up pictures. Also trimmed. Uptown 6:00 p.m. but stores closed, so I could not get what I wished. Bought bunch of flowers for Sister Ellsworth—beauties at five cents.

Wrote Gysin Drugleo, J. B. Buzzard, M. E. Pangburn, Gallatin, Missouri. See No. 33. Also Ed. O. Olson and few lines to Edda. Uptown at 5:45 p.m., but too late to get what I wished. Bought flowers—five cents—for Sister Ellsworth. Spent the evening in the office writing. Bed about 10:15 p.m.

## June 27, 1907, Thursday, Chicago [p. 118]

Rose about 6:30 a.m. Prayer and songs. Breakfast: rice, raisins, and bread. Fixed up cash account. Joseph S. Black, Deseret, [Utah]—nine buttons and view of Adam-ondi-Ahman. Ira J. McKell, Spanish Fork—postcard, two pictures.

A peculiar feeling with me all day. Went uptown to purchase material for finishing pictures and did not get back until near 3:00 p.m. Dinner and made masks for printing and painted pans for developing. Put in light glass for Sister Ellsworth. Supper there.

Received pictures of my family tonight, which gave me much satisfaction. Letter from my wife in which she tells me heard I was coming home before I filled my mission. This is something new to me. No such a thought has come into my mind. Letter made me feel very peculiar and almost vexed.[308]

---

307. Literally, the fiftieth day—a Jewish holiday when, according to the New Testament book of Acts, the Holy Ghost descended upon the disciples of Jesus. Many Christian groups believed the experience could be replicated. Apparently, the Salvationists associated the activities of the meeting with the pentecostal outpouring mentioned in Acts.

308. Apparently, Anderson's delay in arriving in England caused some people in Springville to think he would not complete his mission. Because Anderson had received financial contributions from Springville friends and family to begin his mission, this report would surely add to his personal anxiety.

## June 28, 1907, Friday, Chicago [p. 118]

Rose about 7:00 a.m. Song, prayer, breakfast. Got some beans and fixed for dinner. Wrote to Edda. Also Lowry and my wife.

Printed and developed during afternoon. Evening on Madison Street and got bread etc. and called at Salvation Army headquarters, but not there. President Ellsworth returned this evening. Greeted everybody very warmly. Prayer, bed about 10:30 p.m.

## June 29, 1907, Saturday, Chicago [p. 119]

I rose before 5:00 a.m. this morning and looked up correspondence in relation to Ordway order. Not feeling very well. Not enough sleep.

Wrote John B. McLallen, Breckenridge, Missouri; Harvey Goodson, postcard, Breckenridge, Missouri; A. J. Seeley, postcard, Kingston, Missouri; Elder Carl Madsen, Nauvoo. It was near 11:00 a.m. when I got correspondence done and pictures packed up.

President Ellsworth and Apostle George A. Smith[309] came into priesthood meeting. Brother Smith told me to meet him 1:30 to 2:00 p.m. and he would look at views and give me what information he could about Palmyra, [New York], Sharon, [Vermont]. I made notes of the points he gave. I ask him if I should sail on the vessel that sails on the third. He said, "No. Keep on with the work." And if I was to quit, he would wire me. If I had no word from him, it would be right for me to keep on with the work. He was interested in the views and made suggestions about the views at Palmyra, [New York], Sharon, [Vermont], Kirtland, [Ohio], Seneca Lake, [New York], etc. Also, Sister Smith[310] made some suggestions; and President Ellsworth will give me names of those who will help with the work.[311] I told Apostle Smith that I had thought of writing to President Penrose[312] of the [p. 120] English Mission and tell him why I was so long in coming, what I was doing, etc. He said to do that.

Bath about 6:00 p.m. Berries bought by Elders Flake and Rasmusson.[313]

Haun's Mill stone: I spoke to Brother George A. Smith about this. He said he would make a note of it and speak to the Presidency when he got home. I wrote to John B. McLallen to see if could get it, and maybe we could send it to Salt Lake.[314]

## June 30, 1907, Sunday, Chicago [p. 120]

Beautiful day. Rose about 6:00 a.m. Straightened up where I had been working, also kitchen, and prepared for Sunday School. Professor Mills, teacher—1st, 2nd, and 3rd chapters Helaman.[315] Brother Foster sang.

Service at 11:00 a.m. President Ellsworth related his experiences at Kirtland, Palmyra, and Sharon, which was very interesting to me.

Attended evening service at 7:30 p.m. Started a letter to Brother Walter Thornburg. Wrote up my journal. Rested most of the afternoon and slept part

---

309. George Albert Smith (1870–1951), an ordained LDS Church apostle (1903). He had just returned from visiting Church historical sites and had finalized the purchase of the Smith family farm in Manchester, New York.

310. Lucy Emily Woodruff Smith (1869–1937).

311. The information found in Appendix Two may be the notes from these discussions, which Anderson originally recorded on the last few pages of his diary.

312. Elder Charles William Penrose (1832–1925), an ordained LDS Church apostle (1904). In 1907, he was serving as president of the LDS British Mission.

313. The next paragraph was inserted under Sunday, 30 June 1907, with the indication that the paragraph belongs under 29 June.

314. Apparently, this stone is now located in the town park in Breckenridge, Missouri. A second stone was discovered later in a house foundation near Haun's Mill and is now on display at the LDS Independence Visitors Center in Independence, Missouri.

315. Lesson 53, "Lost Blessings Regained," *Sunday School Outlines, Second Intermediate Department, Second Year Book of Mormon, 1907–1908* (Salt Lake City: Deseret Sunday School Union Bookstore, 1907), 30.

of the time. Practiced singing with the elders. Raining about 10:00 p.m.

## July 1, 1907, Monday, Chicago [p. 121]

Rose about 5:30 a.m. Finished letter to Brother Thornburg. Developed a good many (fifty) five by seven prints and about one dozen ten by eight. Much warmer than usual.

Elders Hansen of Logan, [Utah], and Clawson of Providence, [Utah], Elder Larsen of Cleveland, [Utah], and Elder Burt called on their way home. It was 8:45 a.m. before I got through with washing the prints. With Elder Campbell, visited the Salvation Army to see if views had been sold.

Sang several songs and retired. Elder Campbell and I made bed of quilts on the floor. He could not sleep where he had been rooming. Between sixty and sixty-five views in batch.

## July 2, 1907, Tuesday, Chicago [p. 121]

Rose about 5:30 a.m. Much cooler this morning. Breakfast: green peas and pettijohn wheat. Saw the first two rats I have seen in their native state.

Mailed picture to Brother Peterson's wife. Expressed pictures to M. M. Dahle, Idaho. Wrote to J. F. Bennett,[316] postcard, group at ferry. Wrote to Junius F. Wells, South Royalton, Vermont. Wrote a few lines to Edda. Also my wife. Received a letter from Elder Ed Olson. Also, my letter returned from Brother Junius F. Wells, which I sent to Salt Lake City. [p. 122]

Wrote President Charles W. Penrose, No. 10 Holley Road, Fairfield, Liverpool, England. See letter book. Also, see views sent.

At the request of Elder John Alleman, married [blank] and Olive Develine.[317] These folks were in a

**Miss Post, Mr. Foster, and Miss Chicago**, *Chicago, Illinois, June or July 1907, Anderson Collection, LDSCA. The* Chicago Tribune *announced the selection of the most beautiful woman in Chicago on 24 February 1907. A young working woman, Della Carson, who was a little over twenty-three years old and was from Alton, Illinois, won $100 in the competition. At the time, she was working as a stenographer for $12 a week. The newspaper boldly declared she was a "blue-blooded daughter of Norwegian Vikings." A comparison of this photograph and those in the* Tribune *article, along with Anderson's identification, revealed the young woman's name.*

hurry, and John Alleman was in a hurry. I feel that if I ever had such a task to perform again that I would have prayer and talk to the couple on the sacredness of the obligations they were taking upon them. Finished batch of pictures.

## July 3, 1907, Wednesday, Chicago [p. 122]

I do not now recall just what I did.

---

316. Along with John Hafen (1856–1910) and George Edward Anderson, John F. Bennett (1865–1938) was an apprentice at C. R. Savage's Art Bazaar in Salt Lake City. Later, Bennett founded the successful Bennett Glass and Paint Company. He, along with Junius F. Wells, was instrumental in getting the LDS Church to purchase Anderson's collection from Anderson's widow shortly after his death.

317. Because of Anderson's service as a bishop in Springville, Utah, and/or his calling as an "ordained minister" (that is, a set-apart missionary), he was apparently authorized to perform civil marriages.

*July 4, 1907, Thursday, Chicago [p. 123]*

Rose about 5:00 a.m. Straightened up the prints etc. and, with the elders and sisters, went to Evanston—a town north and a suburb of Chicago.[318] The Sunday School officers had selected this beautiful place under the shade of the trees and on the grass to celebrate the glorious Fourth [of July]. It was a treat to see chickens, cows staked here and there, and barns—something to remind us of country and home life. We played baseball and other games that ladies and gentlemen could take part in—"Last Couple Out," "Three Deep," etc.

An impromptu program was given under the trees: Elder Vance, presiding; prayer, George E. Anderson; singing, "America"; speeches of welcome by Superintendent Sears; recitations; songs; etc. About noon, lunch was spread upon the grass; and the tablecloths were weighted to the ground with the good things of life, which eagerly partaken of by old and young. The long ride, fresh air under God's temples, the trees had sharpened our appetites. I made a picture of the company at lunch.

The crowd adjourned to a nearby road, and races were run. I beat the race for men over forty-five. Made several negatives and played some games. At home about 7:30 p.m. A good many went to White City Parks[319] etc. I stayed and developed negatives. Spoiled one by trying to reduce it. Fireworks on Madison Street were fine.

*July 5, 1907, Friday, Chicago [p. 122]*

Finished a batch of pictures from negatives made yesterday—thirty-one in all.

*July 6, 1907, Sunday, Chicago [p. 122]*

Finished and delivered pictures. Attended priesthood meeting. Uptown and bought plates etc. At 8:00 a.m., with Elders Rasmusson and Harrison, took berth on steamer *Wisconsin* for Milwaukee.[320] See [blank].

*July 8, 1907, Monday, Milwaukee, Watertown[321] [p. 124]*

I slept at Nelson (Sister Ada) Regean's last night. Mr. Regean invited me home with them after church. Rose before 6:00 a.m. Mr. Regean goes to work about 4:00 a.m. Met their son Harrold at breakfast. Had a very pleasant chat with Sister Regean and her husband's mother on tithing, Sunday School, work, etc. Near 10:00 a.m. when I left. A pressing invitation to call again.

At the church just in time to meet Elder Russon, who was on his way to Watertown, [Wisconsin].[322] Purchased ticket and reached Watertown about 12:00 noon. Uncle Ed Olson surprised to meet me. They suggested that we go to the restaurant. I thought better buy a lunch, which we did—fruit, bananas, cheese,

---

318. Adjacent to Chicago's northern border is its oldest suburb, Evanston, which stretches for three and one-half miles along Lake Michigan's shore. Named in honor of John Evans, one of the founders of Northwestern University.

319. Jackson Park, the site of the 1893 World's Fair, a glittering fantasy of an electrically lighted "White City" at the time of the fair, was also known as *White City*. It retained the name following the close of the 1893 World's Fair.

320. County seat of Milwaukee County, located in southeastern Wisconsin on Lake Michigan, where the Milwaukee, Menomonee, and Kinnickinnic Rivers join and flow into Milwaukee Bay.

321. Two autographs appear in the diary at this point: "John Russon, Lehi, Utah, and E. O. Olson, Springville, Utah." Throughout the diary he refers to Olson as *Ed* and *Edd*. We have retained that usage.

322. Located some forty-five miles west of Milwaukee, Watertown was the location of the special experimental education program "Children's Garden," called by the German name *kindergarten*, which is now considered an essential first year of schooling throughout America.

and graham bread—which we ate in the public park.[323] Cool and shady. Made a negative of the monument[324] erected to the soldiers by the town, with us three in the picture. The old [p. 125] gentleman who keeps the park exposing the plate.

Arranged for supper, bed, and breakfast with Mrs. Keaster. A very tidy, pleasant place, and I enjoyed the food. After supper, Elder Russon secured a boat at fifteen cents an hour, and we had a very pleasant ride. Rock River[325] running in shape of a horseshoe around the town. I tried my hands at the oars and found I could do very well.

At the photographer's: Mr. Mattie, a Frenchman who let me develop the negatives. They were not quite dry, although the electric fan dries them very quick.

We then went on to one of the busy corners of the town and held street meeting. Elder Russon presiding. Sang several songs and prayer. Elder Olson, opening remarks, followed by myself and Elder Russon. A very good crowd gathered and remained during the meeting. I sold one of Cowley's *Doctrines*.[326] A police officer spoke very kindly to us and invited us to come back again. At the room, prayer and bed about 10:00 p.m. I slept with Uncle Ed.

## July 9, 1907, Tuesday, Milwaukee, Watertown [p. 125]

Breakfast about 7:00 a.m. Uptown and got negatives and bid President Russon and Uncle Edd goodbye and Godspeed and gave Uncle Edd the kiss that his wife, [Dora Lowry Olson], gave me. They went to Ft. Madison at 8:40 a.m.

I left for Milwaukee about 9:23 a.m. Pass some beautiful homes. Also, some quite large lakes with farms and homes on all sides. Boats of various kinds. Some of the places used as pleasure resorts. Several places the railroad station is opposite and near the lake. Everything looks green and beautiful. [p. 126]

Reached here [Milwaukee] about 11:00 a.m. Watertown must be about 45 miles. Took Fond du Lac Avenue car to 2707 Clark Street, where church is one block south from the end of the line. Key at Brother Lemke's, as the elders not in. They came soon after 12:00 noon. See signatures above.[327]

We had dinner prepared by Elder Tanner: potatoes, green peas, bread and butter, strawberries, and cake. We then visited Juneau Park[328] on the shores of Lake Michigan—a beautiful place, well-kept flowers, lawns, walks winding up and down the shore of the lake. The Chicago and Northwestern Railroad runs next to the lake. Steamers going and coming. Water craft of various kinds in cove. Not far out, a little east of north, a prominent bluff runs out into lake with beautiful homes. Located there is pumping station,[329] which supplies the city with water which is drawn from long distance in the lake. Depot of Chicago Northwestern [Railroad] lies to the south, and farther on the manufacturing industries of Milwaukee— almost hidden in smoke. The tower[330] is 393 feet high, and one feels rather peculiar by the [p. 127] time the top is reached by winding tower stairs.

323. Veterans Memorial Park, bounded by Wisconsin, Milwaukee, South Third, and South Fourth Streets.

324. This Civil War monument was dedicated in 1893 with the inscription "Tribute to Soldiers Dead 1861–1865."

325. River rising from the highlands south of Lake Winnebago and cutting through Watertown, Jefferson, and Ft. Atkinson to enter Lake Koshkonong and eventually overfilling and flowing into the Mississippi River.

326. Matthias Cowley, *Cowley's Talks on Doctrine* (Chattanooga: Ben E. Rich, 1902). The book had several printings, including a Chicago printing in 1905, published by Missions of the Church of Jesus Christ of Latter-day Saints.

327. The following signatures and addresses are located in the diary at this point: "Benj. T. Tanner, Tilden, Idaho, 2707 Clark Street, Milwaukee; John A. Bourne, Farmington, Utah, 2707 Clarke Street, Milwaukee."

328. A large park in downtown Milwaukee bounded by North Prospect and the shores of Lake Michigan.

329. Northpoint Water Tower, located on North Avenue, was built in 1873.

330. Anderson may be referring to the City Hall Building, located at 200 East Wells Street. The building was designed by H. C. Coch in 1893 in the German Renaissance Revival Style. Its 393-foot-tall bell tower holds the third largest bell in the world. See 14 July 1907 diary entry.

I made a view looking northwest. The park is named after Solomon Juneau,[331] who built the first cabin and located on the river. A fine statue of him is one of the prominent sights of the park; and a little farther west is a statue, Leif Erickson of Iceland, who came to America in 1000 A.D.

Evening, we spent with Sister Minnie Minster and husband. An excellent supper with strawberry short-cake was partaken of. Evening was spent in listening to selections on the phonograph, and I related my experiences in Missouri regarding the testimony of the witnesses of the Book of Mormon, which was listened to very attentively by all present. It was near 12:00 midnight when we retired at the church. Sister Minster and husband invited me to stay with them.

## July 10, 1907, Wednesday, Milwaukee [p. 127]

Rose about 6:30 a.m. Bath, breakfast, read, and wrote some in diary. Uptown, left negatives at Mr. Hirsher's for development. Came out very good. Called on Charles F. Netzow Company. Treated us very kindly and sent out Mr. Bert Harris with us for lunch. He has charge of Utah Division [?] [p. 128] Business. Had lived in Idaho, in Jackson Hole, and many other places in the West. Did not believe in any religion. Very enthusiastic over mountains and West in general. Does not think will be here very long; likes the West. Brother Bourne left with him a Book of Mormon and other literature.

Got negatives and at church and balance of afternoon there. Got proof of negative of Juneau Park. It was very fine. A long chat with young people at Steinborn Gallery on views and history of our people.

Supper about 6:30 p.m. and then at the docks where I took the boat for Chicago. About 8:30 p.m. or 9:00 p.m. when we left. I did not take a bed, as I went to sleep in chair; and it was late when I woke up. Brothers Bourne and Tanner are very fine elders and were kind to me—doing all they could to help me around. Secured some good negatives.

## July 11, 1907, Thursday, Chicago [p. 128]

The steamer *Wisconsin* reached Chicago about 6:30 a.m. A heavy rainstorm, so there [p. 129] was some time before I left the vessel. I enjoyed watching the vessel and scanning the horizon for land or sail to the left of us. A large, dark vessel came in sight soon after 5:00 a.m. One of the passengers told me she was from Michigan. After awhile, saw the shoreline to the left, and to the left and behind us, another steamer.

I reached the church about 9:00 a.m. and immediately commenced to arrange for developing. Fixed the negatives, reducing some and retouching and spotting out. Developed a batch of about thirty-four. Not so many blisters as usual. Think have had the hypo too strong.

It was late when I got the pictures through, so I did mounting. But rose early next morning and, with assistance of Elder Rasmusson, finished and sent off quite a number. Surprised that I got no letter from home. A letter from Elder Junius F. Wells; also Ira J. McKell. I will soon get the work through and hope to be in Palmyra on July 24.

## July 12, 1907, Friday, Chicago [p. 130]

Rose about 5:00 a.m. A good night's rest. Breakfast: mush, bread, jelly, and butter.

Elder James Peterson of Riverton, [Utah], left for St. Paul this 7:00 a.m. I sent picture of Fourth [of July] to his wife.

Elder W. L. Wanless left for Lodi, Wisconsin. I sent photos and letter with him and wrote Elder John Russon and sent views. See Letter B.

Elders John A. Bourne and Benjamin F. Tanner, Milwaukee, Wisconsin. Wrote and sent views and card.

Dora L. Olson and sent view of monument in Watertown, Wisconsin.

Wrote John D. Whitmer, "Far West" via Kingston.

Wrote George Swenson, "Far West" via Kingston.

---

331. A French-Canadian fur trader who established his home on a spit of land on the east bank of the south-flowing Milwaukee River. He had been in the area since 1818.

Wrote Elder Carl Madsen Jr., Nauvoo.

A chat with President Ellsworth this evening regarding the work in the Northwestern States Mission. Said expected to put out one hundred thousand copies of the Book of Mormon[332] and then commence to baptize the people. Sold in June: 1,431 Books of Mormon; 6,549 small books; 275 loaned; 78,000 tracts distributed; 2,601 subscriptions, *Liahona*; 41,876 families visited; 6,732 revisited; 1,262 meetings. Feels very much encouraged with the work being done and is enthusiastic about the Book of Mormon and good it will do.

Received a letter from my wife, and very pleased to get it.

## *July 13, 1907, Saturday, Chicago [p. 131]*

I did not get to bed until near 12:00 or 12:30 a.m. last night. Restless. Read the paper. Also wife's letter. Attended priesthood meeting. Also offered some suggestions about exercises and having something to talk about, cleaning the church, etc.

Loaned Brother Edmunds's school and fireside *Knight of Twentieth Century*. Also loaned one to Brother J. Rasmusson. Cook pie plant, beans. Mopped the floor also. Bath and feel much better. Elder Sagers came today. Not very well. Elder James from Salt Lake. Elder Olson from southern Illinois. Bath and washed out some kerchiefs. Bed about 10:15 p.m. Elder James came in late and to bed with me.

## *July 14, 1907, Sunday, Chicago [p. 131]*

Rose 5:15 a.m. Straightened up for sabbath. Sunday School. Wrote Elder H. S. Vance, Flint, Michigan. Wrote A. E. McMullen, Battle Mountain, Nevada. Wrote to Lowry and sent picture of Daniel in the lion's den with the story.[333] Wrote my wife and sent card of City Hall, Milwaukee, Wisconsin. [**p. 132**]

These two elders from Michigan on a visit: George J. Johnson, Preston, Idaho; Hyrum Kidman, Mendon, Utah.[334] Sent *[Improvement] Era*[335] to Sister Smith by Sister Minnie Ward. Wrote to my nephew, Master J. S. Anderson, and sent card of City Hall at Milwaukee, Wisconsin, to Maraes [?] Popper, corner Ninth and I Streets, Salt Lake City. Card of Solomon Juneau, Mother [Anderson], postcard, Grand Avenue, Milwaukee. Marn Anderson, Provo, Utah, postcard, Leif Erickson.[336] Spent the afternoon writing.

Enjoyed conversation with Professor Mills after Sunday School. Fixed dinner: beans, bread and butter, radishes, cake, pie plant. Elders J. M. Anderson and Sagers ate with me.

Warm. Elder John Alleman and President Ellsworth spoke tonight. John traced the gospel restored by Christ and lost and through Dark Ages and later revealed by Prophet Joseph Smith.

---

332. President Ellsworth's publication efforts included a 1905 edition of the Book of Mormon. It was republished in 1906 with 12,000 copies printed and again in 1907 with 27,000 copies. In 1908, a third edition was printed. A large-type edition was published in 1911 and again reprinted in 1912. The Central States Mission (Independence, Missouri) published several editions of the Book of Mormon beginning in 1913, based on the fifth Chicago edition, published in 1912.

333. Anderson may be sending his son material from the Sunday School lesson manual. Lesson 35, "Daniel," *Primary Department Bible Stories, 1906–1907* (Salt Lake City: Deseret Sunday School Union, 1906), 1–4.

334. Elders Johnson's and Kidman's autographs are found on page 132 of Anderson's diary.

335. *The Improvement Era* (1897–1970) was the official publication of the YMMIA; but, by 1900, it was the premier adult periodical of the Church. In 1907, seventeen hundred free copies were sent monthly to the missionaries to be used as tracts.

336. Apparently, Anderson is sending photographic postcards of Solomon Juneau's cabin or statue and Leif Erickson's statue in the Juneau Park in Milwaukee. See 9 July 1907 diary entry.

## July 15, 1907, Monday, Chicago [p. 133]

Rose about 6:30 a.m. Wrote to my wife about pioneer picture.[337] Sent letter to my wife and wrote sixteenth. Also E. A. Richards and money order he sent me. M. E. Crandall, Salt Lake City, a card on the banks of the Mississippi.

Turned the washer for Sister Ellsworth. Do the washing for so many, and it is too much work for the women. Arranged the book for unmounted views of [blank]. A chat with President Ellsworth in regard to sleeping. Also about rent, lodgings at Mrs. Weir's.

Developed and washed a number of prints. Also some kodaks. Bed about 11:00 p.m. Elder Nielson from Freedom, Utah, came yesterday. I used to board with his father in Fountain Green.[338] Very warm today.

## July 16, 1907, Tuesday, Chicago [p. 133]

Rose. Sent book, July [Improvement] Era, B. H. Roberts's speech[339] to H. M. Anschutz, 19 North Fourth Street, Keokuk. I sent E. A. Richards proof of site of Joseph Smith's home, Far West, [Missouri]. Sent proof [Independence] temple lot to Brother Lars Nielson of Fountain Green by his son, Soren C. Nielson, postmaster, Mirabile, Missouri. Wrote Philander A. Page. Also sent photos. Wrote Elders James U. Ralphs and John F. Rassmussen, 302 South Pleasant Street, [Independence, Missouri]. [p. 134] Finished pictures and mounted a number. Got dinner: vegetable soup. Very good. Strawberries for supper tonight.

I have felt that there is something that President Ellsworth does not like.[340] Fixing up view book for President Bennion today. Views that should have gone

to Independence came here today for Sister Fannie Burnham.

## July 17, 1907, Wednesday, Chicago [p. 134]

Rose about 6:00 a.m. Breakfast for Brothers Rasmusson and Nielson and self. Prepared vegetable soup for dinner. Printed batch of five five-by-seven [—], forty-seven five-by-seven; and developed nine eight-by-ten.

Went down town in the evening to F. A. Kerns and for bread.

President Ellsworth went to Independence, [Missouri], today. Elder Sagers of Tooele County, [Utah], went home this evening. Sick with appendicitis. Elder Stephens came in from Michigan today. Elder James had watch taken. About $25. Sister Peterson from Ogden received telegram that her sister was dead and left for home. Elder Stephens ate supper and dinner with us. Bed about 10:30 p.m. Letters from Elders Madsen and Roberts. Also Mrs. Balson.

## July 18, 1907, Thursday, Chicago [p. 135]

Rose 5:30 a.m. Sponge bath. Breakfast: mush, potatoes, toast, honey, and rolls. Elder Cragun ate with us. I worked up the pictures this morning and then went uptown to get some photo stock, albums, etc. In Montgomery Ward Tower,[341] 394 feet, twenty-five stories. Get an excellent view from this point. Could not see far over the city. Wind blew smoke over the town. Elevator from basement to twelfth story. Walk to front and east end of building and elevator lifts you to the twenty-fifth story. The breeze was cool

---

337. Anderson's famous photograph of nearly four hundred surviving pioneers of 1847 taken on 24 July 1897 for the Pioneer Jubilee Celebration held at Temple Square, Salt Lake City.

338. Anderson traveled by horse and buggy to remote villages in Utah, like Fountain Green, between 1884 and 1907 with his traveling tent gallery and often stayed with local residents.

339. B. H. Roberts's reply to the Salt Lake City Ministerial Association's review was printed in the Improvement Era, 10 (July 1907): 687–743. See 13 June 1907 diary entry and footnote.

340. See 25 July 1907 diary entry for a possible explanation.

341. Located on the northwest corner of East Madison at 6 North Madison Avenue, the Montgomery Ward and Company Building is known today as the Tower Building.

and refreshing. It was a wonderful sight to look at the great buildings, various styles of architecture. Stopped at the nineteenth story and sent postal card to Lowry, Ellwood Anderson, Mrs. Ellen Stain—Montgomery Ward and Company[342] pay the postage.

Found some fine albums for views. Home about 4:00 p.m. A lunch and then got frames for "Golgotha." Elders had meeting. Elder Edmunds spoke on the *Ecclesiastical History*.[343] Read *Deseret News* of July 15. Bed after working up cash account.

## July 19, 1907, Friday, Chicago [p. 135]

Rose soon after 5:00 a.m. Elder President[344] Cragun slept with me. Made bed on benches and chairs, cushions, and quilts. Sponge bath. Breakfast. Assorted views. Packed negatives and out to 209 East Fifty-Seventh Street. Mr. C. L. Hull, to whom Mr. John F. Decker of Cramer recommended me [p. 136] to get transparencies[345] made, said could not do them today or before Monday. Had a long talk with him on religion. Does not believe in Christianity. Would throw minister out of doors. Daughter nine years old has never been in church. Gave him tract, "Plan of Salvation." Would like more literature.

Visited Jackson Park, site of [1893] World's Fair.[346] Some of the buildings still standing. In the German building;[347] used for refreshments now.

Some rain this morning; also this afternoon. Did not get back to the room until near 5:30 p.m. Supper and, after bread, had a talk with Mrs. Drechett about transparencies.

Out on Milwaukee and Paulina and held a street meeting with John Alleman. Lady stayed. Accepted a tract and ask us when and where we would hold meeting and wished us good night and God bless us. I find it a hard task to speak to a moving audience. We did not sing. Brother Alleman read from Acts 17, "The Unknown God." Offer [blank].

## July 20, 1907, Saturday, Chicago [p. 136]

Rose about 6:00 a.m. Breakfast. Finished a batch of postals and views. While developing and printing, made soup of vegetables. All seemed to enjoy it. Cleaned up the room. Wiped the linoleum.

President Cragun asked me to go on the street with him, Sister Russell, Brother J. M. Anderson. Meeting on Chicago and Paulina. One of the best meetings I have been to. There was a good [p. 137] crowd, and attention was paid. They wished to have another song. Opening song: "High on the Mountain Top."[348] Prayer by Elder Cragun. Singing: "O My Father." President Cragun asked me to speak. Sister Russell followed. Then, President Cragun gave them a gospel sermon. They ask for a song. Elder Anderson sang "I Know That My Redeemer Lives."[349] Only sold two books.

Home about 9:45 p.m. Tired. Elders Dahle and Harris ate supper with us.

---

342. Anderson uses the abbreviation *Mont.G.W&Co* here.

343. Anderson may be referring to B. H. Roberts's book, *Outlines of Ecclesiastical History* (Salt Lake City: G. Q. Cannon and Sons Company, 1893); a third printing, published in Salt Lake City by Deseret News Press in 1902, was probably the one available at the time.

344. Anderson's courtesy title of *Elder President* depicts Elder Cragun as both a missionary and a conference president.

345. The transparencies typically were 3¼ inches by 4¼ inches and were used with a lantern slide projector.

346. Officially known as the World's Columbian Exposition of 1893 to celebrate the four-hundredth anniversary of Columbus's arrival in America. It officially opened on 11 May 1893 and closed on 30 October 1893.

347. Most buildings were torn down or moved after the fair closed. The German Building, however, was the costliest and purportedly the finest foreign building at the fair. The German government spent $820,000 on its exhibits, which included the construction of this German-styled structure that was still standing when Anderson visited Jackson Park (553 acres), which had been gradually converted to a park and golf course after the closing of the fair.

348. An LDS hymn written by Joel H. Johnson (1802–82) in 1856.

349. Popular Protestant hymn written by Samuel Medley (1738–99). The music, however, was composed by Latter-day Saint Lewis D. Edwards (1858–1921) in 1901.

*July 21, 1907, Sunday, Chicago [p. 137]*

Rose about 7:00 a.m. Breakfast. Moved things into west part of church.

Sunday School a little late. First song had been sung. Enjoyed the remarks of Elder Thornstoff, Armour's representative in Germany. He met some of the leading people who spoke well of Mormons' beliefs.

Services at 11:30 a.m. Elder Jensen of Logan and Elder Hall, a student, speakers. Afternoon fixing up my letters and papers and writing to my wife and Edda and Lowry.

Evening at meeting, I was called to speak by Elder Stark. Remarks were on the Word of Wisdom—principally how Joseph Smith's work coincided with science. Elder Cragun followed, endorsing what I had said. Made our bed on the floor, and it was better than the bed.

*July 22, 1907, Monday, Chicago [p. 138]*

Rose about 6:00 a.m. Put on the mush, fixed up the negatives and my things in the cupboard, and finished letters to my wife, Lowry, and Edda. Wrote to Mrs. Batson; also to Miss Fannie Burnham; also John B. McLallen; and fixed up pictures.

Went to the residence of Alta Swart, who died Friday last. Attended the funeral held in LDS church at 1:15 p.m. President Ellsworth presiding and speaking. Quartets and music by elders and choir. Services will do much good.

Very warm this morning. Cooler this afternoon. Visited Fidelity Portrait Company, and they will try and do copying of negatives for me at 10:30 a.m. tomorrow. 5:00 p.m., developed postal cards and about fifteen, ten by twelve. Read paper while they were washing. About 11:40 p.m., went to bed. Elder Cragun and I making our bed on the floor, as usual.

*July 23, 1907, Tuesday, Chicago [p. 138]*

Rose about 6:00 a.m. Brother Nielson got breakfast. Wrote my wife this morning and this evening—some things I had forgotten.

I felt very much worried and downcast over the way Brother Rasmusson talked about there not being room for so many, and I told him how [p. 139] I had felt when he spoke about it at noon. In the evening, he came to me and said he was sorry and that he had spoken as he did and wished to make it right and offered me his hand, saying he was out here to do good and not to hurt anyone's feelings.

From 2:30 p.m. to 5:30 p.m., assisted in making 3 1/4 by 4 1/2 negatives, five by seven negatives, and eight by ten from my cabinet—must have made about sixty. I changed the plates while Mr. [blank] exposed the plates.

Evening: washed up the dishes. Wrote letter and diary. Wrote Elder J. F. Rasmusson postcard, George Edward Anderson [—]. Wrote J. Wellington Seeley, John McLallen, Far West in view.[350] Bed about 10:20 p.m. after prayer with elders.

*July 24, 1907, Wednesday, Chicago [p. 139]*

Rose soon after 5:00 a.m. Bath. Made our list for views of railway for Mr. Ordway. Wrote wife. President Cragun invited me to breakfast. Washed dishes. Wrote postscript to wife. Finished batch forty-three, eight by ten; thirty-one, five by seven; one, five by seven; one, eight by ten [—].

I thought I had better eat with the elders and try and forget the past. I could see it would cause feelings if I left off now. Would call for explanation and would likely wound Brother Rasmusson's feelings. So I ate and felt that I could learn to school my feelings;[351] and it was best. [p. 140]

Developed a batch of pictures during the

---

350. Anderson may be sending John McLallen's photograph to him in Breckenridge, Missouri. Because Anderson was unable to print negatives while visiting the McLallen home, he wrote McLallen's name and mailing address on the negative.

351. See 3 August 1907 diary entry and accompanying footnote about Anderson's "schooling his feelings."

forenoon and afternoon. Prepared dinner rice with help of President Cragun. Brothers Rasmusson and Nelson late coming in. Having better success with the developing of the pictures. Ordered a picture of pioneers for office to be sent to President Ellsworth.

At 6:00 p.m., took elevated railroad for Logan Square[352] and went to 1385 Monticello Avenue and found Sister Hannah Sorensen Hyldalls at 1340 Longdale Avenue. Spent the evening or until 10:00 p.m. talking with her about her leaving the Church. Apostasy was the charge. She said the question of the sabbath was the only one which was discussed when she was at the bishop's. Could not tell why she done as she did at the time, but now can understand it and see the hand of providence in it. If she had remained a Mormon, would not have come to Chicago; and the difference that existed between her children, especially Peter, would not have been reconciled. Waited on him during his sickness of two years. Quit drinking beer. His brothers helped and paid his expenses. Julia Peterson was brought into the Church. Her finances $18, $11. Reverend Hansen and his going to Utah[353] and her defense of the Mormon people. Her children angry and told her to be quiet. The struggle she had to overcome her feelings and know what to do. Her son of Elsinore, [Utah], and wife here. And many other items discussed. Home and bed about 11:00 p.m.

### July 25, 1907, Thursday, Chicago [p. 141]

Rose early; took a sponge bath. Finished fourteen postcards, thirty-six, eight by ten. Breakfast with the elders.

President Ellsworth told me a report being circulated in the Central States Mission that I had pro-

posed to a Miss Chism of Nauvoo and that I could arrange for her to marry in polygamy.[354] I could fix that matter all right.

Told President Ellsworth that I had never had such a conversation with any lady—that I had never talked with Miss Chism. I would not know Miss Chism from the others that I met at Nauvoo. I had never been in her company that I knew of unless it was when others were present. I had been introduced to a number and could not remember the names.

I ask President Ellsworth to point out the girl on the Nauvoo picture. He did. I remember her face but never remember talking with her unless it was she that was present at Brother Nelson's. Then I only talked to the company, and I remember Brother Nelson said he believed I had been asleep as I was reading the paper.

President Ellsworth said he had been to Nauvoo and talked with Miss Chism, and she said she had never been alone with me, and he thought the conference president had misunderstood her. Said he would write President Bennion and not to worry about it. Said Apostle George A. Smith said he thought I would be gone from here about three weeks to get through with Kirtland and Palmyra and all the places.

I was troubled over that yarn. Could not work to advantage.

Good success with pictures. Packed eight by ten negatives. Elders met tonight. Bed about 10:30 p.m.

### July 26, 1907, Friday, Chicago [p. 142]

Rose 5:00 a.m. Bath. Cold, so had to cover up last night or towards morning. Exercise a few moments with breathing.

Fasting this morning. Prayer that I might under-

352. Located at the intersection of Kedzie, Logan, and Milwaukee Boulevards. Named for Civil War General John Alexander Logan (1826–86), who also founded the Grand Army of the Republic and originated Decoration Day—known today as Memorial Day.

353. During the second half of the nineteenth century and the beginning of the twentieth century, many Protestant churches supported and sent "Christian" missionaries to Utah to evangelize the Latter-day Saints and to reform LDS society.

354. This was a transition period for the LDS Church (1904–11). The Church was attempting to curtail new plural marriages being performed by Church members. Such a charge would naturally cause real concern on Anderson's part. Elders John W. Taylor and Matthias F. Cowley of the Quorum of the Twelve Apostles were not sustained at the April 1906 general conference of the Church because they would not comply with the First Presidency's policy on this issue.

stand the peculiar situation I am in and why President Ellsworth speaks as he does.

Wrote to Mrs. Sarah [Whitmer] Kerr, Kingston, [Missouri], and sent photo of Oliver Cowdery [painting] and postcard, J. Whitmer. Also ask her if she would let oil paintings go to J. Hafen,[355] Springville, to be renewed. Elder Benjamin T. Tanner, 2707 Clark Street, Milwaukee, about package of photos lost—card.

Finished and developed paper. Finished nine postcards, Elder Curtis; five, Hope Russell; eighteen, Elder Alleman; ten, George Edward Anderson; eight, five by seven; seventeen, eight by ten.

In afternoon, went out and bought bananas, one dozen, five cents; bread, five cents; and pie, six cents; and broke my fast in park that lies several blocks east of church.

Evening: cleaned shelves, stove, mopped linoleum, bottles, and put material that I wish to use away. I have left kitchen etc. much cleaner and tidier than when I came. It was near 11:00 p.m. when I went to bed.

July 25 and 26: Talked with President Cragun about the report at Nauvoo. Said he had heard nothing about it when there. Yesterday, I spoke to Sister Laura Bennion to see if she knew who the girl was. Said if they knew these girls, they would not believe such a report—that her impression was that they were not tidy, neat as she would like to see when they came to Nauvoo.

July 26: Brother Rasmusson ask me to sample cake. I got [—] milk, and it was very good.

## July 27, 1907, Saturday, Chicago [p. 143]

Rose soon after 5:00 a.m. Bath. Cold so that extra blanket was comfortable before daylight.

Painted trays. Fixed and separated views. Uptown. Turner Brass Works. Bought glasses. Out to Joseph H.

Smith's, but did not find at home. To see Mr. Callahan about ticket. Many places I went to do business closed at 12:00 noon and 1:00 p.m.

Supper with elders. Washed dishes, cleaned closet, and then separated and packed my things so I could tell which go home etc. It was 11:00 p.m. before I went to bed.

## July 28, 1907, Sunday, Chicago [p. 143]

Cool the past two or three nights. Bath. Cleaned up the rooms near where I was working.

Sunday School. Feeling downcast, but much better after school. Instructive lecture on the Book of Mormon from Professor Mills on traditions of American Indians—about four brothers coming to this land and younger usurping authority and becoming king. The story of the Aztecs and their god. Cortez. Human sacrifice. It resembled the visit of the Savior to this continent, as related in the Book of Mormon. Attend service after Sunday School.

With President Cragun, went home and had dinner with Sister Bromley out at Logan Square. She paid our fare on the elevated railroad. Her husband did not reach home before we left. At depot to meet him, but did not come. I told Sister Bromley about her son-in-law and wife and my visit with them. Brother Cragun operated the Gramophone[356] which, by the way, is a very good one. So many records. President Cragun (see page 145) [p. 145] played and sang some of our songs, and I tried to learn. Conversation with Sister Bromley about her conversion, her father and mother, etc. Looked through album and found a number of familiar faces. See Boyer, Paul Ludlow, and William B. Lowry, my wife's brother.[357]

Evening meeting: Elder Dahle, Sister Bennion, and President Ellsworth the speakers. Elder Anderson singing "O My Father." The president of the branch

---

355. John Hafen (1856–1910) was a well-known Utah landscape artist who had been trained in Paris, with Church support, to help prepare him to paint the murals in the Salt Lake Temple. Closely associated with Anderson in Springville, Hafen died in 1910 before Anderson returned home from his mission.

356. Trademark used for an early phonograph invented by Emile Berliner beginning in 1894.

357. William Brown Lowry (1857–1943) served in the Northern States Mission from 8 September 1902 to 31 August 1904.

(Elder Johnson) also spoke. President Ellsworth read a number of Mormon hymns. Spoke of the favorites of leading brethren. Prophet Joseph Smith had President John Taylor sing "A Poor Wayfaring Man of Grief"[358] just before the mob commenced firing into the [Carthage] Jail. The effect of song—they were inspired. Enjoyed the talk very much. Awakened many thoughts and reflections in my mind. After meeting, started letter to my wife.

## July 29, 1907, Monday, Chicago [p. 144]

Rose before 6:00 a.m. Wrote to my wife and sent likeness[359] of Elders Madsen, Roberts, Sister Alleman, and Bennion.

Elder John A. Bourne, 2707 Clark Street, Milwaukee, and sent views. Learned that the package that was lost is in post office at Milwaukee.

It was near noon when I got through with letter to my wife. Went to see Sister Behringer, 630 West Twenty-First Street, and made negative of little baby boy she had taken to raise. It is about two months old and was in a pitiable condition when she took it. Had not been washed and was sore and raw from its back down on to the legs. Also, a thick scab on its head. By the use of sweet oil and absorbent cotton, its body is now healed, the head natural, and the yellow color gone. When she took it, the doctor did not think it would live two days. Her daughter, Ida Behringer, has been a great help to her mother in caring for the babe.

Sister Behringer has another boy four years old February 16. Dates his birth from the time she found him on the banks of the River [blank], Pittsburgh, Pennsylvania, fifteen below zero. This child met with an accident, running a pen knife into the ball of the eye when a year old. The doctors said eye must be taken out. Sister Behringer said she could not live and see that child with a hole in place of his eye and would not let the doctors touch him but brought him home and prayed for him with her daughters, getting faith from the mission of Christ and the healing of the sick, blind, etc. in his day and that could be done in this day.

The ball came or formed in the eye in two weeks but was red and inflamed and brown for a year when it changed to the color of the other eye. She gave me picture of this child when was a year old, and now he is four years old. **[p. 145]**

Told me of the babies found chloroformed and the bones of twelve that had been burned in a furnace etc.[360] Has two daughters, one away at school. Her husband fond of children and willing for her to take the last baby. He does not go to church because he says not good enough. Drinks beer and says should quit that before he goes to church.

Uptown, visited A. C. McClurg's; also Deardorf's. In evening, developed negatives at Do Soc [?]. Also, showed views to President Ellsworth and wife and Alonzo Lewis and mother. He wishes a full set of the views. Bed about 11:00 p.m. Out and had a bite to eat before bed.

## July 30, 1907, Tuesday, Chicago [p. 146]

Rose about 6:00 a.m. Out and got lunch after straightening up things. Out and had breakfast in Jefferson Park—tomatoes, graham bread. Wrote up journal. In town in the afternoon and made some purchases. Out about 5:15 p.m. Takes considerable time to shop in Chicago.

Evening: made proofs of Sister Behringer and showed them to her and had a pleasant chat. They

---

358. A popular hymn written by James Montgomery (1771–1854) and introduced to the Saints in Nauvoo. A favorite song of the Prophet Joseph Smith, it gained special prominence in the LDS Church because John Taylor sang it twice in Carthage Jail on 27 June 1844 shortly before the mob attacked and martyred Joseph and Hyrum Smith.

359. Popular term for *photograph*.

360. The *Chicago Tribune* of 1 July 1907 reported the findings of Dr. Randolph W. Holmes, chairman of a special committee of the Chicago Medical Society, who stated that at least 150 illegal "baby" hospitals existed in Chicago and that these hospitals may have killed between five and six thousand newborns. Apparently, Sister Behringer is referring to this report.

***German Edgar and Rachel Smith Ellsworth Family****, Chicago, Illinois, 31 July 1907, courtesy of Homer
Ellsworth, Lehi, Utah. Left to right: Blanche, Ruth in a baby buggy, Mary Rachel, German E., and German S.
Ellsworth. Anderson notes in his diary, "Fixed instrument and went out and made picture of President Ellsworth
and family in park east of church."*

made a lunch for me. Back to the church about 9:30
p.m. Went to Aberdeen Bakery and got a loaf of graham [bread].

Prayer with elders. President Cragun called my attention to pioneer picture in *[Deseret] News.*361 It is very good,
and the description will be a help to me in business.

## July 31, 1907, Wednesday, Chicago *[p. 146]*

Rose soon after 5:30 a.m. Bath. Fixed instrument
and went out and made picture of President Ellsworth
and family in park east of church. Had to seek shelter,
as it rained some. Soaked a number of pictures of
cards. Got views and books straightened out.

All afternoon listing views, packing negatives, etc.
Received a letter from my wife. President Cragun left
for southern Illinois this p.m. with Brother J. Morgan
Anderson as companion. Developed two negatives at
Fidelity Portrait Company. Bed about 10:15 p.m. My
prayer was answered in Brother Burt's putting pioneer
picture in *[Deseret] News.* **[p. 147]**

## August 1, 1907, Thursday, Chicago *[p. 147]*

Rose 5:30 a.m. Shave. Cool enough, so covered up
before morning. Prayer.

I was out last evening and tried to find Alonzo
Lewis, but late and did not get answer to bell. On way

361. The *Deseret News* of 24 July 1907 reproduced Anderson's pioneer photograph. See 15 July 1907 diary entry. The
caption states in part, "The accompanying picture is reproduced through the courtesy of Mr. Anderson of Springville who
holds the copyright."

back, music in street—harp and violin. Enjoyed it. Making out invoices and packing and listing negatives, merchandise, etc. Breakfast about 8:30 a.m. Developed two negatives of President Ellsworth.

To see Alonzo Lewis and delivered set of views and book to him. Wrapped and listed goods I will send home. Wrote on postal cards and sent to my wife. Hungry and got bananas. Ate mostly bread and tomatoes today. Enjoyed very much. Bed about 11:30 p.m. Rain this p.m.

## August 2, 1907, Friday, Chicago [p. 147]

Cool this morning. Rose 5:30 a.m. Out to Jefferson Park and made several negatives of John Alleman. Breakfast: rye bread, milk, cheese, sugar. Continued packing up. Wrote Elder George V. Harris, Independence, Missouri, and card of George Edward Anderson and five views.

At the building of Salvation Army and made several sales of views. Left those ordered and not sold with barber. Packing and listing negatives and getting ready to leave.

## August 3, 1907, Saturday, Chicago [p. 148]

Rose 5:00 a.m. Bath. Cool last night. Wrote H. M. Anschutz, 19 North Fourth [Street], Keokuk, [Iowa]. Expressed to him yesterday eight by ten negative of Nauvoo. Also *Deseret News* pioneers [picture]. Wrote Brother Osburn Richins. Also President Bennion, and spoke of the report that had been circulated in Central States Mission.

At Fidelity Portrait Company place and ordered frames. Also at the Cramer Dry Plate Company and left negatives, and they will ship them with plates I ordered.

Took valise down to LaSalle Depot[362] and made other preparations to go. I did not get off on the 9:15 p.m. train; but, with assistance of President Ellsworth and Elder John Alleman, I took the Lake Shore at 10:30 p.m., reaching Cleveland next morning.

Settled up with President Ellsworth for board, lights, and use of church (rooms in back of church), washing, etc. Also Brothers John Alleman, Curtis, and Sister Russell. Cleaned up the room where I had the goods packed etc.

Elder James Peterson[363] again talked very unpleasant to me. I did not answer back. I have felt very hurt over the way he has treated me but have said very little. He came and ask forgiveness before, and I think he will see the position he is in at the present and regret how he spoke and acted when gone. It was one of the hardest things I have had to do to stay at the church after he talked the way he did. I made a sacrifice of my feelings, and I hope made myself stronger for the rebuffs and slurs a missionary gets; but it comes hard from one that is in the same work. "School thy feelings, oh my brother."[364]

## August 4, 1907, Sunday, Cleveland [p. 149]

Last night at the stop near the White City,[365] Chicago, a colored lady with little girl about four or five years took seat by me and put the little girl to

---

362. Located at 414 South LaSalle Street between West VanBuren and West Harrison Streets, LaSalle Street Station was built in 1903 and was one of Chicago's six major depots.

363. In the diary entries for 23 July and 24 July 1907, Anderson reveals a conflict between himself and Elder Rasmusson. That conflict seems to fit the context of this diary entry of 3 August 1907. The diary entry of 3 August, however, clearly uses Elder Peterson's name rather than Elder Rasmusson's.

364. An LDS hymn written by Charles W. Penrose (1832–1925) in 1860–61 as Penrose was finishing a decade of missionary work in England. Originally written as a poem, it had been made into a popular Church hymn exhorting singers and listeners to practice self-mastery. Penrose had been accused falsely by a fellow missionary of a misdeed, which had caused much heartache.

365. The site of the Columbian Exposition.

*Jefferson Park*, *Chicago, Illinois, 2 August 1907, Anderson Collection, LDSCA. The view shows Elder John W. Alleman from Springville, Utah, who is frequently mentioned in Anderson's diary.*

sleep on the opposite seat. Rather crowded me, but I read the paper and got close to the window and slept a good part of the journey. The baby girl had a teddy bear. They left the train before we reached Cleveland, [Ohio].[366] I called the attention of the child to the rising sun, which looked like a ball of fire. Cool wave last night, for I could not have car windows up.

Got off at the [Cleveland] Erie [Railroad] Depot. Upstairs from the river bed and got breakfast at Saunders Hotel and left grips. Shave and changed pants, shirt. Could not find [LDS] Sunday School, so at service in the Catholic Church[367] not far from the Public

366. County seat of Cuyahoga County, located in northwestern Ohio, on the southern shore of Lake Erie, at the mouth of the Cuyahoga River.

367. The Cathedral of St. John the Evangelist, located at 1007 Superior Avenue. The building was completed in 1852 and seats 1,250 people.

Square.[368] About twelve, took Wade Park and Detroit car and found Sister H. E. Harrison and niece, Miss Jennie Newmarch,[369] at 270 Wade Park Avenue; and they invited me to stay there and assisted me in locating Elders Joseph R. Hicks, Raymond, Alberta, Canada; George L. Spangenler, 1972 Washington Avenue, Ogden, Utah. They room at 2708 Jay Avenue. Came up and spent the evening with us.

Elder William Behunin of Castle Dale, [Utah], wished me to call on Sister Harrison. Find a number of the elders I am acquainted have made this their home and come to recognize and call Sister Harrison their "Cleveland mother." Sister Whipple also here. Elder Mecham, Sister Clara Snyder, and Mr. Sawyer called in the evening. I told Sister Harrison I would go to the hotel. She said no—they could give me an extra bed. Bed about 11:00 p.m.

## *August 5, 1907, Monday, Cleveland [p. 150]*

Rose about 6:00 a.m. Stormy, dull, and foggy. Met Elders Spangenler and Hicks at Saunders Hotel. Out at 8:15 a.m. While waiting, wrote to my wife. Elder Spangenler going to Kirtland with me, but so stormy concluded not to go. So went back to Sister Harrison's, and I packed up large pictures. Elder Spangenler assisting.

After dinner, Elder Spangenler went to town; and I crated a [.]odeor bureau. It was 7:30 p.m. before I got through. Elder Hicks came and helped me move it. It was near 8:30 p.m. when we had supper. Sister Harrison is going to move to Salt Lake, and I felt that I

should help her. She has been so kind to the elders. Jennie Newmarch, her niece, lives with her.

Mrs. Corbin called this p.m. She wished to be kindly remembered to Sister Jennie Whipple. Recently lost her daughter Jessie. Very tired, so soon fell asleep when I sat down. Find Sister Harrison has many relatives and acquaintances in Utah that I know. A fine lady. I am glad I could assist her. Boxed the globe she had done and wheat in [blank]. I did not do much writing or work for myself today. I was too busy.

## *August 6, 1907, Tuesday, Cleveland [p. 151]*

Rose 5:00 a.m. Wrote up diary. Sun shining. Breakfast about 7:30 a.m. Quite a chat with Sister Harrison about [1893] World's Fair, Chicago, Utah, etc. Wrote up my diary and fixed up cash account and at 11:00 a.m. took the Wade Park car and rode to Willoughby,[370] two and one-half miles from Kirtland, about 12:15 p.m. Put my instrument in corner where sign showed directions to Kirtland and other towns.

Bought bananas, five cents, for dinner. When I returned, a gentleman who told me he was Fred Viall,[371] relative of Schramm's Drugstore under McCormick Building,[372] Salt Lake City, asked me to ride. Took me to within one-half mile of Kirtland and where I could plainly see the first temple erected to our God in this dispensation.[373] "Had enjoyed the visit and would now let me out so could get back home in time for dinner." I asked him to have a banana. Did not wish to interfere with dinner.

Short distance out of Willoughby, we crossed the

---

368. A ten-acre "village green," the Public Square is the most visible legacy of the city's New England founders. It marks the center of the city of Cleveland and, by 1907, had moved from a common grazing area and meeting place to a park with two memorials erected—a statue of Moses Cleveland unveiled in 1888 and the Soldiers and Sailors Monument dedicated on Independence Day in 1894. Interestingly, the Public Square was the site of the first successful demonstration of electric streetlights in 1879.

369. Jennie Pamela Newmarch (1885–1950), daughter of Clara A. Harrison Newmarch (1863–?); Clara and H. E. Harrison were sisters.

370. Willoughby was also known as Chagrin prior to 1834.

371. Anderson spells this name *Viel* and also *Viall*. Apparently, he was referring to Fred Viall, a local resident.

372. Located on the corner of Main and First South Streets in Salt Lake City. Still standing today. "F. C. Schramm, Druggist" occupied the street-level corner space that fronted on Main and First South Streets.

373. The Kirtland Temple, the first Latter-day Saint temple, was dedicated on 27 March 1836.

*Kirtland Temple*, *Kirtland, Ohio, August 1907, Anderson Collection, LDSCA. The chair in the foreground has been traditionally associated with Patriarch Joseph Smith Sr. and/or the Prophet Joseph Smith Jr. Built between 1834 and 1836, the Kirtland Temple is the first major structure erected by the LDS Church. It is a monumental and substantial building, illustrating the devoted labor and sacrifice of the first few thousand LDS Church members. Although some other religious groups in northern Ohio also built sturdy and well-crafted meetinghouses during this period, most local churches were modest, wood-frame structures. In contrast, the Kirtland Temple is unusually large and substantial. Its walls are constructed of stone covered with plaster, in harmony with Joseph Smith's 1833 City of Zion plan that called for buildings of solid-masonry construction. The expectation that their first meetinghouse would be a "temple," a sacred structure reminiscent of the biblical temples where divine revelations were received, inspired the early Saints to create an impressive symbol of their faith.*

Chagrin River. [p. 150] On south side of this bridge is where Reorganized Church baptizes. North of bridge is where it is said the Prophet drove stakes and put plank under the water and said, "Now see me walk on water."[374] Rocks—no stake drove there. [p. 151]

Beet patch on each side of the road. Farmer was cutting off tops with scythe[375] and women gathering and preparing them for market. Mr. Viall born here. His father, now dead, lived here when our people called Kirtland home. Did not belong to any religion. His father had expressed himself that he thought the early leaders of the Mormons were "fakers." His father knew Joseph Smith and Brigham Young.

I soon found myself going down hill and east towards temple. Sat down, ate bananas. A word of prayer and thought of when our people were here seventy to eighty years ago.[376]

Crossed the east branch of the Chagrin River and soon came to Chillicothe Road, which leads south to the temple.[377] See page 38. [p. 38] This road continues through the state and was the road our people left on when driven out. At the corner, we turn south. Stands the two-story brick "Johnson Hotel"[378] now occupied by Mr. John Schupp as a dwelling. Mrs. Schupp tells me the place was built by Peter French. Mrs. Schupp's father, Samuel Brown, bought the place from Jake Ivins. Mrs. Schupp was born here forty-one years ago. Her father has owned the place about forty-six years. Thinks the place must have been used as a store, as she found a sign in attic: "Christopher Quinn putting up hay today."

The road north crosses the east branch of the Chagrin River and bears to the left after crossing the bridge and leads to Mentor, and the Garfield home,[379] etc. Across the street north is the old N. K. Whitney

374. This widely spread folktale has been quite persistent—even appearing in a 1976 non-LDS publication. A story of a Latter-day Saint elder pretending to walk on water first appeared in the *Philadelphia Saturday Courier* in 1830. Eventually, Joseph Smith was connected with the story; and, in one version, when the plank broke, he fell in the river and drowned.

375. An implement used in cutting agricultural products like hay, composed of a long, curving blade fastened at an angle to a long handle.

376. Joseph Smith arrived at Kirtland on 1 February 1831. The Latter-day Saints gathered there until 1838 when more than sixteen hundred left, most gathering at the new LDS Church center in northwestern Missouri.

377. Anderson included the following comments at this point in the diary: "Johnson Hotel, N. K. Whitney, Home, August 6, 1907. Mrs. Sarah Jane Whitney. Continued from page 151 and 182."

378. The inn was originally built by Peter French and was the first brick building in Kirtland. It served as a church and a community center following its purchase by the United Order in 1833. It is a nonextant building of significant historical importance because the first patriarchal blessings were given there and because members of the Quorum of the Twelve left on their first mission from this building. Later, it was given to John Johnson (1779–1843) and was known as the Johnson Inn. Johnson settled in Hiram, Ohio, in 1818 and converted to Mormonism in 1831. Joseph and Emma Hale Smith resided in their home in Hiram for one year between September 1831 and September 1832. Following the Saints' exodus in 1838, Johnson remained in Kirtland and died there on 30 July 1843.

379. U.S. President James A. Garfield (1831–81) lived in a one-story farmhouse built in 1832 and known as Lawnfield. Garfield bought the house in 1876. It is located at 8095 Mentor Avenue in Mentor, Ohio.

home.[380] Now owned, F[red] H. Sanborn, blacksmith. Unmarried, and his father, A[lden] E. Sanborn, and mother, Sarah Jane Sanborn, and sister [Nellie M. Sanborn] live with him. Mrs. Sanborn has a piece of the scroll work from the temple (which she secured when it was repaired) for Susa Young Gates[381] and Patriarch John Smith.[382] Mrs. Sanborn recalls the visit of Sister Gates and Brother Smith with much satisfaction and prizes very highly the Christmas edition of the *[Deseret] News* and other papers sent by Patriarch Smith and Sister Gates. Ivan Sickle, John R. Coe, Howard Johnson, and Charley Morley and Riley Harris have owned and lived in the house. See page 153.

[**p. 153**]

Across the street east from N. K. Whitney home is the building where N. K. Whitney ran a store. J[ohn] F. Wells has had a store here for twenty-four years and has lived in Kirtland thirty years. Post office is located here and has been for many years with Mr. Wells as postmaster, except when Democratic president. Mr. Wells will retire from business, having sold the place to Henry Hooper. Mr. Hooper has leased the place to John Sleemim,[383] who will continue the merchandise business.

Mr. Wells would like to visit Utah and get acquainted [with] the descendants of Titus Billings,[384] who was his mother's brother.[385]

Joseph Smith [III], president, Reorganized Church, born in this building upstairs.[386] In the center of street is a trough for horses etc. to drink. Piped from spring. From here, we soon commence to ascend the hill, passing the home of the Prophet. Now occupied by Mrs. McFarland on the right. On the left, a blacksmith shop. A little farther up and on the brow of the hill is the old cemetery,[387] and west and north in the flat is the farm owned by Emma Smith. Now has a good crop of wheat in the shock.

On reaching the temple, I set my load down and rested on the grass for three-fourths of hour. Then across the street to the Kirtland Hotel,[388] and Elder Albert E. Stone[389] of the Reorganized Church showed me through the temple. From the tower, we get a beautiful view [**p. 154**] and an idea of the situation of Kirtland. It is decidedly a pretty place—one of the most beautiful I have ever seen. Reminds me of the creek bottom and benches just below the mouth of Hobble Creek Canyon[390] if you forget the great [Wasatch] Mountains in the background.

380. Newel Kimball Whitney (1795–1850), early convert to Mormonism, chosen to be bishop of the Church in Kirtland in December 1831. His home is located on the northwest corner of Chillicothe and Kirtland-Chardon Roads.

381. Susa Young Gates (1856–1933), daughter of Brigham Young, a writer, publisher, advocate for women's achievements, educator, missionary, and genealogist. Anderson spelled the name *Susie*.

382. John Smith (1832–1911), eldest son of Hyrum and Jerusha Barden Smith, LDS Church patriarch from 1855 until his death in 1911.

383. Anderson's spelling is unclear. We think he spells the name *Sleemim*. Period maps spell the name *Sleeman*.

384. Titus Billings (1793–1866), baptized in Kirtland, moved to Independence, Missouri, in 1832 and eventually immigrated to Utah.

385. Salomi Billings Wells (1799–1833).

386. Joseph Smith III was born in the early morning of 6 November 1832 in the northwest corner of the upper room.

387. Located on the west side of Chillicothe Road. Many Saints, including Mary Duty Smith (Joseph Smith's grandmother), Jerusha Barden Smith (Hyrum Smith's wife), Oliver Granger, and John and Elsa Johnson (early Mormon converts and benefactors of Joseph and Emma Hale Smith) are buried here.

388. George W. Robinson (1814–78) operated a hotel in this building, which opened in October 1837. The hotel stood here until it was razed in 1936. It was replaced in 1959 by the current RLDS chapel across the street from the temple.

389. Albert E. Stone (1857–1931), local RLDS member who apparently was a caretaker at the Kirtland Temple at the time.

390. Located in Utah Valley, Utah County, near present-day Springville, Utah, Anderson's hometown.

***Kirtland Temple****, Kirtland, Ohio, August 1907, Anderson Collection, LDSCA. The east end of the Kirtland Temple is the main entrance facade. An ornamental cornice decorates the eaves of the roof and makes the gable end into a triangular pediment, like the front of a Greek temple. The two entrance doors correspond to the two aisles in the building. The dedicatory inscription on the front of the temple contains the phrase HOUSE OF THE LORD as well as additional information proclaiming the ownership of the RLDS Church in 1907, which has preserved, restored, and displayed the building to the public, allowing people like George Edward Anderson to walk through the building and to contemplate the historical significance and the dedicated craftsmanship of the builders. The iron railing on the tower was installed in 1904 and replaced an earlier railing. Originally, the dedicatory inscription may have read: "HOUSE OF THE LORD Built by the Church of Latter Day Saints, A.D. 1834." The Kirtland Temple was officially dedicated on 27 March 1836.*

***Kirtland Temple***, *Kirtland, Ohio, August 1907, Anderson Collection, LDSCA. In its general shape, the Kirtland Temple followed a simple American meetinghouse tradition—a rectangular structure covered with a gabled roof with a bell tower. The details of the building are a mixture of several styles. The quoins (exposed stone blocks on the corners) and dormer windows in the attic are survivals of the eighteenth-century Georgian style. The elliptical arches over the doors, the central windows above them, the large elliptical window in the gable, and the general form of the domed tower are typical of the early twentieth-century Federal style. The pointed arches of the other windows around the building and on the tower show the influence of the popular Gothic Revival. Despite the stylistic diversity of its parts, the design of the temple achieves a kind of provincial elegance and unity.*

From the [temple] tower, was pointed out to me the home of the Prophet to the north. Sidney Rigdon's[391] across the road southeast, and of which I made a view in the evening. William Smith's[392] a little east of south. Frank Steffe and wife [Rosanne], old (Germans) gentleman and lady, live there for sixteen years past. Bought the place from Joseph Plaisted[393] for $1,300. A good many repairs had been made to the place. Flowers and a well-kept lawn made it cozy.

Father Steffe was going to work at 6:30 a.m. the morning of the seventh when I made a view of the place. Sixty-eight years old and never satisfied unless something to do (gardener). Mother Steffe seventy-six years old and does all her work, and her home is neat and tidy inside as well as out. Belongs to the Reorganized Church and wished to know if I had a knowledge of the work in this dispensation. Said a street used to go just west of the house, and the home had been built to face that street. See picture and temple.

Hyrum Smith's[394] south of the temple and a little south and west of William Smith's. R. C. Wilson [p. 155] lives here. Is a farmer. A little farther west and across the street north is the home of Carlos Smith,[395] which has been added to and changed considerable. About two blocks farther west and on the south side of street, under great apple tree, is a little white cottage said to have been owned by Ezra Thayer.[396] Also Hiram Page.[397] Mrs. B. F. Hulmes[398] has lived in it for twelve years. It is owned by a Mr. [Joseph] Squires of Brooklyn of New York. [George W.] Manley owned it before, and Gree before Manley. Mrs. Mary M. Lewis, a neighbor, is in picture with a nephew of Mrs. Hulmes, Will Boyne, little fellow. See picture.

After coming down off the temple, Elder Stone accompanied me to hill, northeast and across river. Made view, which showed the east fork of the Chagrin River, broom fields[399] and valley, the temple on the opposite hill. A few of the houses could be seen here and there between the trees. Away in the south lies south Kirtland and Gildersleeve Mountain,[400] from which the rock was quarried for temple.[401] Elder Stone said several who had visited Kirtland, direct from Holy Land, said the situation reminded them of Jerusalem and valleys and hills. [p. 156]

---

391. Sidney Rigdon (1793–1876), Baptist minister in Mentor, Ohio, was involved with the Disciples of Christ and was eventually baptized by LDS missionaries in 1830. He became Joseph Smith's scribe and counselor in the LDS Church's First Presidency.

392. William Smith (1811–93), brother of Joseph Smith Jr. and chosen in 1835 to be a member of the original Quorum of the Twelve Apostles. The home Anderson mentions is located on the corner of Chillicothe and Joseph Streets.

393. Anderson spelled the name *Plaisteil*. We have provided the correct spelling.

394. Hyrum Smith (1800–44), brother of Joseph Smith Jr., one of the Eight Witnesses of the Book of Mormon and a member of the committee that supervised the construction of the Kirtland temple. Anderson spells the name *Hiram*; we have corrected his spelling. The traditional location of Hyrum Smith's home is the west side of Chillicothe where Joseph Street intersects Chillicothe Road. This building no longer stands, but another building on the east side of Chillicothe has been identified as an alternative site and is so marked today in Kirtland.

395. Don Carlos Smith (1816–41), brother of Joseph Smith Jr., president of the high priests quorum in Kirtland, and managing editor of the *Elders' Journal*, the Church's newspaper in Kirtland in 1837.

396. Ezra Thayer (1787–1856), member of the committee formed to purchase land for settlement in Kirtland, 1833. Thayer later joined the RLDS Church.

397. See 10 May 1907 diary entry.

398. Emma Hulmes, wife of Benjamin Franklin Hulmes.

399. Broomcorn is a variety of sorghum, having a stiff, erect, much-branched flower cluster, the stocks of which are used to make brooms.

400. The rise south of Kirtland is named after Samuel D. Gildersleeve, who lived in the area in the 1840s and 1850s.

401. The Claudius Standard Stone Quarry is located approximately two miles south of the temple and is situated on the west side of Chillicothe Road.

***Interior of the
Kirtland Temple**,
Kirtland, Ohio, August 1907,
Anderson Collection, LDSCA.
The view is of the upper court,
showing the west pulpits. RLDS
custodian Elder Albert Stone
kindly allowed Anderson
not only to tour the building
but also to take several
photographs of the interior.*

***Interior of the
Kirtland Temple**,
Kirtland, Ohio, August 1907,
Anderson Collection, LDSCA.
The view is of the lower court,
showing the west pulpits. These
pulpits and the window behind
displayed the most extraordinary
decorative details inside the
temple. Curved pulpits framed by
fluted pilasters bore the initials of
the various priesthood offices. In
the temple, Joseph Smith and
Oliver Cowdery witnessed a
spectacular vision of the resur-
rected Jesus on 3 April 1836.*

**Sidney and Phebe Brook Rigdon Home**, *Kirtland, Ohio, 6 August 1907, Anderson Collection, LDSCA. One of the most significant converts to Mormonism, Sidney Rigdon served as Joseph Smith's scribe and counselor in Ohio, Missouri, and Illinois.*

Back to hotel about 6:30 p.m. and made several views of homes before supper. Sidney Rigdon's home is now occupied by two families and has been changed considerable. The south is much the same as of old. Frank Brockway, south side. [RLDS] Apostle U. W. Greene,⁴⁰² north end. Hyrum Smith's house does not show the care and attention that other homes do on the outside. It may be much better on the inside.

U. W. Greene and G. T. Griffiths,⁴⁰³ [RLDS] apostles, are at conference, Akron, Ohio. [RLDS] Apostle W. H. Kelley⁴⁰⁴ in Boston. Lives in Lamoni, [Iowa], but retains his membership in Kirtland. Is

402. Ulysses W. Greene (1865–1935), called to the Council of Twelve Apostles, RLDS Church, in 1902. Anderson spells the name *Green.*

403. Gomer T. Griffiths (1856–1950), called to the Council of Twelve Apostles, RLDS Church, in 1887.

404. William H. Kelley (1841–1915), called to the Council of Twelve Apostles, RLDS Church, in 1873.

**Parley Parker and Thankful Halsey Pratt Home**, *Kirtland, Ohio, 7 August 1907, Anderson Collection, LDSCA. This photograph contributes to our visual knowledge of an early Kirtland home of which we did not previously have knowledge. The Pratts were early converts to Mormonism. Thankful died in Kirtland on 25 March 1837, just a few hours following the birth of her only child. She was buried in the cemetery near the Kirtland Temple. Parley wrote, "Farewell, my dear Thankful, thou wife of my youth, and mother of my firstborn; the beginning of my strength—farewell." He married Mary Ann Frost shortly thereafter, but by 7 May 1838, the Pratt family had abandoned their home in Kirtland and had moved to the new LDS Church center in Far West, Missouri. Apparently the man shown standing in the photograph is Newton P. Crawford, who owned the home at the time of Anderson's visit.*

brother of [Presiding RLDS] Bishop [Edmund Levi] Kelley of Independence.

Bank stood on northeast corner of temple block.[405] Safe is in Historical Western Reserve Society, Cleveland. Printing house northwest, rear [?] of lot, near Keziah [Jenkins] Turk's.[406] Fine brick schoolhouse on the Chillicothe Road between north and south Kirtland. Population [blank].

---

405. The Kirtland Safety Society Bank was established on 2 November 1836. It was reorganized as the Kirtland Safety Society Anti-Banking Company when LDS Church leaders were unable to obtain a bank charter. Its failure in 1837 caused much internal dissent within the Church and external prosecution and persecution by local non-Mormons.

406. This printing house mentioned by Anderson was the Church's printing house during the 1830s and was located to the rear of the temple on the west side.

**William and Caroline Amanda Grant Smith Home**, *Kirtland, Ohio, 7 August 1907, Anderson Collection, LDSCA.*
*Shows Frank and Rosanne Steffe, local RLDS members, standing in front of the home. Anderson again captured an early*
*Mormon Kirtland home that has now disappeared. William Smith, a brother of the Prophet Joseph Smith, was chosen as a*
*member of the Quorum of the Twelve Apostles in 1835.*


**Hyrum and Jerusha Barden Smith Home**, *Kirtland, Ohio, 7 August 1907, Anderson Collection, LDSCA. The view shows the home at the tradi-*
*tional site on the west side of Chillicothe Road. Today, a house on the east side is marked as Hyrum Smith's home. Jerusha Barden married Hyrum Smith*
*at Manchester, New York, in 1826. An early convert of Mormonism, she followed her husband to Kirtland, Ohio, where she died in October 1837.*

## August 7, 1907, Wednesday, Kirtland [p. 152]

Theodor Redler and wife, recently from Germany, came to stay here because House of the Lord belonged to the Reorganized [Church]. Thought maybe both the Utah Church and Reorganized Church were wrong—had lost the gifts; neither were crying repentance. Has a friend, Gustave Fisher, who joined Utah church and went to Utah about two years ago. Would like to hear from. Had quite a talk with this brother and wife last night. He speaks very well for being here six or seven months. Is not satisfied, I can tell from his conversation.

Made several views before breakfast. Found the place where temple etc. is reflected in Chagrin River. Wind disturbed the surface too much to get view in the morning. Made exposure in the evening, but rings, stream running, etc. did not give a perfect reflection.

[RLDS] Elder Albert E. Stone asked me why President Young[407] did not print the revelation on plural marriage in the Doctrine and Covenants.[408] I ask him why the Manifesto was not printed in Doctrine and Covenants[409] and read to him the affidavit of William Law and wife [Nancy] as published in *Nauvoo Expositor*, June 7, 1844.[410] He asked to copy it, which he did. Mr. Squire's daughter ask me about statement I made [about] Joseph Smith [III] going to friends in Nauvoo to ask advice about accepting the leadership of the [RLDS] Church.[411] [p. 157]

This afternoon, made negative of N. K. Whitney home, store,[412] also Johnson Hotel. See memorandums, August 6. Also view of reflections. Also view of Mr. N[ewton] P. Crawford's home, formerly Parley P. Pratt's. An instructive duet with him. Said the place had belonged to Jared Carter.[413] Came into his possession nine years ago. Had put on porches. Repainted and repaired inside and out. Also graded up walks etc. For years, the festivities of Kirtland had been held in that house.

Had been pleased at the outcome of the Smoot case.[414] If it had been otherwise, would have established a precedent that would have shattered the Con-

---

407. Brigham Young (1801–77), a member of the original Quorum of the Twelve Apostles, chosen in 1835. Later became LDS Church president following the death of the Prophet Joseph Smith.

408. Actually, Brigham Young did publish section 132 (revelation on marriage) in the 1876 edition of the Doctrine and Covenants.

409. The 1890 Wilford Woodruff Manifesto, which announced the end of new plural marriages in Utah, would be printed in the 1908 edition of the Doctrine and Covenants.

410. William Law (1809–92) was appointed a member of the LDS Church First Presidency in 1841. Opposition to plural marriage led to his removal from the presidency and the Church in 1844. He organized a church opposed to Joseph Smith and was involved in the publication of the *Nauvoo Expositor*. He and his wife published statements, in the only edition of the *Expositor*, that Joseph Smith had shown them a revelation dated 12 July 1843, which we now know as section 132 of the Doctrine and Covenants. Obviously, Anderson used the Law affidavits to prove the LDS Church's claim that Joseph Smith, not Brigham Young, was the author of the revelation on marriage, which included the doctrine of plural marriage. The RLDS Church, at the time, argued that Brigham Young, not Joseph Smith, instituted plural marriage in the Church.

411. Joseph Smith III attended the RLDS Church conference at Amboy, Illinois, in April 1860, where he accepted the invitation to become president of the RLDS Church.

412. Located north of the temple and situated on the northeast corner of Chillicothe and Kirtland-Chardon Roads. The store is significant, not only because Joseph and Emma Smith lived there for some time but also because it was the place where several revelations, including the Word of Wisdom (the Mormon health code), were received and where the School of the Prophets was held.

413. Jared Carter (1801–49), early convert to Mormonism, a member of the Kirtland high council in 1837, and a member of the committee to oversee the construction of the Kirtland Temple. He did not immigrate to Utah.

414. The U.S. Senate finally agreed to seat Utah Senator Reed Smoot, an LDS Church apostle, in February 1907, following a three-year investigation into the Church.

***Kirtland Temple**, Kirtland, Ohio, 7 August 1907, Anderson Collection, LDSCA. The view shows the reflection of the temple in the Chagrin River. Anderson notes in his diary, "Found the place where temple etc. is reflected in Chagrin River. Wind disturbed the surface too much to get view in the morning. Made exposure in the evening. . . . Did not give a perfect reflection."*

stitution. Would like to visit Utah. Buried wife [Lizzie] a week ago. Ezra Bond,[415] neighbor, could give me information about old times if here. On vacation for a few weeks. Mr. Crawford is blacksmith. Shop on the south of house. Also justice of peace for number of years.

Made view of cemetery and temple from cupola of barn of McFarlands.[416] This was formerly schoolhouse. Also view of Mrs. [Viola] McFarland's home (Prophet's). One of the best-kept and finished places in Kirtland.[417] A number of visitors at Mrs. McFarland's. Her father eighty-four years old. Very kind. Husband dead.[418]

Busy all day getting views, conversation at blacksmith shop, fixing tripods. Chat with Mrs. Sarah Jane Sanborn and daughter about people, blood atonement, Adam God, polygamy, etc.[419]

---

415. Ezra Bond's family moved to Kirtland in 1834 when he was nearly ten years old. His father, Ira Bond (1798–1887), was an early convert to Mormonism who remained in Kirtland following the Saints' departure in 1838. Except for one year, Ezra maintained his residence in Kirtland and obviously could have been an excellent resource, as mentioned in Anderson's diary entry.

416. A frame structure measuring thirty-six feet by fifty feet.

417. Known as "Temple Hill Place" at the turn of the century.

418. Milton S. McFarland died on 17 February 1904.

419. The LDS Church received much unwelcome news coverage during the Smoot hearings in Washington (1904–7) as newspapers throughout the country reported on LDS history and doctrine—often without sympathy and with much prejudice. Much of the sensational material published in the press centered around LDS temple ceremonies and other misunderstood doctrines and teachings of the LDS Church (such as blood atonement, the Adam-God theory, and polygamy).

**Kirtland, Lake County (Geauga County in 1830s), Ohio**, *6 or 7 August 1907, Anderson Collection, LDSCA.*
*General view of Kirtland from the northeast showing Chillicothe Road leading up the hill to the temple. Anderson notes in his diary,*
*"Made view, which showed the east fork of the Chagrin River, broom fields and valley, the temple on the opposite hill."*

***Newel Kimball Whitney Store**, Kirtland, Ohio, 7 August 1907, Anderson Collection, LDSCA. Newel K. Whitney opened his first store in Kirtland in a log cabin in 1823. By 1827, he built this frame structure in which he operated a mercantile business and a post office. On 1 February 1831, Joseph and Emma Smith arrived in Kirtland from New York, having traveled overland by sleigh. Joseph sprang from the sleigh and entered the store. Extending his hand to the gentleman as though he were a familiar acquaintance, Joseph said, "Newel K. Whitney! Thou art the man!" A somewhat astonished Whitney said, "You have the advantage of me. I could not call you by name as you have me." Joseph replied, "I am Joseph the Prophet. You've prayed me here, now what do you want of me?"*

***Newel Kimball and Elizabeth Ann Smith Whitney Home***, *Kirtland, Ohio, 7 August 1907, Anderson Collection, LDSCA. Probably sitting in front are Alden E. and Sarah Jane Sanborn. Their unmarried children, Fred H. and Nellie M. Sanborn, are standing. The Sanborn family lived in the home when Anderson visited.*

## August 8, 1907, Thursday, Kirtland, Willoughby, Cleveland [p. 158]

Rose soon after 5:30 a.m. Through the fields northwest and north and northeast to find a point to get view of Kirtland, Chagrin River, dam, etc. Found a good place on ridge north of dam; but trees, foliage, etc. obstructed the view. Heavy dew so that feet and pants wet.

On hill just a little north of east of temple, made a view of temple and hill. Mr. Sanborn's new automobile was here. Broke. Could not move it—sprocket chain broke. Near 9:30 a.m. when I got back to hotel, so I did not ask for breakfast.

A chat with Mrs. Keziah [Jenkins] Turk. Lives just west of temple in house formerly occupied by Oliver Granger.[420] Her mother[421] belonged to the Church. She had never belonged. Was as well informed, or

---

420. Oliver Granger (1794–1841), early convert to Mormonism, moved to Kirtland in 1833. He was a member of the Kirtland high council and was appointed agent for the Church in Kirtland after moving to Missouri in 1838. He located in Nauvoo briefly when he was called to return to Kirtland to serve as Church agent until his death in 1841.

421. Could be Mary E. Jenkins (1828–?), baptized in Kirtland in 1842.

***Joseph and Emma Hale Smith Home***, *Kirtland, Ohio, 7 August 1907, Anderson Collection, LDSCA. Anderson notes in his diary, "One of the best-kept and finished places in Kirtland." The McFarland family posed in front of the home, which they occupied at the time.*

*Kirtland Temple and Cemetery*, *Kirtland, Ohio, 7 August 1907, Anderson Collection, LDSCA. Anderson notes in his diary, "Made view of cemetery and temple from cupola of barn of McFarlands." Many Latter-day Saints are buried in the cemetery under the shadows of the temple, including Mary Duty Smith, the Prophet Joseph Smith's grandmother; Jerusha Barden Smith, Hyrum Smith's wife; Oliver Granger; and John Johnson.*

better, than anyone I met on Church history. Her husband got his name *Turk* from some of his ancestors' being captured by the Turks, and the name *The Turk* given. Said the house built by Jared Carter. Then Parley P. Pratt's. Was more pretentious than most. A grocery underneath it and a number of steps lead up to the upper part. Jared Carter was a Baptist minister in Vermont. Had a blind son, a poet.[422] Came by canal boat. See poetry Mrs. Turk has. **[p. 159]** Said he became an infidel because prayed for home and did not get it.

Recalled with much pleasure the visit of President Joseph F. Smith and party as they were returning from monument,[423] and appreciated the papers, letters, Christmas *[Deseret] News*, etc. received. Regretted very much not at home when President Smith and party

422. Carter's sons: Orlando, Clark, Jared, David, and Joseph. At the time of his death in 1850, his family lived in DeKalb County, Illinois.

423. The party arrived in Kirtland on 27 December 1905 on their way back to Utah from Vermont, where President Smith had dedicated the Joseph Smith Memorial Monument on 23 December 1905.

***Kirtland Hotel***, *Kirtland, Ohio, August 1907, Anderson Collection, LDSCA. One of the early hotels in Kirtland, it apparently opened in 1837 when George W. Robinson, a son-in-law to Sidney and Phebe Brook Rigdon, advertised it in the local newspaper.*

called, as they were going to Europe.[424] Found the card under the door and remembered passing the party near Willoughby, but did not recognize them. The $2 bill that came in letter from President Joseph [F.] Smith was a surprise. Said that Utah people going to the temple. Taught school twenty-nine years. Looked back with pleasure on her labors. A sister had called and had sent picture of little boy. Also the *Elder's Journal*[425] etc. That her name was Mrs. F. Smith (Sister Harrison thinks it was Sister Wilson).

After dinner, took a walk south that I might be better acquainted with the town, find the hill the temple is on. Extends to south Kirtland, and the [p. 160] country seems to raise beyond there. I see steeple or spire among houses in south Kirtland and am told it is Congregational Church and that there is only two churches—the Reorganized being the other. Population about [blank]. Membership of Reorganized, ninety.

[RLDS] Elder Albert E. Stone had been at Liberty, Missouri. Stevens owns the handcuffs that were on the Prophet Joseph [in Liberty Jail]. Floor is the cellar floor of the house erected over jail. See inner

424. Joseph F. Smith, his wife, Edna Smith (1851–1926), and LDS Church Presiding Bishop Charles W. Nibley (1849–1931) and family left Salt Lake City on 21 July 1906 but apparently did not visit Church sites in Ohio until they were on their return trip to Utah, where they arrived in September.

425. A periodical of the LDS Southern States Mission published from 1903 to 1907. It was combined with the *Liahona* in 1907 to form *Liahona The Elders' Journal*.

***H. E. Harrison Home,***
*Cleveland, Ohio, 9 August 1907,*
*Anderson Collection, LDSCA.*
*Located at 270 Wade Park*
*Avenue. Mrs. Harrison was*
*known as the "Cleveland mother"*
*by the missionaries who often fre-*
*quented her home. Apparently, Jen-*
*nie Newmarch (Harrison's niece)*
*and Sister H. E. Harrison stand*
*between Elders Q. H. Barrus of*
*Grantsville, Utah, and Elder*
*Joseph R. Hicks of Raymond,*
*Alberta, Canada.*

door of jail. Elder Stone had picture taken with others, and door was held before them.

Member of the board of education told him that the Kirtland Temple had been offered to them for $80. Had been used for a stable, especially the basement. "School of Prophets, as a foundation of the education of the Church, gave strong evidence that we're in favor of education."[426]

Expect to make the Kirtland Hotel a home for the old people of the Reorganized Church. An old gentleman with one arm and Sister Jones there now. [p. 161]

I bade Elder Stone and people good-bye and started for Willoughby. While at the foot of the hill talking to Mr. Wells, Mr. Sanborn drove up and ask me if I wished to ride and took me to Willoughby over a road to the left of the one I came in on. Saw some beautiful homes and farms. Some men, [Charles A.] Otis, [John] Sherwin, [Henry A.] Everette, and others, own property near $100,000.[427] Enjoyed the ride very much.

Willoughby about 6:15 p.m. Could not find photographer, so took car to Cleveland. Then about 7:30 p.m. or 8:00 p.m. supper. Tired. Could not get hypo for less than $10 per pound, so did not develop. Man lecturing on how men get rich. Privilege hear Sister Harrison. Bed about 10:30 p.m.

## August 9, 1907, Friday, Cleveland [p. 161]

Developed negatives, closed windows in cellar with [—], etc. Bath, shaved, cleaned up, just as soon as I got up. Negatives came out very good.

---

426. Joseph Smith, along with other Church leaders, organized from time to time schools for the instruction of adult male members of the Church. The first such school met on 23 January 1833 in Kirtland, Ohio. This school met through the winter and early spring of 1834, usually above the Newel K. Whitney store. The School of the Elders or School of the Prophets met in the late fall to early spring in 1834–35 and 1835–36. The men studied doctrine and secular subjects.

427. This road is today identified as Markell Road, and the area is the exclusive community known as Waite Hill Village. Otis was a steel baron. His farm was known as the Tannenbaum Farm, consisting of 480 acres. Sherwin was a banker, and his farm was known as South Farm, consisting of 390 acres. Everett was involved in the manufacture of streetcars, and his farm was known as Leodoro Farm, consisting of 1,615 acres. All three homes still stand today.

Elder Q. H. Barrus, Grantsville, [Utah], came today. Had dinner with us at Sister Harrison's. Also Elder Hicks.

Downtown in the evening about 5:30 p.m. to see about trunk. Had it transferred to Cleveland and Buffalo Steamship Company. Made negative of Sister Harrison's store and house today. Tired. Bed about 10:30 p.m. Miss Morrisie [?] at Sister Harrison's.

## August 10, 1907, Saturday, Cleveland [p. 162]

Rose 5:00 a.m. Used Danderine.[428] Cleaned combs, brushes etc. Used Danderine last night also. Spent the forenoon and until after 2:00 p.m. writing up journal for Kirtland and Cleveland, getting letters ready, etc. Tried to get negative of Sister Harrison and cats.

Packed negatives and at 6:30 p.m. left Sister Harrison's for dock of Cleveland and Buffalo [Steamship Company] docks. A gentleman assisted me to the car, and two boys carried one each grip to boat. Had some difficulty in getting draft[429] cashed. Two gentlemen on boat cashed it. The agent or purser not allowed to take drafts or cash. Got excursion ticket just before boat started. Would not check my trunk on excursion ticket, so I had to leave it with the pillow Sister Boyer gave me. I spent a fair night, sleeping most of the time from 9:00 p.m.

## August 11, 1907, Sunday, Buffalo, Niagara Falls [p. 162]

On board the steamboat *City of Erie*. Beautiful morning. I woke daylight but sleep again until near 6:00 a.m. Wash, shave, about 5:30 a.m. We could see land to the left.

A very fine boat. Many passengers. I suppose took advantage of the cheap rates. Looked over the boat pretty well last night. Writing this on the upper deck and can see land plainly on the north and east at 6:10 a.m. Buffalo[430] about 7:30 a.m. Eastern Standard Time.[431] I put my grips in wareroom[432] of dock and went to find the elders at 93 West Eagle. Had rooms moved to [p. 163][433] the Star Theater Building with L. N. Gornee. Elder Sisam went to depot and assisted me with my grips to New York Central Depot. I check my telescope to Palmyra, No. 145410, Ticket No. 4383. Cost me $1.82, ninety-one miles. My trunk at Cleveland and could not do anything to have it checked here, so I sent check to Cleveland Transfer Company, Cleveland, Ohio, asking them to send to Buffalo. Check it if they could; if not, send by express C.O.D.[434]

I then went to Star Theater Building and met Elders VanNoy and Richman. They are laboring in Canada and are going to visit Kirtland with Elders Sisam and Miller by way of Detroit this 5:15 p.m.

---

428. Apparently a brand name for a cleaning agent.

429. A written order from one person to another, requiring the payment of a stated amount of money.

430. County seat of Erie County, located in northwestern New York at the eastern end of Lake Erie as it narrows into the Niagara River.

431. Standard time in the fifth time zone west of Greenwich, England, in the eastern part of North America. In the 1880s an internationally agreed upon set of twenty-four time zones was established to cover the world. The following autograph appears here: "Elder Alma N. Sisam, East Jordan, Utah."

432. A room for storing or displaying goods or wares.

433. The following autographs appear on this page: "Elder T. L. VanNoy, Thayne, Uinta County, Wyoming; Elder T. G. Richman, Teton City, Idaho; Elder A. V. Miller, Murray City, Utah."

434. Abbreviation for *cash on delivery*.

Elder Sisam bought my ticket to return to Cleveland—$1.50. Bought a few bananas, five cents, and five cents cake, and this was breakfast and dinner. Elder Sisam eating bananas with me. 2:00 p.m., took electric car for Niagara Falls, [New York]. Twenty-two miles round trip, fifty cents. Niagara about 3:30 p.m. Left instrument at station and view the falls from the American side. Got instrument and made several negatives from bridge[435] below the falls. One from the Canadian side. Then went above the Horseshoe Falls[436] on the Canada side. Grand, sublime. Cannot describe the feelings one has in gazing up this sight. I thought of the divine hand that had made this. The greatest sight I ever beheld of nature. Canada side is beautiful with shrubs, flowers, [p. 164][437] trees, grass, walks, drives, hotels. Flat about one-fourth to one-half mile wide along the bank of the gorge above this bluff with imposing homes, hotels, etc. A number of small buildings of large cobblestones laid in cement.

Ontario Power Company have large powerhouse in gorge just below Horseshoe Falls. Tube eighteen feet in diameter carries the water. Power is transmitted to Rochester, Rockport, and Syracuse for street, railways, lighting, etc.

Toronto Power Company or Electrical Developing Company have powerhouse above falls. Tunnel thirty-six feet. Send power to Hamilton, Ontario, and other Canadian towns. [Three] boats,[438] *Maid of the Mist, Stars and Stripes*, and *Union Jack* busy making one-half hour trips. People crowd the decks in raincoats.

Water can be seen rushing into the gorge from the American side, showing from the buildings on the banks that the power is used to run factories, mills, etc. of various kinds. Complete rainbow seen from this side. Also from the American side midday morning.

Tried to find Saints, James Silverthorn and John Ellsworth, at the end of Fall Street; but after a long walk, had to give it up. Found a bed at Mrs. H. S. Moffat, 549 Fourth Street, Niagara Falls, New York. Wrote [her] December 25, 1907.[439] Bed, 10:00 p.m.

## August 12, 1907, Monday, Palmyra [p. 164]

Rose about 6:00 a.m. Bath and then bought loaf of graham bread and over at Goat Island[440] and eat my breakfast—potatoes [?] and bread. A fine view of the river and falls and the gorge and iron bridge from here. Down the stairs to the bottom of the American Falls—254 steps, 330 feet, length of incline[441] [—]. [p. 165] Here we see a complete rainbow formed in the spray from the falls. See circular giving description.

An excellent place to write, so I wrote up for yesterday and up 9:30 a.m. today. Museum seems to have a great many relics, mummies, etc.

Thousands of people came here yesterday. The streets, stores, refreshment stands, souvenir places crowded. On the American side, the grass is wore off, as many thousands use it. Railroads, electric cars, automobiles, etc. bringing the crowds every few moments.

To see Mrs. Moffat and pay for lodging. I only had twenty cents change and could not change check, so I will send her a picture of falls or stamps for fifty cents for lodging.

Left falls shortly after 11:30 a.m., going south along the east bank of the Niagara River. Many factories. Buffalo about 1:00 p.m. Could not hear anything from my trunk at Cleveland and Buffalo[442] [Steamship Company] Docks, also at New York

---

435. The Full View Bridge collapsed in 1938.

436. The Canadian, or Horseshoe Falls, has a curving crest-line of about 2,600 feet, over which the cataract tumbles 162 feet.

437. At the top of this page, Anderson wrote the following: "Niagara, grandest waterfall in the world."

438. The diary here reads *two boats*, which we have changed to *three* because Anderson apparently names three boats.

439. Apparently, Anderson added this sentence at a later date to confirm that he wrote Mrs. Moffat at that time.

440. The falls are in two principal parts (Horseshoe Falls and American Falls), separated by Goat Island.

441. The American Falls are 167 feet high and 1,000 feet across.

442. Anderson used the abbreviation *C and B.*

*Sacred Grove, Manchester, New York, 13 August 1907, Anderson Collection, LDSCA. Anderson took at least two photographs in the grove during his visit in 1907. This one is identified as No. 3 in the lower left-hand corner. The boy is barely visible in the middle of the picture by the base of a large tree just before the clearing. The second image, identified as No. 3A by Anderson in the lower left-hand corner, has the additional notation by Anderson and is also identified as "Sacred Grove Manchester N.Y." in the lower center of the photograph and "G.E.A. Photo Springville Utah" in the lower right.*

Central Railway. Very warm by the time I got things to the depot. Pretty well warmed through.

3:15 p.m., for Palmyra, reaching there about fifteen minutes to 6:00 p.m. Left all but one grip in depot and crossing the tracks on the right, then the first road to right and leading to the west brought me to Palmyra[443] proper.

The main street, on which the business houses and fine residences, runs east and west. I walked west on Main to Stafford Street. Then about one and one-half miles south to the Smith homestead.[444] One hundred forty acres and for many years owned by S. T. Chapman. [—][445] who recently sold the place to our people through George A. Smith.[446] Mr. [William Avery] Chapman gave to Mr. Clemons [?] to be treated for inflammatory rheumatism.[447] Found Mr. [p. 166] Clark Austin, who has charge of the place. Gave me such information as I ask.

Could not give me lodging, so I walked back to Palmyra, reaching there about 11:30 p.m. Tired, but satisfied with what I accomplished. Enjoyed glass milk

at Mr. Austin's before I started for Palmyra. While resting, fell asleep; and just as I got up, met a man carry flour or groceries his shoulder. Bed at Powers Hotel.[448] If I had know just where I was etc., was tired enough to sleep on ground and was warm enough.

## August 13, 1907, Tuesday, Palmyra [p. 166]

Called me about 5:30 a.m. Was awake, shave, shoes cleaned, got instrument, and walked to the Smith homestead, reaching there about 8:30 a.m. Raisins for breakfast.

Visited the grove.[449] Mr. Austin's boy, Hugh (twelve years old), pointed out the place or tree near where it is said the boy prophet had the vision. Went all around the place and decided where the best points to make the pictures, views, etc. Made view of Mr. Austin cutting grain with self-binder.[450]

A very windy day. Also, clouds passing over the sun. I set the camera and waited for opportunity to get negatives. Made several negatives and drove into

443. Palmyra, Wayne County, New York, located twenty miles southeast of Rochester. Named for the ancient Syrian city.

444. Joseph Smith Sr. (1771–1840) and Lucy Mack Smith (1775–1856) moved to the Palmyra area in 1816 from Vermont. The Smiths moved into a log home near the framed Smith homestead in late 1818. The frame home is located two miles south of the Palmyra town center in Manchester Township.

445. At this point in the diary, Anderson wrote the following: "now wa his son." The "wa" may represent William A. Chapman, Seth T. Chapman's son.

446. LDS Apostle George Albert Smith purchased the Chapman farm, which includes the original one-hundred-acre Smith farm, on 10 June 1907 for $16,000. Later, on 7 December 1916, he deeded the farm to the LDS Church for $1.

447. Apparently, William A. Chapman sold the farm when his rheumatism prevented him from working it properly.

448. Located on west corner of Fayette and Main Streets. Built in 1835–36. Also known as the Eagle or Palmyra Hotel.

449. Located at the west end of the Smith farm is a wooded area of substantial age that has been traditionally identified as the site of the First Vision since the LDS Church purchased the property. Chapman played a role in establishing this site as the traditional location of the First Vision.

450. The machine is a self-binding reaper. It was widely used between 1880 and the 1930s. Its invention began with the McCormick reaper in 1834 and developed through several stages of improvement, with the twine knotter being added in the early 1870s.

***Joseph and Lucy Mack Smith Farm***, *Manchester, New York, 13 August 1907, Anderson Collection, LDSCA. Anderson notes in his diary, "Made view of Mr. Austin cutting grain with self-binder." The machine is used for harvesting grain. It is pulled by horses, and all moving parts are driven by the main drive wheel (bull wheel). It cuts the grain and elevates it by canvas belts to a table where it is bunched and tied into a bundle. The bundles are then placed in stacks or piles like those seen in the background of the picture. From this point, the grain can be collected easily to take to the threshing machine.*

Palmyra and changed plates at Mr. Elton's gallery.[451] He gave me $1.00 until I could get draft for $9.95 cashed. Bought bread graham, cakes, etc. and broke my fast on cookies and old-fashioned brown bread.

Out to farm before Mr. Cook was ready for buggy and rode with him about mile toward Hill Cumorah. Walked about a mile. Called on half a dozen different people before got a place to stop. Stayed at the

---

451. George M. Elton established a photography gallery on Main Street in the Exchange Building (now known as the E. B. Grandin Building, where the Book of Mormon was published) on the third floor. He worked here for fifty-five years until his death in 1927.

Sampson farm[452] just under "Mormon Hill."[453] Clemons has charge. Showed them the views etc. and told the history of Mormon Hill.

## August 14, 1907, Wednesday, "Mormon Hill" or Hill Cumorah [p. 167]

Rose before sunup, and by the time the rays lit up the landscape, I had my camera from the other side of the hill (where I left it last night) and ready to make pictures. Made several negatives from different points.

Mr. T. J. Clemons called me to breakfast. Was near 7:00 a.m. Breakfast; then made negatives of Mr. Clemons's children, also his neighbors.

One or two more negatives of the hill and visited the top and Mr. Clemons's boy [Charles] took me to the place where it [is] said the plates were found—the "Gold Bible." Highest hill in this part. Commences to rise away south and is highest near the north end. Here it ends rather abruptly, and the descent on the northwest and east is quite steep and, being covered with grass, slippery. About a block from the north end, trees are found and form quite a grove farther south and a little below ridge. Very few trees near and around the north end. See photos. Years ago, I am told by Mr. Elton, photographer, the hill had considerable timber on, and for many years a long, scraggly tree stood near the top. Oaks are being cut near the north and west side.

Admiral Sampson's farm lies on the east of the hill and takes in most of the hill. Manchester lies about three or four miles a little west of south of hill. The country to the north with farmhouses and orchards, field of grain. The wooded hills that here and there are cleared and cultivated made a beautiful landscape. Need the painter's hand to do it justice and fix the colors.[454]

A long chat with Mr. Clemons about the gospel and its restoration. He told me what he had heard of Joseph Smith and others digging for the plates. "Black sheep let down one night and frightened off his companions. He stayed and sprinkled the blood of the sheep around the hole and told his companions that would keep away the evil spirits; they would not come back. Next night, Joe Smith found the plates."[455] [p. 168]

Conversation about John the Baptist. I told him of his visit to Joseph Smith, etc., etc. Left him a tract. His boy, Charles Clemons, with me on the hill. Made a negative of their children.

Talk with Mr. Purdy, a Quaker.[456] Said Joseph Smith did not have a good reputation among his neighbors. "Mr. Ford had told him he was acquainted with Joe Smith as a boy, and he was 'vile and profane' etc. Did not see how any good could come from such a man." I explained that many good and glorious truths had come from Joseph Smith, and he said he heard different. Last night, when I spoke to him, he was radical. Today, when I left, said he had no ill will towards me and realized he would soon go to the other side and there had peace come to his mind through the gospel as found in the New Testament

---

452. Admiral William T. Sampson purchased this farm in the 1870s from the Robinson family. Following Sampson's death in 1902, the farm eventually fell into the hands of Pliney T. Sexton.

453. Known as *Mormon Hill* on U.S. topographic maps from 1898 to 1952, when its name was changed to *Hill Cumorah*. The Hill Cumorah is located on the east side of the Canandaigua Road, approximately three miles south of the Smith farm and four miles south of the town of Palmyra. It is one drumlin of a number of north-south-oriented drumlins south of Lake Ontario.

454. Like other photographers of the period, Anderson was frustrated by the fact that his photographs could not replicate the natural colors of his view.

455. A folk tradition circulated by non-LDS residents.

456. A member of the Society of Friends, which arose in seventeenth-century England and America. The name *Quaker* reflected the physical impact of their inner struggles to yield all self-will to God and to the admonition to "tremble at the word of God." They were known for their simplicity of life, nonviolence, and commitment to social justice. A long tradition of anti-Smith-family feelings existed among some local Quakers in the Palmyra area beginning in the 1820s.

***Hill Cumorah****, Manchester, New York, August 1907, Anderson Collection, LDSCA. Anderson notes in his diary, "Admiral Sampson's farm lies on the east of the hill and takes in most of the hill." The Hill Cumorah is an important feature in LDS geography and history. The drumlin, a natural feature created by the deposition of clay, gravel, and rocks as the slowly advancing ice passed over some small obstruction, is located in Manchester Township, New York, four miles southeast of the town of Palmyra and three miles south of the Joseph and Lucy Mack Smith farm.*

**Hill Cumorah**, *Manchester,*
*New York, August 1907,*
*Anderson Collection, LDSCA.*
*Like other photographers at the turn*
*of the century, Anderson was frus-*
*trated by the fact that his views*
*could not reflect the colors of*
*nature. He notes in his diary on*
*14 August 1907, "The wooded*
*hills that here and there are cleared*
*and cultivated made a beautiful*
*landscape. Need the painter's hand*
*to do it justice and fix the colors."*

**Hill Cumorah**,
*Manchester, New York,*
*August 1907, Anderson*
*Collection, LDSCA. The*
*hill was known as*
Mormon Hill *on U.S.*
*topographic maps from*
*1898 to 1952, when its*
*name was changed to* Hill
Cumorah. *By 1928, the*
*LDS Church had purchased*
*more than three hundred*
*acres at this site to preserve*
*it as a historical landmark.*

*A View from the Hill Cumorah, Manchester, New York, August 1907, Anderson Collection, LDSCA.* On the night of 21 September 1823, Joseph Smith was visited by the angel Moroni, who showed Joseph, in a vision, a hill where was deposited an ancient record inscribed on metal plates that had the appearance of gold. On the following day, young Joseph went to the hill, where he met the same messenger and found the ancient record in a stone box on the west side of the hill. For four years, Joseph Smith returned to the hill each September to receive instruction from the heavenly messenger. Joseph received permission to take the ancient record in 1827.

and as understood by Quakers or Friends. Has son a minister in Quakers and one in the house studying for and a Methodist minister.

I left there about noon and carried my instrument etc. to the Smith farm, and from there I rode to town and got draft cashed and paid Mr. Elton and [Mr.] Powers. Changed plates and saw Mr. Pliney T. Sexton,[457] who said could copy the proofs from the first edition of the Book of Mormon. Also talked with him about the Prophet Joseph Smith. Told him of my visiting David Whitmer's folks, also Hiram Page, their testimony, etc. Generally believed by early settlers in this neighborhood that it was a fraud—was what Mr.

Sexton had gathered in conversation with old settlers. Spoke of peep stone found at Johnson's[458] where they were digging well. Joseph Smith used it. Others could not, so gave it to him.

Mr. Elton told me I could come in and develop negatives in the morning. A pleasant gentleman and a fine photographer. Some of the best subjects I have seen illustrated by him.[459]

## August 15, 1907, Thursday, Palmyra [p. 169]

Last night on way out to Chapman or Smith home, I stopped in and saw the tent shows. A large

---

457. Local banker Pliney T. Sexton obtained the Book of Mormon proof sheets from John Gilbert, typesetter of the Book of Mormon. Eventually, these proof sheets were obtained by Wilford C. Wood and are currently on display in the Museum of Church History and Art, Salt Lake City, Utah. Among the Anderson photographic collection is a photograph of these sheets taken at this time.

458. Johnson is probably the 1907 owner of the Chase farm, where Joseph Smith found a brown stone while digging a well there in 1822.

459. Elton was an internationally recognized photographer who won numerous gold medals for his work. He was also associated with George Eastman in nearby Rochester, New York.

**Main Street**, *Palmyra, Wayne County, New York, August 1907, Anderson Collection, LDSCA. The view is of Main Street. Anderson has written the letters* B.M. *on a third-story window of the old Grandin Bookstore, known in 1830 as the Thayer and Grandin Brick Row or Block, to designate the area where the Book of Mormon had been published in 1830. In June 1829, Joseph Smith and Martin Harris contracted with the owner and editor of the* Wayne Sentinel, *E. B. Grandin, to print five thousand copies of the Book of Mormon for $3,000. Grandin was one of the few printers in western New York capable of producing such a project. Apparently, he employed at least sixteen persons between August 1829 and March 1830 to publish the newspaper, his job-work, and the Book of Mormon. The printing office was located at the west end of the upper level of the recently constructed three-story brick building on Palmyra's Main Street.*

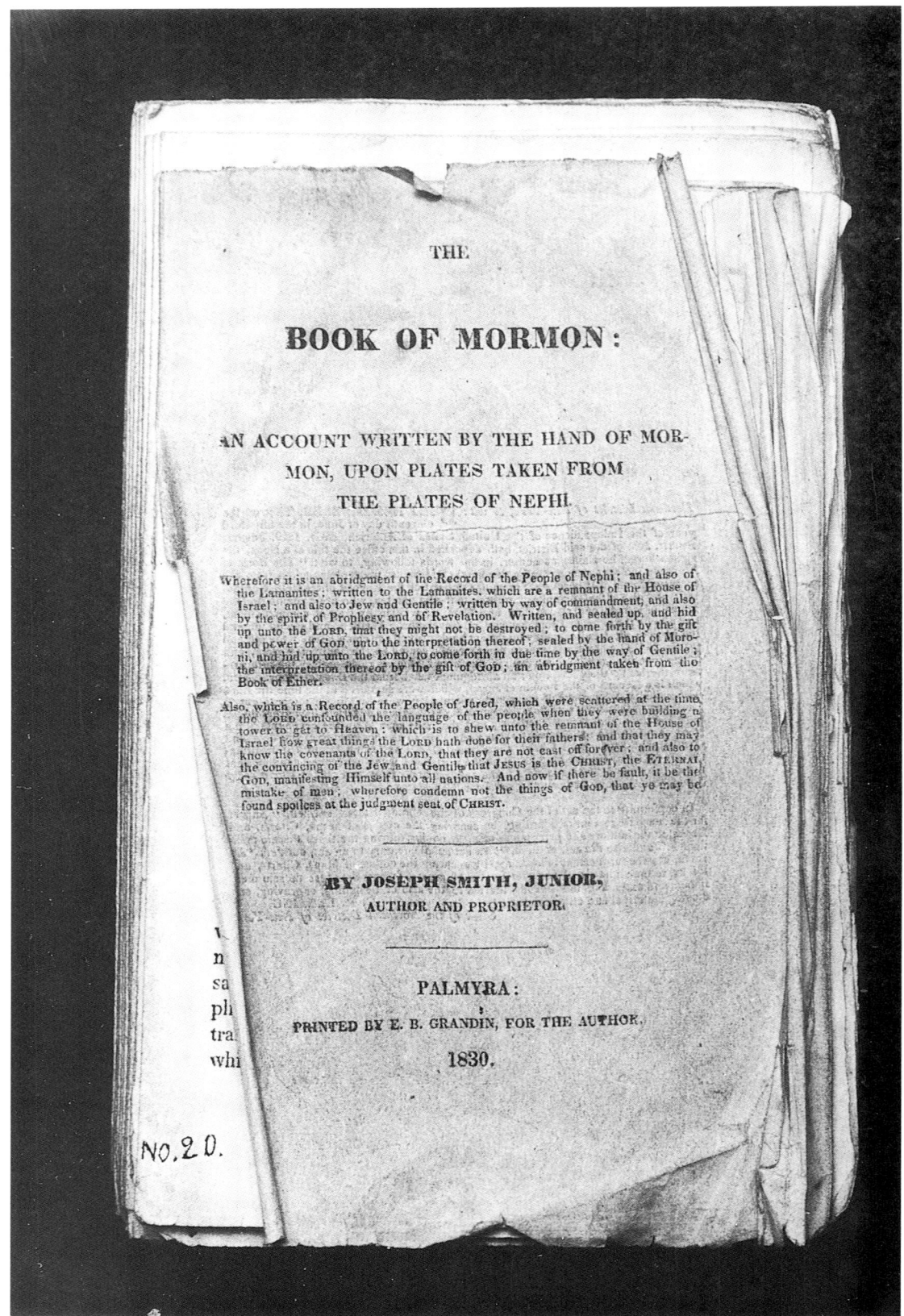

***Book of Mormon Proof Sheets***, *Palmyra, New York, August 1907, Anderson Collection, LDSCA. Anderson photographed these*

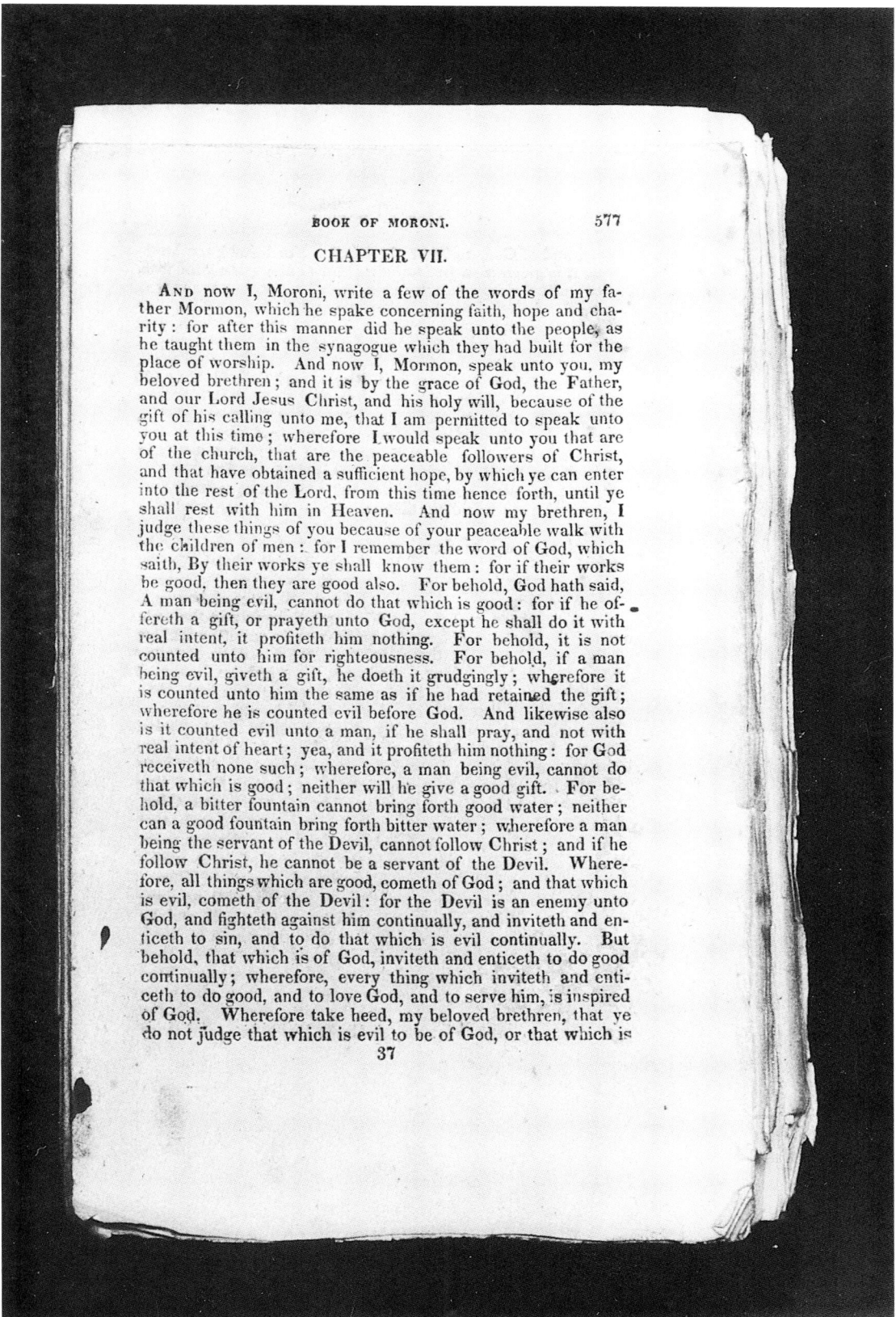

BOOK OF MORONI.                    577

## CHAPTER VII.

AND now I, Moroni, write a few of the words of my father Mormon, which he spake concerning faith, hope and charity: for after this manner did he speak unto the people, as he taught them in the synagogue which they had built for the place of worship. And now I, Mormon, speak unto you, my beloved brethren; and it is by the grace of God, the Father, and our Lord Jesus Christ, and his holy will, because of the gift of his calling unto me, that I am permitted to speak unto you at this time; wherefore I would speak unto you that are of the church, that are the peaceable followers of Christ, and that have obtained a sufficient hope, by which ye can enter into the rest of the Lord, from this time hence forth, until ye shall rest with him in Heaven. And now my brethren, I judge these things of you because of your peaceable walk with the children of men: for I remember the word of God, which saith, By their works ye shall know them: for if their works be good, then they are good also. For behold, God hath said, A man being evil, cannot do that which is good: for if he offereth a gift, or prayeth unto God, except he shall do it with real intent, it profiteth him nothing. For behold, it is not counted unto him for righteousness. For behold, if a man being evil, giveth a gift, he doeth it grudgingly; wherefore it is counted unto him the same as if he had retained the gift; wherefore he is counted evil before God. And likewise also is it counted evil unto a man, if he shall pray, and not with real intent of heart; yea, and it profiteth him nothing: for God receiveth none such; wherefore, a man being evil, cannot do that which is good; neither will he give a good gift. For behold, a bitter fountain cannot bring forth good water; neither can a good fountain bring forth bitter water; wherefore a man being the servant of the Devil, cannot follow Christ; and if he follow Christ, he cannot be a servant of the Devil. Wherefore, all things which are good, cometh of God; and that which is evil, cometh of the Devil: for the Devil is an enemy unto God, and fighteth against him continually, and inviteth and enticeth to sin, and to do that which is evil continually. But behold, that which is of God, inviteth and enticeth to do good continually; wherefore, every thing which inviteth and enticeth to do good, and to love God, and to serve him, is inspired of God. Wherefore take heed, my beloved brethren, that ye do not judge that which is evil to be of God, or that which is

37

*pages of the proof sheets from the Book of Mormon, which at the time were in the possession of a local Palmyra banker, Pliney T. Sexton.*

***Egbert B. Grandin Bookstore and Printing Office***, *Palmyra, New York, August 1907, Anderson Collection, LDSCA. Anderson has not only written in his identification number, information about the site, and his complete name and address but also has written* **B.M.** *on a third-floor window to identify the E. B. Grandin printing office. The entrance to George Elton's Gallery is a little right of center. Note the display of oval portrait photographs near the entrance.*

crowd. I did not go inside. Did not have the money to spare. Found instrument got heavy, so I rested under a tree near the road and concluded to sleep there, which I did. Cool before morning, so covered with camera cloth.

Rose soon after daylight and at Smith farm and made several negatives. Some milk at Mrs. Austin's and made a very good breakfast on graham bread and cake. Mr. Austin invited me to take dinner with them, and I enjoyed the potatoes, gravy, bread, butter, milk, pie, etc.

So much haze and dust I could not get the pictures I desired. Developed a number of negatives at Mr. Elton's. Some not very good. He thought overtimed.[460] Graham bread for lunch and bed at the Exchange Hotel.[461]

## August 16, 1907, Friday, Palmyra [p. 169]

Rose soon after daylight. Bathed feet and part of body. Took a walk out north of Palmyra to see if could find Martin Harris home or farm. Bought quart milk and made breakfast. In town and haircut. Then at gallery and developed negatives. Raining during afternoon. Very smoky and misty this morning.

Fixed plate holder and kits and tripod this p.m. at the shop. A long chat with Mr. Elton about our missionary work, what we believed, etc. Also, a long chat with him about the prize pictures he has made. A number of medals from the National Photography Association.[462]

Would like to get the views I can see in my mind's eye. Bought graham bread, cakes, and cheese and made a good lunch. At Exchange Hotel and worked up cash account. Retired about 10:15 p.m.

## August 17, 1907, Saturday, Palmyra [p. 170]

Rose about 5:30 a.m. Shave and cleaned up. Packed instrument to Smith homestead, reaching there about 7:30 a.m.

Made view of [Smith] home[463] and in grove and general view of farm. Smoky and very windy. Could not get the effect of light and shade I wished.

About 11:00 a.m., started for Hill Cumorah. Hugh Austin wished to go with me. His father willing. Made negative of Armington School House, but this cannot be the schoolhouse that the Prophet Joseph Smith attended school as it bears inscription "Union District No. 10, Manchester, 1846."[464] The schoolhouse beyond this about mile to the west and one-half south was erected in 1840.[465]

I told Mrs. Clemons at the Sampson house east of the Hill Cumorah that I would make another negative of the children, as the other was blurred. She did not feel like getting them ready. Had washed clothes.

---

460. Anderson refers here to film, rather than paper. "Overtimed" may refer to *overexposed* (shutter open too long). It may also refer to taking too long in developing.

461. Located on the north side of Canal Street at the intersection of Railroad Avenue (known as Park Drive now) and Canal Street. Constructed originally in the 1830s, the hotel had a warehouse located at the west end of the building. The warehouse was utilized during the heyday of the Erie Canal.

462. Anderson uses the abbreviation *N.P.A.* here, which we assume stands for the *National Photography Association*, which was founded in 1868. Its name was changed to Photographic Association of America in 1880.

463. Located on the east side of Stafford Road, this 1½-story frame home was occupied by the Smiths from 1825 to 1829. The family moved into a small log home located on the west side of Stafford just north of the Palmyra Township line in 1818. The Smiths lived in this log home during the significant period covering the time of the First Vision (1820) and the appearance of the angel Moroni (1823).

464. Local tradition at the turn of the century associated the Armington School with the Smith family and Oliver Cowdery, but that tradition is incorrect.

465. Anderson has given the incorrect date of 1840. The schoolhouse was erected in 1848. This is the actual site of the school where Oliver Cowdery taught and where the Smith children attended. The original frame structure from the 1820s–1830s period was moved and incorporated into the house directly south of this 1848 cobblestone schoolhouse that sits on the original foundation.

*Joseph and Lucy Mack Smith Home, Manchester, New York, 19 August 1907, Anderson Collection, LDSCA. The view is taken toward the north. Joseph Smith's vision on the evening and morning of 21–22 September 1823 occurred in the garret of the Smith family log cabin across the street and just north of the Palmyra Township line. Nevertheless, this white frame home is of historical significance to Latter-day Saints. In this home, Joseph Smith received several revelations, hid the Golden Plates, and lived until he moved to Harmony, Pennsylvania.*

Made another negative of hill and returned to Smith farm about 4:00 p.m. Very windy and do not think negative of farm will be successful. Made negative of creek and boys fishing. Table made by President Young.

## August 18, 1907, Sunday, Palmyra [p. 170]

I rose about 6:00 a.m. Fixed up my camera and found Martin Harris[466] farm. Now owned by Mr. Bush, and for upwards of fifty-one years known as the "Mormon Hill" farm.[467] Recently came into possession of Mr. Shaw. Beautifully located, running north and south and immediately north of the New York Central [Railroad], about two miles northwest from Palmyra on the state road running to Manchester. [p. 171]

Cave Hill,[468] two miles south of Palmyra on Canandaigua Road, east side on the Miner farm. Made this cave for translating the plates.[469] Was heavily timbered or in a forest at the time.

---

466. Martin Harris (1783–1875), who assisted Joseph Smith as a scribe during the translation of the Book of Mormon, paid the costs of its publication, and became one of the Three Witnesses of the Book of Mormon.

467. Located one and one-half miles north of Palmyra. Martin Harris mortgaged 151 acres to pay for the publication of the Book of Mormon.

468. A man-made cave on Miner's Hill. The cave has been connected with Joseph Smith by non-LDS area residents.

469. This was a folk tradition circulated by local non-LDS residents.

NO.5.

***Joseph and Lucy Mack Smith Home***, *Manchester, New York, 19 August 1907, Anderson Collection, LDSCA.*
*The Smith family occupied this farm in 1818 or 1819. They built a small log home two miles south of Palmyra Village down*
*Stafford Road toward Manchester. They purchased a one-hundred-acre, heavily forested tract of land just over the line in Manchester Township.*
*Within a decade, the Smith family fenced the land, cleared sixty acres, built a barn, a cooper's shop, and animal shelters, planted*
*a garden, started a large apple orchard, and developed meadows and fields. They also built a one-and-a-half-story frame home they*
*occupied in the spring of 1825. This white frame building stands today on the east side of the road across the street from the Sacred Grove.*

***Interior of Joseph and Lucy Mack Smith Home***, *Manchester, New York, August 1907, Anderson Collection, LDSCA. The view is of a bedroom in the Smith home.*

***Interior of Joseph and Lucy Mack Smith Home***, *Manchester, New York, August 1907, Anderson Collection, LDSCA. Photograph taken inside the Smith home. The table in the foreground purportedly was made by Brigham Young. Anderson noted: "Heavy mahogany table made by Brigham Young."*

**Small Country Lane Leading to the Sacred Grove**, *Manchester, New York, 17 August 1907, Anderson Collection, LDSCA. Across Stafford Road from the Joseph and Lucy Mack Smith home is a "small country lane" leading to the Sacred Grove. Hathaway Brook, which flows north beginning near the Hill Cumorah, through the Smith farm into the Erie Canal in Palmyra, can be seen in the view. Anderson notes in his diary, "Made negative of creek and boys fishing." The Sacred Grove can be seen on the north side (right side) of the fence.*

***Hathaway Brook, Joseph and Lucy Mack Smith Farm***, *Manchester, New York, August 1907, Anderson Collection, LDSCA. This view shows a small brook on the farm, known as Hathaway (Crooked) Brook or Creek. In his autobiography, Parley P. Pratt describes the baptism of several individuals at or near the Smith farm in the fall of 1830. Hathaway Creek may be the location of these baptisms.*

Has cedar tub[470] said to have been made by Joseph Smith Jr. before he was twenty-one years or when he was a big boy or minor. Made for Mrs. Balina White Saunders,[471] wife of Orlando Saunders, one of Mr. Smith's near neighbors; and Mr. Estey took it after the death of old people. Lived with them nine and one-half years and knew them well for about thirty years.

Breakfast this morning from raspberries I picked and milk and bread and egg at home on left hand about mile from Palmyra on left-hand side of the road. Only accepted five cents for milk. Supper: had ginger cookies and cupcakes.

Found old copies of the *Wayne Sentinel* and spent considerable of the afternoon looking through numbers from April 1825 to April 1837 [to] see if any-

---

470. At this point, Anderson is apparently at the home of Jason Estey. At the top of page 171 of the diary, "Jason Estey, Palmyra, N.Y." is written. Although Anderson listed Palmyra, Jason Estey and his wife, Fanny McKnutt Estey, lived just south of Armington Road on the west side of Canandaigua Road in Ontario County, Manchester Township.

471. Anderson spells the name *Sanders* throughout the diary. We have corrected the spelling to *Saunders*.

***Joseph and Lucy Mack Smith Farm**, Manchester, New York, 18 August 1907, Anderson Collection, LDSCA. The view shows the Sacred Grove in the distance. The "small country lane" can be seen on the left of the photograph. Anderson is taking this photograph either from Stafford Road, which runs north from the Smith farm to Palmyra, or just west of it. Hathaway Brook flows through the farm along the fence line, which can be seen separating the two fields in this view.*

thing about the Book of Mormon, Joseph Smith, etc. Father Estey found a number, April 16, 1830, with advertisement of Book of Mormon.[472]

Attended service in Methodist Church and could not keep awake. A good part of sermon I heard was on temperance.[473]

## August 19, 1907, Monday, Palmyra [p. 172]

Last night started from Smith farm and made my bed on new-mown hay under apple tree about a three-fourths mile from the farm and slept until 4:45 a.m. Cold, and camera cloth hardly heavy enough.

William W. Miner lives on the Canandaigua Road from Palmyra, two miles from churches.[474] "Cave Hill" is on his place a little east and running south. Made a photo of where the cave is. Was dug by Joseph Smith Jr. Was a door at the mouth of cave, which was kept up for years.

Martin Harris visited here when Mr. Miner was a boy about twelve or thirteen years. "Went on the hill (cave) a number of times with Martin Harris. He

---

472. Under the heading "The Book of Mormon," this issue of the *Wayne Sentinel* published the entire title page of the Book of Mormon with the following additional material: "By Joseph Smith Junior, Author and Proprietor. The above work, containing about 600 pages, large Duodecimo, is now for sale, wholesale and retail, at the Palmyra Bookstore, by E. B. Grandin." This also appeared in the 9 April 1830 issue.

473. Moderation or abstinence from the use of intoxicating drinks.

474. Known as the "Four Corners," the intersection has a church on each corner—the Presbyterian church, on the east corner of Church and Main, built in 1832; the Baptist church, on the west corner of Canandaigua and Main, built in 1871; the Methodist church, on the west corner of Church and Main, built in 1867; and the Episcopal Church, on the east corner of Canandaigua and Main, built in 1873. Church Street becomes Canandaigua Street at this intersection.

*Joseph and Lucy Mack Smith Farm*, Manchester, New York, August 1907, Anderson Collection, LDSCA. This view of the Smith farm and Sacred Grove is taken toward the northwest. The Sacred Grove is in the distance. The small country lane can be seen leading from the Sacred Grove to the farm buildings in the center of the photograph. The farm buildings were located on the west side of Stafford Road. The Smith white frame home is obscured by the trees in the center right.

*Joseph and Lucy Mack Smith Farm*, Manchester, New York, August 1907, Anderson Collection, LDSCA. The view of the Smith farm and Sacred Grove is taken toward the east. The Sacred Grove is on the left. The "small country lane" can be seen in the center of the photograph leading toward the farm buildings. Apparently, Anderson took the previous image from the distant hill on the right. The Smith white frame home is again obscured by the trees on the left of the country lane.

**Near Joseph and Lucy Mack Smith Home, Manchester Road**, *Manchester, New York, August 1907, Anderson Collection, LDSCA. The view shows a road that passes the Smith home. The Smith family was unable to make the last mortgage payment on the farm in 1825. They remained on it as renters until 1829.*

**District No. 10 Schoolhouse,** *Manchester, New York, 17 August 1907, Anderson Collection, LDSCA. Local tradition at the turn of the century identified this schoolhouse as the site where Joseph Smith had attended school, but Anderson notes in his diary that the date on the building is 1846 and therefore could not be the school Joseph Smith attended.*

**Martin and Lucy Harris Farm,** *Palmyra, New York, 18 August 1907, Anderson Collection, LDSCA. Martin Harris was born in Eastown, Saratoga County, New York, in 1783. He moved to Palmyra in 1792 and became a respected landowner. Lucy Harris was Martin's cousin. They married in 1808. Martin assisted Joseph Smith financially, served as his scribe during the translation of the Book of Mormon, and paid the printing cost of the publication of the book by selling 151 acres of this farm. Martin was one of the Three Witnesses to the Book of Mormon.*

**Martin and Lucy Harris Farm,** *Palmyra, New York, 18 August 1907, Anderson Collection, LDSCA. Anderson notes in his diary, "Beautifully located, running north and south and immediately north of the New York Central [Railroad]." Note the blurred image of the train passing by. The present-day rock house on the Harris property is southeast of this site.*

*The Hill, Martin Harris Farm*, *Palmyra, New York, 18 August 1907, Anderson Collection, LDSCA. Anderson apparently took the previous two photographs from this hill on the Harris farm property.*

always removed his hat when on the hill. Said it was 'this is holy ground, my boy.' God came here. This is like Mt. Sinai and Mt. Zion. At one time, he prayed on the hill, earnestly, for the welfare of the Mormon people—that they might be prospered. There was nothing selfish in the prayer, for he prayed for all mankind. Was thankful for revelation. I was impressed with the prayer and the sincerity of the old man. He stayed at our house several days, maybe a week. He enjoyed the visit very much. He came in peace and did not feel that he was an intruder. He went on the hill every day to offer his devotions."

Hill was wooded at this time, and many names inscribed on the trees near the cave: "Joseph Smith, Barney Brothers, Rigdon, and Martin Harris came to the cave every night in early days." [p. 173]

Major James Henry Petty, First North Regiment, Carolina, knew the Saunders, who were acquainted with the Prophet Joseph Smith's family and had heard Mrs. Saunders say that the Smiths were good neighbors. Also said that Granny Smith[475] said many times that she would have a son who would be a prophet and a great leader. Met Mr. Petty while making view of Cave Hill. See figure pointing with cane. Said had heard Saunders's folks say the Smiths were good neighbors.[476]

Made several negatives at the Smith farm this morning. There before 6:00 a.m. Heavy dew and made my feet wet moving around in the grass.

Crossed the hill east to Mr. Miner's, where I got information recorded above. Had dinner with them and went to town in afternoon and developed negatives at Mr. Elton's gallery, and Mr. Miner came in for

---

475. Lucy Mack Smith (1775–1856), mother of Joseph Smith Jr.

476. Anderson makes a separate entry at this point, as follows: "Dr. Crawford of Blue Rapids, Marshall County, Kansas—his wife exercised spiritual gifts. Call and see him if you ever go to Blue Rapids. W. W. Miner."

***Crossing of the New York Central Railroad,*** *Palmyra, New York, 18 August 1907, Anderson Collection, LDSCA. This crossing photograph was taken by Anderson at the Harris farm, just north of the present-day stone home.*

me and I went out but did not make another negative. Too late.

Drove out to the Sampson place and showed them negative of children. **[p. 174]** Chatted with Mr. Miner and wife until near 10:30 p.m. Then he done his chores, and we retired. Mrs. Miner a very fine lady. Has poor health. She has been a schoolteacher. Has taught languages in Rowland Hall,[477] Salt Lake City. Very kind to me. Invited me to stay overnight. Wished me to ride to town with them. I told them no. Would not make them uncomfortable by crowding in. Mrs. Miner a Presbyterian; Mr. Miner, a Unitarian.[478] Mrs. Miner is going to hospital or sanitarium for treatment.

*August 20, 1907, Tuesday, Palmyra [p. 174]*

Rose before 6:00 a.m. This morning not such a pleasant, clear morning as yesterday. Made two negatives of Mrs. Miner's home. Also spent some time writing and making notes. **[p. 178]**

Continued from page 174. We did not get breakfast until near 10:00 a.m. About 1:00 p.m., went out to Mr. Clemons's and made negative of children and then drove around by the Smith farm. Did not get negative of interior, as Mr. Austin was not home; so went into town and developed negatives and had a chat with Mr. Elton. Slept at Exchange Hotel.

477. Located at 205 East First Avenue, Salt Lake City, Rowland Hall was established in 1880 by the Episcopal Church as a home school and seminary for young ladies, kindergarten to college. Rowland Hall catered to intermountain ranching and mining families. Known today as Rowland Hall–St. Mark's School.

478. An adherent of Unitarian Universalism. The basic foundation of Unitarianism is the belief that deity exists in one person only. Unitarianism stresses the humanity of Jesus. The American Unitarian Association was founded in 1825.

*Wallace and Margaret Cavanaugh Miner Farm,* Manchester, New York, 19 August 1907, Anderson Collection, LDSCA.

*Cave Hill,* Manchester, New York, 19 August 1907, Anderson Collection, LDSCA. Cave Hill is located on the old Miner farm. Miner Road branches off Canandaigua Road, which runs north to Palmyra from the Hill Cumorah. Anderson notes in his diary, "Met Mr. Petty while making view of Cave Hill. See figure pointing with cane. Said had heard Saunders's folks say the Smiths were good neighbors."

*Peter and Mary Musselman Whitmer Farm,* Fayette, New York, 1907, Anderson Collection, LDSCA. Site of the organization of the Church of Christ on 6 April 1830, when at least thirty to fifty believers met together in the log home of Peter and Mary Musselman Whitmer. Some had already been baptized, and six of those present were officially listed as organizing members. The newly organized group called itself the Church of Christ or, in some cases, the Church of Jesus Christ.

*Peter and Mary Musselman Whitmer Farm,* Fayette, New York, 1907, Anderson Collection, LDSCA. The log cabin where the Church was organized had disappeared before Anderson arrived in 1907. The buildings in this view are of a later period than when the early Saints gathered here on the first Tuesday of April 1830.

**Seneca Lake,** *Seneca County, New York, 1907, Anderson Collection, LDSCA. In June 1829, Hyrum Smith, David Whitmer, and Peter Whitmer Jr. were baptized in Seneca Lake. Anderson notes on the photograph, "Converts to Mormonism baptized here, April 11 and 18, 1830, by Oliver Cowdery." Those baptized by Oliver Cowdery on 11 and 18 April were Hiram Page, Catherine Page, Christian Whitmer, Anne Whitmer, Jacob Whitmer, Elizabeth Whitmer, Peter Whitmer Sr., Mary Whitmer, William Jolly, Elizabeth Jolly, Vincent Jolly, Ziba Peterson, and Elizabeth Ann Whitmer.*

*Harmony, Susquehanna County, Pennsylvania, 1907, Anderson Collection, LDSCA. Joseph Smith arrived in Susquehanna County, Pennsylvania, for the first time in November 1825. He boarded with Isaac Hale in Harmony Township while employed by Josiah Stowell, who was at that time attempting to find an ancient Spanish mine where coins had presumably been minted and buried. Joseph's brief stay had considerable influence on his own life and on the beginnings of Mormonism. Four important events occurred in or near Harmony. Joseph met his future wife, Emma Hale (Isaac's daughter); he completed much of the Book of Mormon translation; he received several divine revelations and visitations; and he had early associations with individuals in the area who would prove important for the Church of Christ that was established in 1830.*

## *August 21, 1907, Wednesday, Palmyra [p. 178]*

At Mr. Elton's, developed negatives and named and numbered them. Lunch: brown bread and tomatoes. After dinner, called on William Shannon, ninety-three years old. Helped build the first railroad coaches run on the first railroad in America. See note and copy. [p. 179]

Sent paper to Andrew Jenson about first edition of Book of Mormon.[479] Tried to find other papers with notice about Book of Mormon, but could not. Found one or two other issues and sent to my wife.

Evening out to Clark Austin's and had a chat with him about Joseph Smith.[480]

[end sheet of diary] Salt Lake City, March 4, 1907, For my brother, Geo. Ed. Anderson, from Joe and Camilla.[481]

---

479. Anderson may be referring to the 16 April 1830 *Wayne Sentinel* issue he found on 18 August.

480. The diary ends with what appears to be a list of photographs (some taken following Anderson's departure from the Manchester area), historical notes, and, in one case, a photographic-process chemical formula. That information is contained in Appendix Two.

481. Camilla Josephine Anderson Popper (1875–1925), Anderson's sister, who married Joseph Popper (1875–?).

**Joseph and Emma Hale Smith Home,** *Harmony, Pennsylvania, 1907, Anderson Collection, LDSCA. The center part of the structure is the original Smith dwelling.*

***Harmony Property Deed Signed by Joseph and Emma Hale Smith,***
*Anderson Collection, LDSCA. Joseph and Emma purchased 13½ acres
from Isaac Hale and a small, uncompleted home from Emma's brother,
Jesse Hale. In this home, the translation of the Book of Mormon began.
Joseph and Emma moved from Harmony in 1829 but apparently did
not sell their property at that time. The photograph shows the signed deed
transferring their ownership to Joseph McKune in 1834.*

**Joseph and Emma Smith Home,** *Harmony, Pennsylvania, 1907, Anderson Collection, LDSCA. The McKune Cemetery can be seen beyond the Smith home on the left.*

**A Young Woman,** *Harmony, Pennsylvania, 1907, Anderson Collection, LDSCA. A photograph of an unknown young woman. The Joseph and Emma Smith home can be seen in the background.*

***Isaac and Elizabeth Hale Tombstones,*** *Harmony, Pennsylvania, 1907, Anderson Collection, LDSCA. The cemetery is located near the Smith home. Gravestones of Isaac and Elizabeth Hale, Emma's parents, can be seen clearly.*

**Alvin Smith Tombstone**, *Harmony, Pennsylvania, 1907, Anderson Collection, LDSCA. Shows the grave marker for Joseph and Emma's first child, Alvin, who died on 15 June 1828.*

***Susquehanna River,*** *Harmony, Pennsylvania, 1907, Anderson Collection, LDSCA. In May 1829, Joseph Smith and Oliver Cowdery reached a section in the Book of Mormon translation that discussed baptism. They left the small home for a wooded area near the riverbank. As they prayed for guidance on the subject, an angel (John the Baptist) appeared and gave them the authority to baptize, which they did in the nearby river.*

***Susquehanna River,*** *Harmony, Pennsylvania, 1907, Anderson Collection, LDSCA. One of the longest rivers of the Eastern Seaboard of the United States, the Susquehanna is about 444 miles long and, with its tributaries, drains an area of 27,570 square miles. Because of the numerous rapids and other obstructions, it never served as an important waterway. It rises in Otsego Lake in central New York State and winds through the Appalachian Mountains in New York, Pennsylvania, and Maryland before flowing into the head of Chesapeake Bay at Havre de Grace, Maryland.*

**"Money Hole,"** *Harmony, Pennsylvania, 1907, Anderson Collection, LDSCA. According to tradition, Joseph Smith was employed by Josiah Stowell to dig for silver here in 1825. As the Smith family struggled to make the payments on their farm, Joseph Smith and his father accepted employment in Pennsylvania in an attempt to find a buried treasure. Young Joseph convinced Stowell to give up the venture. Joseph eventually moved to Chenango County, New York, where he continued to work for Stowell and others.*

**New York–Pennsylvania State Line,** *1907, Anderson Collection, LDSCA. The Prophet Joseph Smith indicated that somewhere between Colesville, New York, and Harmony, Pennsylvania, Peter, James, and John—the New Testament disciples of Jesus— appeared on the banks of the Susquehanna River to restore priesthood keys and rights to him and Oliver Cowdery. The photograph is taken from Pennsylvania looking into New York.*

*Nineveh (Colesville Township)*, Broome County, New York, 1907, Anderson Collection, LDSCA. Anderson's view is looking south toward the small community of Nineveh. The town is located across the Susquehanna River from the old Joseph Knight farm. Most of the Knight farm is obscured by the hill on the left of the photograph. Part of the original 142-acre farm, however, bordered the river and therefore may be in view just beyond the bridge that spans the river in this photograph. Members of the Knight family became closely associated with Joseph Smith and were among the earliest converts of Mormonism. With tremendous sacrifices, the Knight family followed Joseph Smith from New York to Ohio, Missouri, and Illinois and later followed Brigham Young to Utah.

*Pickerel Pond, Joseph and Polly Peck Knight Farm*, Colesville, New York, 1907, Anderson Collection, LDSCA. Young Joseph Smith worked for Joseph Knight, who operated carding machinery and a gristmill in addition to his farm. Pickerel Pond, either all or part of it, was located on the Knight farm.

**Tunbridge Gore,** *Orange County, Vermont, 1907, Anderson Collection, LDSCA. The view is a fall scene, contrasting the following photograph. The Prophet Joseph Smith's parents, Joseph and Lucy Mack Smith, met and married in Tunbridge. They remained near their extended family for six years on their own farm before they made their first move in 1802 to Randolph, a neighboring village seven miles west, to open a store. In Randolph, Joseph Smith Sr. also invested in a trading venture that ultimately failed. It was a significant turning point in the family's finances.*

***Tunbridge Gore,*** *Orange County, Vermont, 9 February 1908, Anderson Collection, LDSCA. The view is a winter scene, contrasting the previous photograph. Joseph and Lucy Smith were forced to sell their share of the farm in Tunbridge—an event that blighted the family fortunes for the next thirty years. Lucy Mack Smith said they made the sacrifice to avoid the "embarrassment of debt," which was brought about when a partner in the China trading venture cheated Joseph Smith Sr. During the next fourteen years, they moved many times. The Smith farm in Tunbridge Gore was the birthplace of Alvin, Hyrum, Sophronia, and Samuel Smith.*

*Tunbridge Hill Cemetery,* Orange County, Vermont, 1908, Anderson Collection, LDSCA. Anderson took many photographs of cemeteries of historical significance for the LDS Church and for the Smith family. The tombstones, like the ones at Tunbridge Hill, contained information about the extended Smith family.

*Schoolhouse,* Royalton, Vermont, 1907, Anderson Collection, LDSCA. Traditionally identified as the place where Joseph Smith Sr. taught school. After they lost the Tunbridge farm, the Smiths became tenant farmers and moved whenever the farm they rented was sold or a better opportunity arose. Royalton was not far from the Smiths' Tunbridge relatives and thus provided some security. While the Smith family was in Royalton, two boys were added to the family—Ephraim and William. Joseph Smith Sr. had several dreams or visions during this period. In one particular vision received in 1811 in Royalton, he was traveling in a field covered with dead, fallen timber. He interpreted the vision as a sign the world was dead to the knowledge of "true religion or plan of salvation."

NO.52.

*Harvey Smith Home,* South Royalton, Vermont, 13 November 1907, Anderson Collection, LDSCA. Apparently, Harvey Smith was a relative of the Prophet Joseph Smith and an early convert to the Church. The owners of the home in 1907 posed with their oxen.

**Solomon and Lydia Gates Mack Homesite,** *Sharon, Vermont, 1907, Anderson Collection, LDSCA. The Macks were the maternal grandparents of the Prophet Joseph Smith. A current marker at this site states, "Solomon Mack home. The Solomon Mack farm. 100 acres was purchased by him in 1804. An extra house on it was rented to his son-in-law, Joseph Smith Sr. This old cellar is all that remains of the Solomon Mack home. Nearby may be seen [the] foundation for the outbuildings."*

**Memorial Cottage and Joseph Smith Memorial Monument**, *Sharon, Vermont, 31 October 1907, Anderson Collection, LDSCA. Joseph Smith's family lines all run through New England. His ancestor, Robert Smith, came from England during the Puritan "great migration" to settle in Topsfield, Massachusetts, north of Boston. Joseph Smith's maternal ancestors lived in Connecticut, New Hampshire, and Vermont. His parents, Joseph and Lucy Mack Smith, moved to the farm of Solomon and Lydia Gates Mack, his maternal grandparents, in Sharon, Vermont, shortly before his birth on 23 December 1805.*

NO. 6A.

**Joseph Smith Memorial Monument,** *Sharon, Vermont, 1907, Anderson Collection, LDSCA. Dedicated on 23 December 1905, the one-hundredth anniversary of the birth of the Prophet Joseph Smith. The doctor who delivered Joseph Smith Jr. is reportedly Dr. Joseph Adam Denison. According to a Denison family tradition, a diary entry in Dr. Denison's diary reported the birth of a son at the Smith home in December 1805. A note, written at a later time, was pinned to the 23 December 1805 diary entry stating, "If I had known how he was going to turn out I'd have smothered the little cuss."*

**Joseph Smith Memorial Monument,** *Sharon, Vermont, 1907, Anderson Collection, LDSCA. The view is a closeup view of the monument. The inscription reads, "Sacred to the memory of Joseph Smith, the Prophet, born here 23rd December, 1805; martyred, Carthage, Illinois, 27th June, 1844." In the spring of 1905, Junius F. Wells, on assignment from the LDS Church First Presidency, arrived in Sharon, Vermont, to pinpoint the site of the Solomon Mack farm and to purchase the land for the Church. Soon thereafter, the land was bought, and a decision was made to erect a monument on the one-hundredth anniversary of the Prophet Joseph Smith's birth. Two local firms, R. C. Bowers Company and the firm of Marr and Gord, were given the contract to furnish and to erect the monument. It was dedicated by Joseph F. Smith, LDS Church president and nephew of the Prophet Joseph Smith, on 23 December 1905.*

***Interior of Joseph Smith Memorial Cottage,*** *Sharon, Vermont, 1907, Anderson Collection, LDSCA.*
*The view shows the interior of the cottage. The hearthstone was recovered from the foundation of the old Joseph Smith and Lucy Mack Smith cabin.*

**Lebanon, New Hampshire,** *6 January 1908, Anderson Collection, LDSCA. A general view is shown. Between 1803 and 1811, all the Smith family moves were in a tiny circle around Tunbridge, Randolph, Royalton, and Sharon. The circle then enlarged when they relocated twenty miles across the Connecticut River to Lebanon, New Hampshire, in 1811. Here, several Smith children received formal educations, but the family returned to Vermont when sickness depleted their savings.*

**Squire Murdock Farm,** *Norwich, Vermont, 23 January 1908,*
*Anderson Collection, LDSCA. The Joseph and Lucy Mack Smith*
*family moved to this rented farm from Lebanon, New Hampshire,*
*in 1814. Finally, the Joseph and Lucy Mack Smith family sepa-*
*rated themselves from family and friends in 1816 following*
*another failed harvest and moved to Palmyra, New York, some*
*three hundred miles west, for a new beginning.*

# George Edward Anderson's Notes
# Made from *An Illustrated Historical Atlas of*
# *Caldwell County, Missouri*

1.  [**p. 47**] Mormon emigration from Jackson County. John Whitmer sent special revelation. Approved the site. Jerusalem new home in the wilderness.

2.  Far West. Caldwell County organized on the 26th day of December 1836 with seat of justice at Far West. High rolling prairie, visible from long distances in all directions. At time of Mormon War, largest town in state north of Missouri, 2,500.

3.  The Mormons. The early history of county is inseparably connected with the Mormons. See history, "Illiterate Fanatic." A few able men and eloquent. Parley P. Pratt, Oliver Cowdery, Sidney Rigdon, and others.

4.  Mormon Settlements. Along Shoal Creek, Livingston County, Daviess and Clinton Counties. See No. 5A, page 49. [**p. 49**]

5A. Mormons largely outnumbered the Gentiles. They elected to all offices of honor and trust persons of their own faith. Smith was careful that the persons selected should be subservient to the will of himself and apostles. The Gentiles complained that it was impossible for them to obtain a fair hearing before the Mormon magistrates and juries, that the trials were farces, that the leaders taught and the members acted on the principle that Gentiles had no rights which a Mormon was bound to respect, and that not the merits of the case but the creeds of the contestants determined which way the scales of justice would turn.

Whether these complaints were true or false, they were believed by many, and naturally excited deep indignation against the Mormons. Tales of debauchery, theft and murder were told of them, and their expulsion from the county demanded. These bitter feelings engendered brawls and riots. Crowds of excited fanatics pelted obnoxious Gentiles on the streets of Far West with clubs and stones. In retaliation, armed Gentiles rode into public meetings where their lawless conduct was being denounced, seized the speakers, and afflicted the lash until blood trickled down their backs. Both sides ceased to resort to legal methods for the enforcement of their rights amidst so much excitement. The civil [**p. 50**] authorities were powerless to enforce the laws and punish offenses. [**p. 47**]

5.  Mormon Leaders. Sixteen mentioned. Philo Dibble among the sixteen. Distinguished for their business qualifications.

6.  The Temple. To erect a magnificent temple, one-tenth of all time, labor, and earnings to be devoted to the building of temple.

7.  Mormon War. Deluded followers of Joe Smith as a people were honest, sober, and industrious, but object of the leaders was to obtain power and make money.

8.  Mormon exodus in November. Old and young, sick and feeble, delicate women and suckling children, almost without food and clothing, [p. **48**] were compelled to abandon their homes and firesides. Valued farms traded for a yoke of oxen, an old wagon, or anything that would furnish transportation. . . . Many walked. . . . Chilly blast of winter. New asylum Nauvoo. Population reduced from 6,000 to less than 1,000 by exodus of Mormons.

    David Whitmer, the Bozarths, George Walters, Abner Scovell, Avery Smith, and others remained and have retained the respect of all for their good qualities and acts.

    Visions. If that strange people, who built Nauvoo and Salt Lake, who uncomplainingly toiled across the great American desert . . . had been permitted to remain . . . how different the history of Far West. Instead of being a farm with scarcely sufficient ruins to mark the spot, they would have been a rich and popular city, along which would be pouring the wealth of the world. Instead of an old dilapidated farmhouse, there would have been magnificent temples to which devout Saints from the farthest corners of the world would have made their yearly pilgrimages. But the bigotry and the intolerance of the Saints toward the Gentiles and especially the dissenters from the new revelations of Joe Smith rendered such a consummation impossible.

# George Edward Anderson's Notes at the End of His Diary

**[p. 174] Topsfield, Essex County**

- Sixteen miles nearer Boston than Sharon [we cannot be sure what Anderson may have meant by this statement since Topsfield is significantly closer to Boston than Sharon, Vermont]. Home of Robert Smith. Brick monument of first Samuel Smith in cemetery. [p. 175]

**Sharon, South Royalton**

- Monument and cottage. General view. Sharon. Hearthstone. Inscription on monument.

- Mr. Robinson, who [blank]. Old home where Smiths lived. Now owned by Mr. Eaton. Fine spring. Ruins of old cellar and chimney here. William and Ephraim born here. Ephraim buried at South Royalton.

- Old Mack home in hollow below cottage near where waterpipe crosses hollow.

- Old Mack or Smith farm in Tunbridge about five miles from Robinson farmhouse.

- Tunbridge, first home, then Sharon, then Royalton of Smiths.

- Schoolhouse where the Prophet's father taught school. On the road to monument. [p. 176]

**Fayette, New York, Seneca County**

- Conference, January 2, 1831.

- Farm of Peter Whitmer. See old tree now standing.

- See Chester Reed, old gentleman member of the Church, about one or two miles from McDougall post office. Will assist and give what information can. Apostle George A. Smith and President Ellsworth told me.

- Woods near Peter Whitmer's where angel showed Three Witnesses the plates.

- David Whitmer's home.

- Seneca Lake. [p. 177]

## New York

- Athalia Rigdon, now Athalia Robinson of Friendship, Allegheny County, New York, 1900. Present when her father received the Book of Mormon.

## Palmyra

- Building where Book of Mormon published. Two stores from where Admiral Sampson's cannon [is located]. Five thousand copies by Egbert Grandin.

- First leaves of Book of Mormon. Also store that held first leaves.

- Press that was printed on in Deseret News Building, Salt Lake City.

## Hill Cumorah

- Book of Mormon cave and convex stones. See them.

## Smith Homestead

- Old log house now owned by William Avery Chapman.

- Death of Alvin, who desired his parents to occupy it.

- No settee and heavy mahogany table made by Brigham Young.

## Sacred Grove

- First prayer, one-fourth mile from house, five to eight acres.

- Small creek used for early baptisms.

## Colesville, New York

- Thirteen baptized.

- Prophet arrested and acquitted at South Bainbridge. [**p. 178**]

## Manchester, New York

- Eight Witnesses saw the plates near the Smith residence. [**p. 179**]

## Mentor, Ohio, Geauga County

- Sidney Rigdon, Campbellite preacher, October or November 1830. Baptized—had a large following.

- Mentor is 30 miles from Bainbridge, Geauga County.

- Book of Mormon presented by Elders Parley P. Pratt, Ziba Peterson, and others.

- Athalia Rigdon. See New York, page 177.

- See testimony of John W. Rigdon, H. of C., page 122. [**p. 180**]

## Kirtland, Ohio, Geauga County

- See dedication of Joseph Smith Monument, pages 68 and 69.

- Cleveland. Electric car for Willoughby.

- Ulysses W. Green[e], one of the apostles of Reorganized [Church].

- John H. Lake, a former apostle [of Reorganized Church]; now one of the evangelists.

- Albert E. Stone, who takes charge of edifice.

- "Inner court" or main room. Personages on breastwork of the pulpit. Doctrine and Covenants section 110.

- Upper room. School of Prophets.

- Higher apartments where classes of the priesthood assembled. From the roof, a fine view.

- Fine work in the main room. Pulpits for the Melchizedek and Aaronic Priesthoods.

- President Brigham Young and his brother, Joseph Young, were workmen on that building. Marks of skill.

- The Glazing.

- Register names. [**p. 181**]

- Water 10 oz.; edinol 30 gr.; sul. soda ½ oz. anhydrus; carb. soda 200 gr. anhydrus; bromide solution to keep the whites clear; mix in order given.

## Kirtland, continued

- Inscription: House of the Lord, Built by the Church of Jesus Christ of Latter Day Saints 1834. Reorganized Church of Jesus Christ of Latter Day Saints in Succession by Decision of Court February 1880.

- Hyrum Smith's home; also Sidney Rigdon's.

- Keziah Turk—see what she remembers of old times.

- Whitmer's [Whitney] store.

- Residences of the Johnsons. [p. 182]

## Cleveland

- Garfield Monument. See interior. Monument to memory of Union soldiers.

- Euclid Avenue. Shaking Quakers near Cleveland.

## Kirtland, continued

- Sidney Rigdon lived at [Mentor]. Revelation to Parley P. Pratt and Ziba Peterson concerning the Lamanites brought them first to Kirtland. See Mentor, page 179.

- 1838: Prophet and Saints left Kirtland.

- Prophet and Sidney Rigdon left January 12, 1838. Horseback act, mob violence.

- May 4, 1839: Oliver Granger to go to Kirtland and preside and Saints from eastern states to gather there.

- October 3, 1840: Almon W. Babbitt appointed to preside at Kirtland. May 22, 1841, was chosen president, Kirtland Stake of Zion.

- Thursday, April 6, 1843: Decided all Saints should remove to Nauvoo.

- September 1845: Saints persecuted and temple taken possession of.

- Bank, Kirtland Safety Society, November 2, 1836. [p. 183]

- Revelation on Word of Wisdom, February 27, 1833.

- Cornerstone[s] of temple laid July 23, 1833. Rededicated [Dedicated] March 27, 1836, Sunday.

- Elder Edward Stevenson preached in Kirtland Temple, April 7, 1870.

- Prophet and wife arrived at Kirtland February 1, 1831. Welcomed at home of Newel K. Whitney.

- Shaking Quakers near Cleveland, Ohio.

- Hiram, Portage County. Prophet moved here and revised the scriptures and many important revelations received while here at home of John Johnson. See page 55, brief history. Tar and beaten.

- Joseph Smith [III], president of the Reorganized Church, born on November [6], 1832.

- School of Prophets, 1832–1833.

# Bibliography

### Contemporary Newspapers Consulted

*Boston Sunday Globe*

*Chicago Tribune*

*Deseret Evening News*

*Deseret News*

*Kansas City Times*

*Liahona*

*Liahona The Elders' Journal*

*Philadelphia Saturday Courier*

*Saints Herald*

*Salt Lake Tribune*

*Springville Independent*

*Wayne Sentinel*

### Unpublished Materials

Early Church Information File, Family History Library, The Church of Jesus Christ of Latter-day Saints, Salt Lake City, Utah (LDSFHL).

George Edward Anderson Manuscript Collection, 1901–28, Archive Division, Church Historical Department, The Church of Jesus Christ of Latter-day Saints, Salt Lake City, Utah (LDSCA).

"Historical Records and Minutes." Central States Mission Collection, LDSCA.

"Historical Records and Minutes." Colorado Mission Collection, LDSCA.

"Historical Records and Minutes." Indian Territory Mission Collection, LDSCA.

"Historical Records and Minutes." Northern States Mission Collection, LDSCA.

Journal History of The Church of Jesus Christ of Latter-day Saints, LDSCA.

"Missionary Registers, 1860–1959." Missionary Department Collection, LDSCA.

Name Authority Cards, Library-Archives, Reorganized Church of Jesus Christ of Latter Day Saints, Independence, Missouri (RLDSCA).

*Saints Herald* Obituary Index, RLDSCA.

Temple Index Bureau, LDSFHL.

U.S. Federal Census, 1900 and 1910, Ohio, Illinois, New York, Missouri, LDSFHL.


## Books and Periodicals Consulted

"Address to the World." *Improvement Era* 10 (May 1907): 481–95.

Alexander, Thomas G. *Mormonism in Transition: A History of the Latter-day Saints 1890–1930.* Urbana: University of Illinois Press, 1986.

Allen, James B., and Glen M. Leonard. *The Story of the Latter-day Saints.* Salt Lake City: Deseret Book, 1992.

Anderson, George Ed. "Boy in the Picture of the Sacred Grove." *Improvement Era* 23 (May 1920): 638–40.

Anderson, Richard L. "Clarifications of Boggs's 'Order' and Joseph Smith's Constitutionalism." In *Regional Studies in Latter-day Saint Church History, Missouri.* Provo, Utah: Department of Church History and Doctrine, Brigham Young University, 1994.

———. "Joseph Smith's Ancestors." In *Historical Atlas of Mormonism,* 4–5. New York: Simon & Schuster, 1994.

Appleberg, Marilyn. *I Love Chicago Guide.* New York: Collier Books, Macmillan, 1993.

Barrett, Lamar C. "Adam-ondi-Ahman." In *Encyclopedia of Mormonism,* 1:19–20. New York: Macmillan, 1992.

Black, Susan Easton, comp. *Early Members of the Reorganized Church of Jesus Christ of Latter Day Saints.* 6 vols. Provo, Utah: Religious Studies Center, Brigham Young University, 1993.

———, comp. *Membership of The Church of Jesus Christ of Latter-day Saints: 1830–1848.* 50 vols. Provo, Utah: Religious Studies Center, Brigham Young University, 1989.

Blair, Alma R. "Conflict in Missouri." In *Historical Atlas of Mormonism*, 46–47. New York: Simon & Schuster, 1994.

———. "The Haun's Mill Massacre." *BYU Studies* 13 (autumn 1972): 62–76.

Blocker, Jack S., Jr. *American Temperance Movements: Cycles of Reform.* Boston: Twayne Publishers, 1988.

Blum, Ida. *Nauvoo: An American Heritage.* Carthage, Ill.: Journal Printing Co., 1969.

Brown, S. Kent, Donald Q. Cannon, and Richard H. Jackson. *Historical Atlas of Mormonism.* New York: Simon & Schuster, 1994.

Cannon, Donald Q. "Commerce, Illinois." In *Historical Atlas of Mormonism*, 52–53. New York: Simon & Schuster, 1994.

———. "Nauvoo (1842)." In *Historical Atlas of Mormonism*, 54–55. New York: Simon & Schuster, 1994.

Cannon, Sean J. "Expulsion from Missouri." In *Historical Atlas of Mormonism*, 48–49. New York: Simon & Schuster, 1994.

Cook, Lyndon W. *The Revelations of the Prophet Joseph Smith: A Historical and Biographical Commentary of the Doctrine and Covenants.* Salt Lake City: Deseret Book, 1985.

Cook, Thomas L. *Palmyra and Vicinity.* Palmyra, N.Y.: Press of The Palmyra Courier-Journal, 1930.

Cornwall, J. Spencer. *Stories of Our Mormon Hymns.* Salt Lake City: Deseret Book Co., 1968.

Cowley, Matthias. *Cowley's Talks on Doctrine.* Chattanooga, Tenn.: Ben E. Rich, 1902.

Cutler, Carl. *Queens of the Western Ocean: The Story of America's Mail and Passenger Sailing Lines.* Annapolis, Md.: United States Naval Institute, 1961.

"David." *Primary Department Bible Stories, 1906–1907.* Lesson 35, 1–4. Salt Lake City: Deseret Sunday School Union, 1906.

Davidson, J. Brownlee, and Leon Wilson Chase. *Farm Machinery and Farm Motors.* New York: Orange Judd Co., 1913.

Dear, Mary Cleora, comp. *Two Hundred Thirty-Eight Years of the Whitmer Family, 1737–1976.* Richmond, Missouri: Beck Printing Co., 1976.

*Deseret News 1991–1992 Church Almanac.* Salt Lake City: Deseret News, 1990.

*The Doctrine and Covenants of The Church of Jesus Christ of Latter-day Saints.* Salt Lake City: The Church of Jesus Christ of Latter-day Saints, 1989.

Druis, Perry R. *The Saloon: Public Drinking in Chicago and Boston 1880–1920.* Chicago: University of Illinois Press, 1983.

Durham, Michael S. *The Smithsonian Guide to Historic America: The Desert States.* New York: Stewart, Tabori & Chang, 1990.

Durham, Reed C. "The Election Day Battle at Gallatin." *BYU Studies* 13 (autumn 1972): 36–61.

*Encyclopedia Britannica: A Dictionary of Arts, Sciences and General Literature.* New York: Charles Scribner's Sons, 1904, 16:825–28.

*Encyclopedia Britannica: Micropedia, Ready Reference.* 12 vols. Chicago: Encyclopedia, Inc., 1993.

Enders, Donald L. "New York State." In *Historical Atlas of Mormonism,* 12–13. New York: Simon & Schuster, 1994.

———. "Palmyra, New York." In *Historical Atlas of Mormonism,* 10–11. New York: Simon & Schuster, 1994.

———. "Sacred Grove." In *Encyclopedia of Mormonism,* 3:1247–48. New York: Macmillan, 1992.

Esshom, Frank. *Pioneers and Prominent Men of Utah.* Salt Lake City: Utah Pioneers Book Publishing Co., 1913.

Evans, John Henry. *The Birth of Mormonism in Picture: Scenes and Incidents in Early Church History.* Salt Lake City: Deseret Sunday School Union, 1909.

Flake, Chad J. *A Mormon Bibliography: 1830–1930.* Salt Lake City: University of Utah Press, 1978.

Foner, Eric, and John A. Garraty, eds. *The Reader's Companion to American History.* Boston: Houghton Mifflin Co., 1991.

Francis, Rell G. *The Utah Photographs of George Edward Anderson.* Lincoln: University of Nebraska Press, 1979.

Gentry, Leland H. "LDS Communities in Caldwell and Daviess Counties." In *Encyclopedia of Mormonism,* 2:925–27. New York: Macmillan, 1992.

Golby, J. M. and A. W. Purdue. *The Monarchy and the British People, 1760 to the Present.* London: B. T. Batsford Ltd., 1988.

Grenville, J. D. S. *A History of the World in the Twentieth Century.* Cambridge, Mass.: The Belknap Press of Harvard University Press, 1994.

"Helaman's Army of 2,000 Young Men." *Sunday School Outlines, Second Intermediate Department, First Year Book of Mormon, 1907–1908.* Lesson 48, 27. Salt Lake City: Deseret Sunday School Union Bookstore, 1907.

Henisch, Heinz K., and Bridget A. Henisch. *The Photographic Experience 1839–1914: Images and Attitudes.* University Park: Pennsylvania State University Press, 1994.

*Historical Atlas of the United States.* Washington, D.C.: National Geographic Society, 1988.

*The History of Caldwell and Livingston Counties, Written and Compiled from the Most Authentic Official and Private Sources, Including a History of Their Townships and Villages, Together with a Condensed History of Missouri; a Reliable and Detailed History of Caldwell and Livingston Counties—Their Pioneer Record, Resources, Biographical Sketches of Prominent Citizens; General and Local Statistics of Great Value; Incidents and Reminiscences.* St. Louis: Natural Historical Company, 1886.

"History of Tithing." *Young Men's Mutual Improvement Association Manual, 1907–1908.* Lesson 6, 34–40. Salt Lake City: The General Board of the Y.M.M.I.A.

Holzapfel, Richard Neitzel. "The Church on the Early 19th-Century Frontier." In *Historical Atlas of Mormonism,* 6–7. New York: Simon & Schuster, 1994.

————. "Establishing Zion in Preparation for the Second Coming." In *Watch and Be Ready: Preparing for the Second Coming of the Lord,* 105–33. Salt Lake City: Deseret Book, 1994.

————. "Pennsylvania." In *Historical Atlas of Mormonism,* 16–17. New York: Simon & Schuster, 1994.

————. "Stereographs and Stereotypes: A 1904 View of Mormonism." *Journal of Mormon History* 18 (fall 1992): 155–76.

Holzapfel, Richard Neitzel, and T. Jeffery Cottle. "Capturing the Past: G. E. Anderson's 1907 Photographic Mission to Missouri," *Restoration Studies V.* Independence, Mo.: Herald Publishing House, 1993: 216–39.

————. "The City of Joseph in Focus: The Use and Abuse of Historic Photographs." *BYU Studies* 32 (winter-spring 1991): 249–68.

————. *Old Mormon Kirtland and Missouri: Historic Photographs and Guide.* Santa Ana, Ca.: Fieldbrook Productions, 1991.

————. *Old Mormon Nauvoo and Southeastern Iowa: Historic Photographs and Guide.* Santa Ana, Ca.: Fieldbrook Productions, 1991.

————. *Old Mormon Palmyra and New England: Historic Photographs and Guide.* Santa Ana, Ca.: Fieldbrook Productions, 1991.

Hopkins, C. Howard. *History of the Y.M.C.A. in North America.* New York: Association Press, 1951.

*Hoye's Kansas City Directory Including Independence.* Kansas City: Hoye's, 1907.

*An Illustrated Historical Atlas of Caldwell County, Missouri.* N.p.: Brink, McDonough, and Co., 1876.

*Images of America: A Panorama of History and Photographs.* Washington, D.C.: Smithsonian Books, 1989.

Jackson, Richard H. "Hill Cumorah." In *Historical Atlas of Mormonism,* 9–10. New York: Simon & Schuster, 1994.

Jenson, Andrew. "Amanda Smith." *The Historical Record* 5 (July 1886): 83–88.

————. *Church Chronology: A Record of Important Events Pertaining to the History of the Church of Jesus Christ of Latter-day Saints.* Salt Lake City: Deseret News, 1914.

————. *Encyclopedia History of the Church of Jesus Christ of Latter-day Saints.* Salt Lake City: Deseret News, 1941.

————. "Haun's Mill Massacre." *The Historical Record* 7 (December 1888): 671–84.

————. *Latter-day Saint Biographical Encyclopedia: A Compilation of Biographical Sketches of Prominent Men and Women in The Church of Jesus Christ of Latter-day Saints.* 4 vols. Salt Lake City: Western Epics, 1971.

"Jesus the Christ to Return." *Sunday School Outlines, Theological Department, First Year.* Lesson 6, 42. Salt Lake City: Deseret Sunday School Union, 1907.

Johnson, Clark V. "Missouri." In *Encyclopedia of Mormonism,* 2:922–25. New York: Macmillan, 1992.

————. "Northern Missouri." In *Historical Atlas of Mormonism,* 42–43. New York: Simon & Schuster, 1994.

Kimball, Stanley B. "Eastern Iowa." In *Historical Atlas of Mormonism,* 58–59. New York: Simon & Schuster, 1994.

Klusmire, Jon. *Colorado.* Oakland, Ca.: Fodor's Travel Publications, Inc., 1993.

"The Last Days of the War." *Sunday School Outlines, Second Intermediate Department, First Year Book of Mormon, 1907–1908.* Lesson 49, 28. Salt Lake City: Deseret Sunday School Union Bookstore, 1907.

Lippy, Charles H., and Peter W. Williams. *Encyclopedia of the American Religious Experience: Studies of Traditions and Movements.* New York: Charles Scribner's Sons, 1988.

"Lost Blessings Regained." *Sunday School Outlines, Second Intermediate Department, Second Year Book of Mormon, 1907–1908.* Lesson 53, 30. Salt Lake City: Deseret Sunday School Union Bookstore, 1907.

Ludlow, Daniel H. *Encyclopedia of Mormonism.* 4 vols. New York: Macmillan, 1992.

Martin, David C. *A Pocket Guide to Nauvoo, Illinois and Nearby Areas.* Nauvoo, Ill.: Martin Publishing Co., 1980.

McGee, Harold. *On Food and Cooking: The Science and Lore of the Kitchen.* New York: Charles Scribner's Sons, 1984.

McKinley, Edward H. *Marching to Glory: The History of the Salvation Army in the United States of America, 1880–1980.* San Francisco: Harper & Row, 1980.

Muse, Vance. *The Smithsonian Guide to Historic America: Northern New England.* New York: Stewart, Tabori & Chang, 1989.

*New Century Atlas, Lake County, Ohio.* Philadelphia: Century Man Co., 1915.

*1902 Pocket Guide to Salt Lake and Vicinity.* Salt Lake City: Smith and Morton, 1902.

Parkin, Max H. "Independence, Missouri." In *Historical Atlas of Mormonism,* 40–41. New York: Simon & Schuster, 1994.

———. "Jackson County and Vicinity." In *Historical Atlas of Mormonism,* 38–39. New York: Simon & Schuster, 1994.

———. "Missouri Conflict." In *Encyclopedia of Mormonism,* 2:927–32. New York: Macmillan, 1992.

*Polk, R. L. & Co's Provo City and Utah County Directory, 1901–1902.* Salt Lake City: R. L. Polk & Co., 1901.

*Portrait and Biographical Record of Clay, Ray, Carroll, Chariton and Linn Counties, Missouri.* Chicago: Chapman Brothers, 1893.

Pratt, Parley P. *Autobiography of Parley P. Pratt.* Salt Lake City: Deseret News Book, 1950.

*Primary Department Bible Stories, 1906–1907.* Salt Lake City: Deseret Sunday School Union, 1906.

Pyper, George D. *Stories of Latter-day Saint Hymns.* Salt Lake City: Deseret Sunday School Union, 1939.

Roberts, B. H. *The Latter-day Saints' Tour from Palmyra, New York to Salt Lake City Through the Stereoscope: A History of the Church of Jesus Christ of Latter-day Saints.* Salt Lake City: Deseret News, 1904; Ottawa, Kansas: Underwood and Underwood, 1905.

———. *Outlines of Ecclesiastical History.* Salt Lake City: G. Q. Cannon and Sons Co., 1893.

Romig, Ronald E. "Temple Lot Discoveries and the RLDS Temple." *BYU Regional Studies: Missouri,* 313–35. Provo: Brigham Young University Press, 1994.

———. "Temple Lot Suit After 100 Years." *John Whitmer Historical Association Journal* 12 (1992): 3–15.

Romig, Ronald E., and John H. Siebert. "Historic Views of the Temple Lot." *John Whitmer Historical Association Journal* 7 (1987): 21–27.

Schnedler, Jack. *Chicago*. Oakland, Ca.: Fodor's Travel Publications, 1993.

"Shrine for Mormon Pilgrims in Vermont." *Juvenile Instructor* 43 (1 July 1908): 246–53.

Smith, Joseph. *History of the Church of Jesus Christ of Latter-day Saints*. 7 vols. 3:183–86. Salt Lake City: Deseret Book, 1978.

Smith, Joseph Fielding. *Blood Atonement and the Origin of Plural Marriage: A Discussion*. Salt Lake City: The Deseret News, 1905.

———. *Proceedings at the Dedication of the Joseph Smith Memorial Monument*. Salt Lake City? 1906?.

*Souvenir of Salt Lake: The City Beautiful*. Salt Lake City: Smith and Morton, 1901.

"Temporal Laws." *Young Men's Mutual Improvement Association Manual, 1906–1907*. Lesson 12, 88–91. Salt Lake City: The General Board of the Y.M.M.I.A., 1906.

Tobler, Douglas F., and Nelson B. Wadsworth. *The History of the Mormons*. New York: St. Martin's Press, 1987.

Tullidge, Edward W. *The Women of Mormondom*. New York: n.p., 1877.

Wadsworth, Nelson B. *Set in Stone, Fixed in Glass: The Great Mormon Temple and Its Photographers*. Salt Lake City: Signature Books, 1992.

———. *Through Camera Eyes*. Provo, Utah: Brigham Young University Press, 1975.

———. "A Village Photographer's Dream." *Ensign* September 1973, 40–55.

Whitmer, David. *An Address to All Believers in Christ*. Richmond, Mo.: David Whitmer, 1887.

Will, Tracy. *Wisconsin*. Oakland: Fodor's Travel Publications, 1994.

Winckler, Suzanne. *The Smithsonian Guide to Historic America: The Great Lakes States*. New York: Stewart, Tabori & Chang, 1989.

———. *The Smithsonian Guide to Historic America: The Plains States*. New York: Stewart, Tabori & Chang, 1990.

Wurman, Richard Saul. *Chicago Access*. Dunmore, Pa.: Harper Collins, 1995.

# Index

Aberdeen Bakery, Chicago, 124

Adam-ondi-Ahman (Mo.), 89–93

Adams, R. D., 20

Adam's altar, 91

Adam's grave (folklore), 91

*Address to All Believers in Christ, An* (pamphlet), 67

"Address to the World," First Presidency, 9, 119

Albany Park, Chicago, 116

Albert Edward, Prince, 115

Alleman, Ida, 20, 35, 41, 49, 61, 114, 119, 121, 137

Alleman, John W., 19, 64, 85, 112, 113, 114, 118, 120, 127, 131, 133, 136, 139, 140

Alleman, Martha Jane, 19

Allgood, Elder, 85

American Falls, Niagara Falls, 163

American Unitarian Association, 191

Anderson, Anne, 39

Anderson, Edda, 2, 118, 125, 126, 127, 134

Anderson, Ellwood, 120, 133

Anderson, Eva, 2, 23, 106

Anderson, George (GEA's father), 103

Anderson, George Lowry, 2, 16, 76, 112, 118, 120, 122, 126, 131, 133, 134

Anderson, Gustave Ed, 114

Anderson, J. Morgan, 115, 120, 121, 131, 133, 136, 138

Anderson, J. S., 85, 131

Anderson, James A., 123

Anderson, L., 124, 125

Anderson, Lilly, 120

Anderson, Marn, 131

Anderson, Mary Ann Thorn, 113

Anderson, Mern, 120

Anderson, Minnie, 31

Anderson, Olive Lowry, 1, 2, 3, 19, 109; GEA writes to, 20, 64, 112, 114, 115, 118, 122, 126, 127, 131, 134; writes to GEA, 106, 114, 120, 125, 131

Anschutz, Harmon M., 64, 106, 118, 132, 139

Anthon, Charles, 74

Anti-Mormon Party, Hancock County (Ill.), 109

Anti-Saloon League, 45

Armington School House, Manchester (N.Y.), 175

Armour and Company, Chicago, 10, 14, 119

Armour, Philip, 119

Austin, Clark, 164, 166, 187, 191

Austin, Hugh, 6, 164, 175

Austin, Mrs., 175

*Automobile,* Anderson's use of term, 39

Aylett, John Argent, 97, 104

Azo paper (photography), 15, 39

Babbitt, Almon W., 218

Balson, Mrs., 132

Baptism, 104, 109

Barney Brothers, 186

Barrus, Q. H., 161, 162

Barton County (Kans.), 22

Batson, John E., 82, 123

Batson, Mrs., 85, 134

Battle Creek (Mich.), 14, 122

Batts, R. W., 45

Behringer, Ida, 137

Behunin, Mrs., 65

Behunin, William, 141

*Ben Hur* (novel), 74

Bennet, William Henry, 20

Bennett, John F., 127

Bennett Glass and Paint Company, Salt Lake City, 127

Bennett's Hall. *See* Spaulding Institute Building, Nauvoo (Ill.)

Bennion, Burvidge David, 31, 32

Bennion, Charlotte Towler, 31, 32

Bennion, Laura, 41, 49, 61, 64, 114, 115, 120, 136, 137

Bennion, Samuel O., 22, 27, 31, 32, 132, 135, 139

Berliner, Emile, 136

Berry, Elder, 75

Bidamon, Emma. *See* Smith, Emma Hale

Bidamon, Lewis, 47, 45, 54, 88

Big Blue River (Mo.), 65, 66

Billings, Titus, 144

Bingham Canyon (Utah), 19

*Birth of Mormonism in Pictures: Scenes and Incidents in Early Church History, The* (book), 4

Bisbee, David P., 76

Bisbee, Mariann Whitmer, 76

Bishop, Mr., 108

Bison (Kans.), 22

Black, Joseph S., 76, 78, 93, 125

Blair, Willard F., 104

Blake, Mr., 23

Blankmeyer, Helen Farwell Van Cleave, 74

Bluff Park, Montrose (Iowa), 41, 108

Bogart, Samuel, 77, 78

Bogart's Battleground. *See* Crooked River Battleground

Boggs, Lilburn W., 40, 76, 85

Bond, Ezra, 154

Book of Mormon: class, 112; John Whitmer's testimony of, 70, 82; manuscript of, 54, 74, 82; news article about, 191; on David Whitmer Monument, 65; Palmyra publishing site, 171; proof sheets, 170, 172, 173; published by Central States Mission, 131; Richmond monument to, 70; witnesses, 7; writing characters, 74

Booth, Ballington, 124

Booth, Maud Elizabeth Charlesworth, 124

Booth, William, 124

*Boston Sunday Globe* (newspaper), 4, 15

Bourne, John A., 130, 137

Boyer, Paul Ludlow, 136

Boyer, Susie, 20

Boyne, Will, 147

Bozarth family, 214

Branch, Jennie. *See* Thomas, Mrs. E. L.

Brandley, Edda. *See* Anderson, Edda

Brandley, Louis Orson, 118

Braymer (Mo.), 95, 97, 104

Breckenridge (Mo.), 85, 95, 96, 104, 126

Briggs, L. T., 120

Briggs, R. J., 124

*British Queen* (ship), 1

Brockway, Frank, 149

Bromley, Sister, 136

Broomcorn, 147

Brown, Samuel, 143

Brown's Mill (Ill.), 109

Buchanan, George W., 70

Buchanan, W. P., 122

Buffalo (N.Y.), 10, 162

Burlington (Iowa), 113

Burlington Railroad, 41, 65

Burnham, Fannie, 31, 132, 134

Burt, Elder, 127

Bush, Mr., 6, 176

Buzzard, J. B., 125

Buzzard, T. B., 89

Cabinet cards, 45. *See also* Postcards

Caldwell County (Mo.), 12, 95

Caleb, Abdel, story of, 76, 103, 108

Callahan, Mr., 136

Cameron (Mo.), 85, 89

Campbell, Elder, 123, 124, 127

*Car*, Anderson's use of term, 39

Cardon, Elder, 35

Carroll County (Mo.), troops, 99

Carson, Christopher "Kit," 21

Carson, Della, 127

Carter, Clark, 159

Carter, David, 159

Carter, Jared, 152; Kirtland home of, 159

Carter, Jared, Jr., 159

Carter, Joseph, 159

Carter, Mrs., 75

Carter, Orlando, 159

Carthage (Ill.), 5, 45, 48, 49, 109, 137

Cathedral of St. John the Evangelist, Cleveland, 140

Cave Hill, Manchester (N.Y.), 176, 186, 188

Central States Mission (LDS), 13, 20, 22, 24, 27, 31, 32, 66, 114, 139

Centropolis (Mo.), 65

Cereal, as health food, 14

Chagrin River (Ohio), 147, 153, 154-55, 157

Chagrin. *See* Willoughby (Ohio)

Chamberlain, John, 80

Chambers, Thomas, 97

Chapman, Mr., 104

Chapman, Seth T., 164

Chapman, William Avery, 164, 216

Chase, Darwin, 75

Chase farm, Palmyra (N.Y.), 170

Cheesman, Walter S., 21

Chicago (Ill.), 113-28, 130-39; Aberdeen Bakery, 124; Albany Park, 116; Armour and Company, 10, 14, 119; Cramer Dry Plate Company, 139; elevated trains, 122, 135, 136; Fidelity Portrait Company, 134, 138, 139; German Building, 133; Home Insurance Building, 115; Jackson Park, 133; Jefferson Park, 139, 140; LaSalle Depot, 139; LDS church building, 114; Logan Park, 116; Logan Square, 135, 136; Montgomery Ward and Company Building, 132; Moody Bible Institute, 124; Photo Jewelry Company, 115, 118, 119; Photo Materials Company, 118; population of, 10; reformers of, 13; Salvation Army Building, 10, 123, 124, 139; Turner Brass Works, 136; Union Park, 121; Union Stockyards and Transit Company, 10, 119; White City Park, 128, 139

Chicago and Northwestern Railroad, 129

*Chicago Illustrated* (book), 118

Chicago Temple Corps Building, 123

*Chicago Tribune* (newspaper), 13, 127

Childress, Alvin, 61

Childress, Mrs., 61

Chillicothe (Mo.), 85, 89, 95, 106

Chipman, Elder, 22

Chipman, Mrs., 65

Chism, Miss, 135

Christ Lutheran Church, Nauvoo, 49

Christensen, A. C., 41, 45, 61, 112

Christian evangelical fundamentalism, 13

Church of Christ (Temple Lot/Hedrickite), 7, 35, 36-37

Church of Christ (Whitmerite), 67

Church of Jesus Christ of Latter-day Saints, The: and baptism, 104, 109; Church Education System, 9; Historian's Office, 12; schismatizing of, 35; transition of, 8-9. *See also individual missions and temples*; Sunday School (LDS)

Citizen's Water Company, Denver, 21

*City of Erie* (steamboat), 162

Claudius Standard Stone Quarry, Kirtland (Ohio), 147

Clawson, Elder, 127

Clemons, Charles, 167

Clemons, Mr., 164

Clemons, Mrs., 175

Clemons, T. J., 167

Clendersen, Benjamin Kimball, 93

Cleveland (Ohio), 10, 13, 140-41, 161-62

Cleveland and Buffalo Steamship Company, 162

Cleveland Erie Railroad Depot, 140

Cleveland Transfer Company, 162

Clevenger, Bell, 78

Coch, H. C., 129

Coe, John R., 144

Color photography, 167

Colorado Mission (LDS), 20

Colorado Springs (Colo.), 20

Colorado State Capitol Building, Denver, 21

Colorado State Historical Society, Denver, 21

Colorado State Natural History Society, Denver, 21

Colorado War Relics Collection, Denver, 21

Columbian Exposition. *See* World's Columbian Exposition

"Come Ye Elders" (hymn), 122

Commerce (Ill.), 40. *See also* Nauvoo (Ill.)

Committee Store, Far West (Mo.), 80

Conferences, LDS (geographic unit), 49

Cook, Mr., 166

Cooperative Retrenchment Association (LDS), 64

Cottle, T. Jeffery, 7, 8

Cowdery, Elizabeth Ann Whitmer, 82, 84, 190

Cowdery, Lucy. *See* Young, Lucy Cowdery

Cowdery, Maria Louise, 82

Cowdery, Oliver, 213; baptized, 197; baptizes in Seneca Lake, 190; death of, 67, 68, 71; and Kirtland Temple, 145; portrait of, 82; Richmond burial site, 68, 70; taught in Palmyra, 175

Cowdery, William, 82

Cowley, Matthias F., 129, 135

*Cowley's Talks on Doctrine* (book), 129

Cox, Sylvester H., 97

Cragun, Wiley M., 115, 132, 133, 134, 135, 136, 138

Craig's Bridge (Mo.), 95

Cramer Dry Plate Company, Chicago, 139

Crandall, M. E., 132

Crandall, Myron, 116

Cravens, E. Holmes, 91, 92, 93

Cravens, John, 93

Cravens, John, Jr., 93

Cravensville (Mo.), 93. *See also* Adam-ondi-Ahman (Mo.)

Crawford, Dr., 186

Crawford, Lizzie, 154

Crawford, Newton P., 150, 152, 154

Creston (Mo.), 89

Crooked Creek (Ill.), 109

Crooked River, Battle of, 85

Crooked River Battleground (Mo.), 76, 77, 78, 79

Cultural Hall. *See* Masonic Hall, Nauvoo (Ill.)

Cummings, Benjamin Franklin, 27, 31, 32, 39

Curtis, G. N., 113, 115, 116, 118, 136, 139

Curver, Mr., 118

Cutler, Alpheus, 81

Daguerre, Louis, 1

Daguerreotypes (photography), 1-2

Dahle, M. M., 115, 127, 133, 136

Darrow, Clarence S., 123

Darrow, Wasel, story of, 116

Davidson, Emma Evlin, 108

Davidson, Margaret Brown, 61, 64

Daviess County (Mo.), 92-94, 99

Davis, Evan V., studio of, 27, 32, 39

Deardoff, Mr., 115

Deardorf home, 137

Decker, John F., 133

*Democrat* (newspaper), 91

Denison, Joseph Adam, 206

Denver (Colo.), 20-22

Denver and Rio Grande Railway, 19

Denver City Water Company, 21

Denver Free Boarding School, 21

Denver Museum of Natural History, 21

Denver Union Water Company, 21

Des Moines rapids, 64

*Deseret News*, 61, 106, 119, 133, 138, 159

*Deseret Semiweekly News*, 108

Develine, Olive, 127

Developing-out paper (photography), 39, 120, 123

Diahman. *See* Adam-ondi-Ahman (Mo.)

Diary, importance of Anderson's, 6-11

Dibble, Philo, 214

Disciples of Christ Church, 147

Districts (LDS), 49

Dockery, Alexander M., 93

Documentary photography, 2

Doniphan, Alexander, Richmond home of, 71

Doubletrees (wagon parts), 113

*Draft*, Anderson's use of term, 162

*Drays*, Anderson's use of term, 114

Drechett, Mrs., 133

Dropsy (physical swelling), 103

Drugleo, Gysin, 125

Duffin, Elder, 97

Duffin, James G., 23

Duke, Wesley V., 23, 35, 39, 65, 66

Dundey, Mrs. E. S., 61, 64

Durphey, James, 76

Duty, Mary Ann, 80

Dymock, England, 109, 110

Eagle (Colo.), 20

Eagle Hotel. *See* Powers Hotel, Palmyra (N.Y.)

Eastern States Mission (LDS), 13, 119

Eastman, George, 116, 170

Eaton, Mr., 215

Edema (physical swelling), 103

Edmunds, D. G., 115, 116, 131, 133

Education System (LDS), 9

Edwards, Lewis D., 133

Edwards, Robert W., 19

Egbert, Bert, 97
*Elders' Journal* (Kirtland newspaper), 147
*Elders' Journal* (mission magazine), 27, 160
Electrical Developing Company, 163
Elevated trains, Chicago, 122, 135, 136
Elevator, Otis, 118
Ellsworth, Blanche, 138
Ellsworth, German Edgar, 114, 118, 119,
    122, 126, 131, 134, 135, 136,
    137, 138, 139, 216
Ellsworth, German S., 138
Ellsworth, Homer, 138
Ellsworth, John, 163
Ellsworth, Mary Rachel Smith, 114, 115,
    117, 119, 122, 125, 132, 138
Ellsworth, Ruth. *See* Knudsen, Ruth
    Ellsworth
Elmira (Mo.), 76, 78
Elton, George M., 166, 167, 170, 175,
    186, 187, 191
Encoe, Gerald, 75
Encoe, John, 75
Encoe, Ollie B., 75
Encoe, Sylvia, 75
*Encyclopedia Britannica*, 106
Engines, 108
England, apostles leave for mission to
    (1838), 81; GEA leaves for mission
    to, 2-3
Entrakin, Bertha, 80, 82
Entrakin, Elmer, 80, 82
Erickson, Leif, 130, 131
Escalators, 10, 118
Estey, Fanny McKnutt, 181
Estey, Jason, 181, 182
Evans, John, 128
Evans, John Henry, 4
Evans, William E., 27, 31, 32
Evanston (Ill.), 128
Everette, Henry A., 161
Evinrude Motor Company, Milwaukee
    (Wis.), 108
Examiner Printing Company Building,
    Independence (Mo.), 25, 27
Excelsior Springs (Mo.), 70
Exchange Building. *See* Grandin, Egbert B.,
    Bookstore and Printing Office,
    Palmyra

Exchange Hotel, Palmyra (N.Y.), 175,
    187
Extermination order of Governor Boggs,
    40, 76, 85

Fager, Dr., 41
Fairbanks, John B., 19, 20
Far West (Mo.), 5, 70, 78, 80-86
Far West Militia, 76
Faul, Charles P., 85, 123
Fayette (N.Y.), 189
Ferat, Charles, 91, 93
Ferrin, James, 60
Fidelity Portrait Company, Chicago, 134,
    138, 139
Fielding, Elder, 125
Finances, mission, 10-11
Finishing process (photography), 75
First Presidency, "Address to the World,"
    9, 119
Fisher, Gustave, 152
Fixing (photography), 119
Flake, Elder, 123, 126
Folklore: Adam's grave, 91; hill cave made
    for translating plates, 176; Joseph
    Smith sprinkles blood of sheep,
    167; Joseph Smith tries to walk on
    water, 143
Follett, King, 75
Ford, Mr., 167
Fort Des Moines (Iowa), 40
Foster, Brother, 126, 127
*Founder of Mormonism* (book), 74
Fountain Green (Utah), 132
Fowler, Elder, 123
Fowles, D. H., 115
Francis, Rell G., 7, 11, 16
Frankland, John, 115
Frilling (photography), 76
Frost, Mary Ann, 150
Full View Bridge, Niagara Falls, 163

G. E. Anderson Art Bazaar, Springville
    (Utah), 3
Gallatin (Mo.), 85, 89, 91, 93-94
Garfield, James A., 143
Gascanue, Haun's Mill site sold to, 95
Gaslight (photography), 39

Gates, Susa Young, 144
*Gentile*, Anderson's use of term, 93
German Building, Chicago, 133
Gibbs, Luman, 75
Gilbert, John, 170
Gildersleeve, Samuel D., 147
Glenwood Springs (Colo.), 20
Gold chloride (photography), 122
Gold Plates, translating of, 176. *See also*
    Book of Mormon
*Golgotha* (painting), 120, 133
Good Health Publishing, Battle Creek
    (Mich.), 122
Goodson, Harvey, 126
Gooley, Mr., 14-15, 104
Goulty, Frank, 45, 49, 60, 64
Graham, Mr. and Mrs., 20
Graham, Sylvester, health food of, 14
Gramophone, 136
Grand Army of the Republic (patriotic
    organization), 21
Grand Junction (Colo.), 19, 20
Grand River (Mo.), 89
Grandin, Egbert B., 171, 216; Bookstore
    and Printing Office, Palmyra, 166,
    171, 174
Granger, Oliver, 157, 218; Kirtland grave
    of, 144, 159
Gray, Mitchell, 95
Gree, Mr., Kirtland home of, 147
Green, Jim, 76
Greene, Ulysses W., 149, 217
Gregory, Spencer, 101
Griffiths, Gomer T., 149
Grimes, Brother, 113
Grimes, Sister, 112
*Grippe*, Anderson's use of term, 101
Gudgill, Jacob, 101
Gudgill, John T., 95
Guffy, All, 95, 109
Guilliman, Minnie, 108
Guilliman, William, 108, 113
Guilliman, Willie (son of William), 108
Gundy, Mrs., 108

Hafen, John, 10, 127, 136
Hale, Elizabeth, Harmony tombstone of,
    195

Hale, Isaac, 193; Harmony tombstone of, 195

Hale, Jesse, 193

Hall, Elder, 134

Hamilton, Clarissa. *See* Young, Clarissa Hamilton

Hancock County (Ill.), 45, 109

Hansen, Elder, 127

Hansen, Reverend, 135

Hardee, Elder, 75

Hardin, Dr., 123

Harmony (Pa.), 12, 191-98; Alvin Smith tombstone, 196; deed, Joseph Smith home, 193; Isaac and Elizabeth Hale tombstones, 195; Joseph Smith home, 192; McKune Cemetery, 194; "Money Hole," 198

Harris, Bert, 130

Harris, George V., 15, 22, 23, 31, 32, 39, 133, 139

Harris, Lorenzo, 115

Harris, Lucy, Palmyra farm of, 185

Harris, Martin, 74-75, 82, 182; Palmyra farm of, 6, 175, 176, 185, 186

Harris, Riley, 144

Harrison, Elder, 128

Harrison, H. E., Cleveland home of, 161

Harrison, Sister H. E., 141, 160, 162

Hathaway (Crooked) Brook, Manchester (N.Y.), 181, 182

Haun's Mill (Mo.), 5, 85, 95, 97-104, 126

Haun, Jacob, 95

Hedlock, Reuben, 110

Hedrick, Elder, 85

Hedrick, Elizabeth A., 35

Hedrick, Granville, 35

Hedrick, John H., 7, 35

Hedrickite Church. *See* Church of Christ (Temple Lot/Hedrickite)

Helm, Meredith, 58

Hensel, H. C., *Night of the Twentieth Century,* 118

Hicks, Jacob T., 74

Hicks, Joseph R., 141, 161, 162

"High on the Mountain Top" (hymn), 133

Hill Cumorah, Manchester (N.Y.), 6, 166, 167, 168, 169, 170, 175,
176, 180, 216

Himes, Almira Amanda, 35

Himes, Andrew, 6, 35

Himes, Joseph Hyrum, 35

Himes, Lucy Minerva, 35

Hirsher, Mr., 130

Historian's Office (LDS), 12

Historical Western Reserve Society, 150

*History of Caldwell and Livingston Counties* (book), 80

Hitchcock, Mr., 108

Hobble Creek Canyon (Utah), 144

Holmes, Randolph W., 137

Home Insurance Building, Chicago, 115

Hooper, Henry, 144

Horseshoe Falls, Niagara Falls, 10, 163

Horton, Fred B., 105, 107, 108

Hotel Nauvoo. *See* Oriental Hotel, Nauvoo (Ill.)

Howard, Elder, 97

Howard, John F. A., 118

Howell, Thomas, 64, 106

Hughes, E. G., 121

Hull, C. L., 133

Hulmes, Benjamin Franklin, 147

Hulmes, Emma, 147

Huntington, Elfie, 11

Huntington, O. B., 10

Hyde, Orson, misidentified home of, 51

Hyldall, Hannah Sorensen, 135

Hyldall, Peter, 135

"I know That My Redeemer Lives" (hymn), 115, 133

Icarian schoolhouse, Nauvoo (Ill.), 53, 56

Illinois, overview of Anderson's travels in, 5. *See also individual sites and cities*

*Illustrated Atlas of Caldwell County, Missouri,* 12

*Illustrated Chicago Today* (book), 118

*Illustrated Historical Atlas of Caldwell County, Missouri,* 80, 82

*Improvement Era* (magazine), 131

Independence (Mo.), 22-39; Examiner Printing Company Building, 25, 27; headquarters for RLDS, 74; Himes family of, 6; Liahona Office Building, 24, 27; mission home
(LDS), 4-5, 27, 30, 31; Owens Building, 24, 27; RLDS Stone Church, 5, 26, 27, 31, 33, 37; South Pleasant Street, 30; Temple Lot, 23, 27, 28-29, 33, 34, 35, 36-37, 38; Visitors Center (LDS), 23, 126

*Independent* (newspaper), 121

*Independent Examiner* (newspaper), 25

Ineles, Mr., 106

Ingrams, Elder, 97

Intensifying (photography), 116

Itasca, Lake (Minn.), 41

Iverson, Elder, 123

Ivins, Jake, 143

Ivins–Smith–Taylor Home, Nauvoo, 43, 41

Jackson County (Mo.), 91

*Jackson Examiner* (newspaper), 25

Jackson Park, Chicago, 128, 133

James, Elder, 131, 132

Jameson (Mo.), 93

Jefferson Park, Chicago, 139

Jenkins, Mary E., 157

Jensen, Elder, 97, 134

Jenson, Andrew, 12, 76, 78, 93, 191

Jessie, Elder, 97

Johnson, Aaron, Nauvoo home of, 50-51

Johnson, Charley, 20

Johnson, Dr. Charles, 82

Johnson, Elder, 137

Johnson, Ella Kerr, 82

Johnson, Elsa, Kirtland grave of, 144

Johnson, George J., 131

Johnson, Howard, 144

Johnson, James Edward, 82

Johnson, Joel H., 133

Johnson, John, Kirtland grave of, 144, 159

Johnson, Mr. (son of Sarah Whitmer), 85

Johnson, Sarah. *See* Kerr, Sarah Elizabeth Whitmer Johnson

Johnson Hotel, Kirtland (Ohio), 143, 152

Johnson's farm, Palmyra, 170

Johnston, N., 115

Jolly, Elizabeth, 190

Jolly, Vincent, 190

Jolly, William, 190

Jones, Joseph, 2, 14, 19

Jones, Rob, 115, 118

Jones, Sister, 161

Juneau, Solomon, 130, 131

Juneau Park, Milwaukee (Wis.), 129, 130, 131

*Jungle, The* (novel), 10

*Juvenile Instructor* (magazine), 4

Kansas City (Kans.), 27

Kansas City (Mo.), 22-23, 27, 39, 65

*Kansas City Times* (newspaper), 65

Kansas River, 22

Kaw River. *See* Kansas River

Kaw Township (Mo.), 65, 66

Keaster, Mrs., 129

Kelley, Edmund Levi, 80, 150

Kelley, William H., 149

Kellogg, John Harvey, on being "chaste in thought," 18

Kellogg, John Henry, 14

Kellogg, William Keith, 14

Kendall family, 112, 113

Kendall, John, 108

Keokuk (Iowa), 64, 106

Keokuk Dam, 41, 50-51

Kerns, F. A., 132

Kerr, Christopher, 85

Kerr, Sarah Elizabeth Whitmer Johnson, 82, 84, 136

Kerr farm, Far West (Mo.), 82, 85

Kidman, Hyrum, 131

Kimball, Ethan, 113

Kimball, Heber Chase, 81, 107; Nauvoo home of, 5, 111

Kimball, Hiram M., 113

Kimball, James LeRoy, 111

Kimball, Vilate Murray, Nauvoo home of, 111

King, Austin A., Richmond burial site of, 74

Kingston (Mo.), 7, 80, 82, 85, 87, 88

Kington, Thomas, 109

Kirtland (Ohio), 142-61, 217-19; Carlos Smith home, 147; Ezra Thayer home, 147; Hyrum Smith home, 147, 149, 151; Johnson Hotel, 143, 152; Newel K. Whitney home, 143-44, 157; Newel K. Whitney store, 144, 152, 156, 161; Old Cemetery, 144, 154, 159; Parley P. Pratt home, 150, 152, 159; RLDS chapel, 144; Sidney Rigdon home, 147, 149; William Smith home, 147, 151

Kirtland and Gildersleeve Mountain, 147

Kirtland Hotel, 160, 161

Kirtland Safety Society Bank, 150

Kirtland Temple, 5, 84, 141, 142-43, 145, 146, 153, 159

KLDS (radio station), 26

KMBZ (radio station), 26

Knight, Joseph, Colesville farm of, 199

Knight, Polly Peck, Colesville farm of, 199

*Knight of the Twentieth Century* (book), 118

Knudson, Ruth Ellsworth, 117, 118, 138

Kodak (camera), 116

Kromeich, Albert, 95

Lagenbocker, Mattie, 20

Lake, John H., 217

Lamb, Brigham F., 22

Lamoni (Iowa), 26, 35, 74

Lane, J. R. (Dick), 97, 101, 103

Larsen, Elder, 127

LaSalle Depot, Chicago, 139

Lathern, Rachel, 20

*Latter-day Saints' Tour from Palmyra . . .* (book), 118

Law, Nancy, 152

Law, William, 152

Lawson (Mo.), 75, 76

Lawson, Sister, 64

Laying on of hands (ordinance), 104

LDS Church. *See* Church of Jesus Christ of Latter-day Saints, The

LDS Sunday School. *See* Sunday School (LDS)

Lebanon (N.H.), 209

Lee, Agatha Woolsey, Nauvoo home of, 60

Lee, John D., Nauvoo home of, 60

Lee, Joseph Smith, 6-7, 35

Lemke, Brother, 129

Lewis, Alonzo, 137, 138, 139

Lewis, Benjamin, 101

Lewis, David, 101

Lewis, Mary M., 147

Lewis, Tarlton, 101

Lexington Junction (Mo.), 65

*Liahona* (magazine), 24, 27, 108, 131

Liahona Office Building, Independence, 24, 27

*Liahona The Elders' Journal* (magazine), 27, 160

Liberty Jail (Mo.), 161

Light glass (photography), 125

*Likeness*, Anderson's use of term, 137

Livingston County (Mo.), troops, 99

Locust Creek (Mo.), 89

Logan, John Alexander, 135

Logan Park, Chicago, 116

Logan Square, Chicago, 135, 136

Long Log Creek (Mo.), 80

Loop (elevated trains), Chicago, 122, 135, 136

Lowe, Thomas C., 23, 27, 35, 39, 65, 66

Lowry, Dora. *See* Olson, Dora Lowry

Lowry, John, Sr., 2, 19, 112

Lowry, Olive. *See* Anderson, Olive Lowry

Lowry, Sarah Jane Brown, 2, 19

Lowry, William Brown, 136

Lutheran North Church, Nauvoo (Ill.), 49

Lyons, Elder, 97

Mack, Lydia Gates, Sharon home site of, 203

Mack, Solomon, Sharon home site of, 203, 207

Mackey, James G., 103

Mackey, John F., 103

Mack farm, Sharon (Vt.), 119, 215

Madsen, Karl, Jr., 41, 49, 60, 61, 64, 112, 113, 115, 118, 123, 126, 131, 132, 137

*Maid of the Mist* (boat), 163

Mail, missionary, 11-12

Manchester (N.Y.), 164-70, 175-84; Cave Hill, 176, 186, 188; District No. 10 Schoolhouse, 175, 184; Hathaway (Crooked) Brook, 181, 182; Hill Cumorah, 6, 166, 167, 168, 169, 170, 175, 180, 216; Joseph Smith Memorial, 6; Sacred Grove, 6, 164-65, 180, 182, 183, 216; Smith farm, 6, 164, 166, 170, 176-77, 178, 179, 181, 182, 183, 216; Wallace Miner farm, 188. *See also* Palmyra (N.Y.)

Manley, George W., Kirtland home of, 147

Mansion House, Nauvoo (Ill.), 41, 46, 45

Manti Temple, Manti (Utah), 109

Manwaring, J. H., 10

Marion (Mo.), 40

Marring (photography), 122

Marshall, Martha, 112

Marshall's Mill (Mo.), 95, 104, 105-6, 109

Martin, Mr., 116, 118

Mary, Virgin (image of), 61

Masking (photography), 122

Masonic Hall, Nauvoo (Ill.), 58

Masonic Lodge, Nauvoo (Ill.), 52

Matheson, "Long Mike," 97

Mattie, Mr., 129

May, Roderick, 32

May Procession (Catholic ritual), 61

McBride, Thomas, 102

McCarthy, Leonora, 9, 22, 27

McClurg, A. C., 137

McCollough, Ray, 78, 80

McComb (Ill.), 110

McCordboug, Albert, 78

McCormick Building, Cleveland, 141

McCormick reaper, 164

McDonald, Absalom, 93

McDonald, Julia, 93

McDonald, Sarah A., 93

McDonald Ford, Adam-ondi-Ahman, 89

McDonough County (Ill.), 110

McDougall Post Office, Fayette, 216

McFarland, Milton S., 154

McFarland, Viola, 144, 154

McFarland family, 159

McKell, Ira J., 115, 118, 119, 120, 121, 122, 125, 130

McKune, Joseph, 193

McLallen, Brother, 104

McLallen, Ed, 104

McLallen, George B., 97, 104

McLallen, George M., 95, 97, 104

McLallen, James E., 97

McLallen, James L., 101

McLallen, John B., 96, 97, 101, 103, 112, 114, 126, 134

McLallen, Mary B., 95, 97

McLallen, Nancy Jane, 95

McLellin, William, 67

McMullen, A. E., 131

McQuarrie, John G., 119

McRae, Alice, 95

McRae, J. C., 101

McRae, Joseph, 22

Mecham, Elder, 141

Medicine Creek (Mo.), 89

Medley, Samuel, 133

Mentor (Ohio), 143, 217

Mesa Temple, Mesa (Ariz.), 15

*Messenger and Advocate* (newspaper), 87

Methodist Church, 75, 84, 93, 182

MIA. *See* Mutual Improvement Association

Miller, A. V., 162

Miller, Francis M., 67

Miller, Mrs., 67

Miller family, 110

Mills, Elder/Professor, 123, 126, 131, 136

Milwaukee (Wis.), 129-30, 131

Milwaukee and St. Paul Railroad, 95

Miner, Margaret Cavanaugh, Manchester farm of, 188

Miner, Wallace, 186, 187; Manchester farm of, 188

Miner, William W., 182

Miner's Hill. *See* Cave Hill, Manchester (N.Y.)

Ministerial Association of Salt Lake City, 119

Minster, Minnie, 130

Minturn (Colo.), 20

Mirabile (Mo.), 78

Missionary work, 13-14

Mississippi River, 41, 64; and baptisms for the dead, 104; Saints camp near (1846), 105

Missouri, overview of Anderson's travels in, 4-5. *See also individual sites and cities*

Missouri Pacific Railroad, 65

Missouri River, 27

Moffat, Mrs. H. S., 163

Montgomery, James, 137

Montgomery Ward and Company, Chicago, 132, 133; St. Joseph, 65

Montrose (Iowa), 41, 64, 106-8

Moody, Dwight Lyman, 124

Moody Bible Institute, Chicago, 124

Mooresville (Mo.), 97

Morley, Charley, 144

Mormon Hill. *See* Hill Cumorah, Manchester (N.Y.)

Mormon Tabernacle Choir, 122

Moroni, Angel, 170

Morten, Brother, 115

Mortensen, Elder, 123

Morton view book, 22

Moses, Elder, 97

Motorboats, 10, 108

Mounting (photography), 39

Mulch, Mr., 58

Murdock, Squire, Norwich farm of, 210-11

Music, and missionary work, 13

Mutual Improvement Association, 64

Nalder, Elder, 97

National Photography Association, 175

*Nauvoo*, definition of, 41

Nauvoo (Ill.), 41-47, 45-64, 106-13; angel statue, 42; brass band of, 109; Brigham Young home, 107; Charles Pitt home, 49, 54; Chauncey Webb home, 110; Christ Lutheran Church, 49; David Yearsley home, 62-63; Emma Smith grave, 5; Female Relief Society, 49,

52; headquarters for RLDS, 74; Heber C. Kimball home, 5, 111; Icarian schoolhouse, 53, 56; Ivins–Smith–Taylor home, 43, 41; John D. Lee home, 60; Jonathan C. Wright home, 49, 50-51; Joseph Young home, 110; Luthern North Church, 49; Mansion House, 41, 45, 46, 52; Masonic Hall, 52, 58; Masonic Lodge, 52; Old Public Green, 113; Oriental Hotel, 41; Orson Pratt home, 49; Oschner Building, 56, 60; Pitt family moves to, 109; Post Office, 41, 43; Printing Office, 41, 43; Red Brick Store, 49, 52, 110; Rose Nickace shop, 56; Smith family cemetery, 44; Smith homestead, 47, 52; Snow–Ashby duplex, 57; Spaulding Institute Building, 60; St. Mary's Academy, 56, 60, 62-63; St. Peter and St. Paul Catholic Church, 42, 53, 55, 61; Water and Bain Streets, 52; Water Street, 50-51; Wilford Woodruff home, 5, 59; wine industry, 56, 62-63. *See also* Commerce (Ill.)
Nauvoo City Council, 52
*Nauvoo Expositor* (newspaper), 59, 152
Nauvoo Expositor Building, 59
Nauvoo House, 42, 47, 52, 54-55
Nauvoo House Committee, 52
Nauvoo Legion, 52
Nauvoo Legion Arsenal Building, 62-63
*Nauvoo Neighbor* (newspaper), 43
Nauvoo Restoration Inc., 111
Nauvoo State Bank, 60
Nauvoo Temple, 42, 49, 107, 109, 110, 112
Nauvoo Temple Block, 41, 53, 56
Nauvoo Temple Committee, 52
Negatives (photography), cleaned, 115; developing, 75
Nelson, James, 64, 112, 113, 135
Nelson, Mr., 20
Netzow, Charles F., 130
Newmarch, Jennie, 141, 161
New York, overview of Anderson's travels

in, 5-6. *See also individual sites and cities*
New York Central Railroad, 6, 163-64, 176, 187
Niagara Falls (N.Y.), 4, 10, 162-63
Nibley, Charles W., 160
Nibley, Ellen June Ricks, 116
Nibley, Preston, 116
Nichols, Levi, 97
Nickace, Rose, 56
Nielson, Lars, 132
Nielson, Soren C., 132, 134
*Night of the Twentieth Century* (book), 118
*1902 Pocket Guide to Salt Lake and Vicinity*, 22
Nineveh (N.Y.), 199
Northern States Mission (LDS), 13, 97, 112, 122, 136
Northwestern States Mission (LDS), 131
Norwich (Vt.), 210-11
"Now Let Us Rejoice" (hymn), 122
Noyes, Eva. *See* Anderson, Eva
Noyes, Lyman Wells, 23

"O My Father" (hymn), 124, 133
Odell, Mr., 104
Ogden (Utah), 19
Ohio, overview of Anderson's travels in, 5. *See also individual sites and cities*
Olson, Dora Lowry, 112, 129, 130
Olson, Edwin Orlando, 112, 122, 123, 125, 127, 128, 129, 131
Ontario Power Company, 163
Oquirrh Mountains, 19
Orchard, Harry, 123
Ordway, W. D., 115, 134
Orem, Mr., 78
Oriental Hotel, Nauvoo (Ill.), 41
Osborne, Elder, 123
Oschner, Joseph, 41, 49, 60
Oschner Building, Nauvoo, 56, 60
Otis, Charles A., 161
Ouray, Chief, 21
*Outlines of Ecclesiastical History* (book), 133
Overexposure (photography), 175
Owens Building, Independence (Mo.), 24, 27

Pace, Elder, 97
Page, Brother, 118

Page, Hiram, 67, 70, 170; Kirtland home of, 147
Page, John E., 81
Page, Miss, 67
Page, Philander Alma, 67, 70, 76, 132
Page, Sarah E. Farris, 67
Page family, 7
Painting trays (photography), 120
Palmer, William J., 20
Palmyra (N.Y.), 163-64, 171-75, 176, 185-87; Exchange Hotel, 175, 187; Four Corners, 182; Main Street, 171; Martin Harris farm, 6, 175, 176, 185, 186; Powers Hotel, 164. *See also* Manchester (N.Y.)
Palmyra Hotel, 164
Palmyra Junction (Mo.), 106
Paltridge's, Nauvoo (Ill.), 114
Pangburn, M. E., 125
Parker, H. Elmer, 95, 97, 104; Caldwell County home of, 103
Parker home, Haun's Mill (Mo.), 97
Parsons, Eliza, 112
Partridge, Edward, 23, 37
Patten, David Wyman, 76, 77, 78
Penrose, Charles William, 126, 127, 139
Pentecost, 125
Pepper Building, St. Joseph (Mo.), 65
Peterson, James, 20, 115, 116, 118, 119, 120, 121, 124, 127, 130, 139
Peterson, John E., 115
Peterson, Joseph, 115
Peterson, Julia, 135
Peterson, Matilda, 115, 132
Peterson, P. P., 115
Peterson, Ziba, 190, 217
Pettman, William, 41
Petty, James Henry, 186, 188
Phelps, Morris, 75
Phelps, William W., 122
*Philadelphia Saturday Courier* (newspaper), 143
Phineas Kimball, Nauvoo property of, 113
Photographic Association of America, 175
Photographs, indentifying and dating, 7-8
Photography: Azo paper, 15, 39; cabinet

cards, 45; cleaning negatives, 115; color, 167; daguerreotypes, 1-2; developing negatives, 75; developing-out paper, 39, 120, 123; documentary, 2; electric fans, 129; finishing process, 75; fixing, 119; frilling, 76; gaslight, 39; gold chloride, 122; history of, 1-2; intensifying, 116; Kodak camera, 116; light glass, 125; marring, 122; masking, 122; mixing chemicals, 120; mounting, 39; overtimed (overexposed), 175; painting trays, 120; pans for solutions, 118; plates, 45; printing-out paper, 39; reducing, 116; sodium hyposulphite, 119; spotting, 15, 39, 116; telephoto lens, 113; telescope lens, 106; trays, 39; view cameras, 3-4; views, 20; washing, 39

Photo Jewelry Company, Chicago, 115, 118, 119

Photo Materials Company, Chicago, 118

Photo Products Company, 120, 122

Pike's Peak (Colo.), 20

Pitt, Charles Robert, 5, 45, 56, 61, 64, 108, 112, 113; Nauvoo home of, 49, 54

Pitt, Charlotte Hill, 45, 109

Pitt, Emma Evlin Davidson, 61, 108, 112; Nauvoo home of, 54

Pitt, Hannah Hill, 109

Pitt, James, 109, 110, 112

Pitt, John, 45, 54, 61, 109, 110, 112

Pitt, Mary, 110

Pitt, Robert Calvin, 109, 112

Pitt, Thomas, 45, 110

Pitt, William, 109, 112

Plano (Ill.), 74

*Plan of Salvation* (pamphlet), 133

Plates (photography), 45

Polygamy, 9, 80, 135, 152

"Poor Wayfaring Man of Grief" (hymn), 137

Popper, Camilla Josephine Anderson, 191

Popper, Joseph, 191

Post, C. W., 14

Post, Miss, 127

Post, Pearl, 116

Postcards, 11, 12. *See also* Cabinet cards

Potter's Slough (Iowa), 105, 107, 108

Powell Brothers Blacksmith Shop, Richmond (Mo.), 75

Powers, Mrs., 170

Powers Hotel, Palmyra (N.Y.), 164

Pratt, Orson, 81; Nauvoo home of, 49

Pratt, Parley Parker, 75, 181, 213, 217; Kirtland home of, 150, 152, 159

Pratt, Thankful Halsey, Kirtland home of, 150

Presbyterian Church, 84

Preemption rights, 92

Price (Utah), 19

Printing-out paper (photography), 39

Prohibition, 45

Pueblo (Colo.), 20, 21-22

Purdy, Mr., 167

Quail, miracle of, 105, 108

Quaker Church. *See* Society of Friends

Quincy (Ill.), 5, 39-40, 41, 106

Quinn, Christopher, 143

Racial discrimination, 9

Railroads, 8. *See also individual railroads*

Ralphs, James A., 5, 45, 49, 132

Ramsey, Brother, 114

Randolph (Vt.), 200

Rasmusson, James, 13, 115, 120, 121, 122, 123, 124, 126, 128, 130, 131, 132, 134, 135, 136, 139

Rassmussen, John F., 5, 45, 49, 132

Rebaptism, 109

Red Brick Store, Nauvoo (Ill.), 49, 52, 110

Redler, Theodor, 152

Reducing (photography), 116

Reed, Chester, 216

Regean, Ada, 128

Regean, Nelson, 128

Reimbold, Father (priest), 61

Reimbold, Mr., 41, 57

Relief Society, in Nauvoo, 49, 52

Reorganized Church of Jesus Christ of Latter Day Saints, 12-13; Far West building, 5, 80; headquarters sites, 74; history of, 35; Independence

Stake bishop, 32; Sunday School, Far West (Mo.), 86; Sunday School, Kingston (Mo.), 85

Restoration Trails Foundation (RLDS), 111

Reynolds, William, 102

Rich, Charles C., 76

Richards, E. A., 123, 132

Richards, Willard, 48, 110

Richins, Osburn, 23, 31, 32, 39, 65, 85, 123, 139

Richman, T. G., 162

Richmond (Mo.), 5, 7, 65, 67-75

Ricks, Joel, 116

Ricks, Susette Cardon, 116

Rieser, Elder, 85

Rigby, M. M. Dahle, 115

Rigdon, Athalia, 216, 217

Rigdon, John W., 217

Rigdon, Phebe Brook, Kirtland home of, 149

Rigdon, Sidney, 186, 213, 217; Kirtland home of, 147, 149, 218; visits Cave Hill, 186

Riley, I. Woodbridge, *The Founder of Mormonism*, 74

Rio Grande Western Railroad, 19, 20, 115

Riverside Mansion. *See* Nauvoo (Ill.); Nauvoo House

RLDS Church. *See* Reorganized Church of Jesus Christ of Latter Day Saints

Roberts, B. H., 119, 132, 133

Roberts, J. C., 49, 60, 61, 64, 85, 112, 113, 123, 132, 137

Robinson, Athalia, 216

Robinson, Ebenezer, 41

Robinson, George W., Kirtland hotel of, 144

Robinson, Herbert, 118

Robinson, Mr., 215

Rock Church. *See* Stone Church, RLDS, Independence (Mo.)

Rock River (Wis.), 129

Rockwell, Orin, 66

Rockwell, Orrin Porter, 66

Rogers, Jacob, 102

Ross, Charles R., 101, 103

Ross, Maud, 113
Rowland Hall, Salt Lake City, 187
Royalton (Vt.), 202
Russell, Hope, 114, 115, 124, 133, 136, 139
Russon, John, 128, 129, 130

Sacred Grove, Manchester (N.Y.), 6, 164, 180, 182, 183
Sagers, Elder, 131, 132
Salt Lake City (Utah), 10, 127, 187
Salt Lake City Ministerial Association, 119
Salvation Army, 13, 125, 126, 127
Salvation Army Building, Chicago, 10, 123, 124
Sampson, William T., 168, 187, 216; Palmyra farm of. 167, 175
Sanborn, Alden E., 144, 157
Sanborn, Fred H., 144, 157
Sanborn, Mr., 161
Sanborn, Nellie M., 144, 157
Sanborn, Sarah Jane, 144, 154, 157
Saunders, Balina White, 181
Saunders, Orlando, 181
Savage, C. R., 8, 127
Sawyer, Mr., 141
Schooler, John, 101
School of the Prophets, 161
Schramm, F. C., 141
Schramm's Drugstore, Cleveland, 141
Schultz, Mr., 92
Schultz, Sister, 39
Schupp, John, 143
Schupp, Mrs., 143
Schweich, George W., 70, 74, 75, 82
Schweich, Josephine. *See* Van Cleave, Josephine Helen Schweich
Schweich, Julia Ann Whitmer, 67, 70, 74, 75
Schweich, Paul, 70
Schweich, Van, 70
Scovell, Abner, 214
Scythe (farm tool), 143
Sears, Brother, 116, 128
Seeley, Andrew Jackson, 82, 84, 85, 126
Seeley, David, 84
Seeley, J. Wellington, 134

Seeley, Oliver, 84
*Seine*, definition of, 108
Self-binder (reaper), 164
Seneca Lake (N.Y.), 190
Seventh-day Adventist Church, 14
Sexton, Pliney T., 170, 173
Shannon, William, 191
Sharon (Vt.), 119, 203, 204-8
Sharp, Thomas, 109
Shaw, Mr., 6, 176
Shearer, Norman, 75
Shehitah (Jewish ritual), 120
Sherwin, John, 161
Shoal Creek (Mo.), 85, 89, 95, 98-99, 104
Shohet (Jewish ritual), 120
Short, John, 70
Shorthorn cattle, 45, 49
Shriner's Temple, Denver, 21
Sickle, Ivan, 144
Silverthorn, James, 163
Sinclair, Upton, *The Jungle*, 10
Sisam, Alma N., 162, 163
Skyscrapers, 10, 115
Sleemim, John, 144
Sloan, Ruben, 78
*Slough*, definition of, 107
Smith, Alice M., 95
Smith, Alvin, 216; birthplace of, 201; Harmony tombstone of, 196
Smith, Amanda Barnes, 95
Smith, Avery, 214
Smith, Caroline Amanda Grant, Kirtland home of, 151
Smith, Don Carlos, 44, 41; Kirtland home of, 147
Smith, Edna, 160
Smith, Emma Hale, 5, 44, 47, 144, 156; Far West homesite of, 80, 83; Harmony home of, 192, 194; Kirtland home of, 158; Nauvoo grave site of, 5, 45
Smith, Emmeline Griswold, 44, 45
Smith, Ephraim, 202
Smith, Evelyn Rebecca, 45
Smith, Frederick Madison, 80
Smith, George A. (1817-79), 3, 81, 114, 118, 126, 135, 164, 216

Smith, George Albert (1870-1951), 3
Smith, Harvey, South Royalton home of, 203
Smith, Hyrum, 44, 45, 47, 48, 109, 190, 218; birthplace of, 201; Kirtland home of, 147, 149, 151, 218
Smith, Jerusha Barden, Kirtland grave of, 144, 159; Kirtland home of, 151
Smith, John, 144
Smith, Joseph Arthur, 45
Smith, Joseph F., 6, 9, 14, 23, 159, 160, 207
Smith, Joseph Fielding, 1
Smith, Joseph H., 136
Smith, Joseph, III, 35, 44, 45, 74, 80, 144, 152, 219
Smith, Joseph: and Alexander Doniphan, 71; baptized, 197; burial site, Nauvoo, 44, 47; in Carthage Jail, 45, 48, 137; defines *Nauvoo*, 41; Far West home site of, 80, 83; folklore about, 143, 167; Harmony home of, 192, 194; heals Saints at Montrose, 64; Kirtland home of, 147, 159; and Kirtland Temple, 143; in Liberty Jail, 160-61; and Lyman Wight, 91; Manchester memorial to, 6; Martin Harris assisted, 185; martydom of, 109; meets Newel K. Whitney, 156; Memorial Cottage, 208; and *Nauvoo Expositor*, 59; Palmyra home of, 182; parents described in encyclopedia, 106; Red Brick Store of, 52; revealed baptism for the dead, 104; in Richmond Jail, 68; Richmond monument to, 70; Sharon monument to, 6, 119, 159, 206; on spirits of animals, 14; visited by angel Moroni, 170; visits Cave Hill, 186; writes John Wentworth, 119
Smith, Joseph, Sr., 44, 143, 200, 204; Manchester farm of, 166, 176-77, 178, 179, 181, 183
Smith, Lucy Emily Woodruff, 126
Smith, Lucy Mack, 44, 186, 200, 204; Manchester farm of, 166, 176-77, 178, 179, 181, 182, 183

Smith, Mary Duty, Kirtland grave of, 144, 159

Smith, Mr., 120

Smith, Mrs. F., 160

Smith, Robert, 204, 215

Smith, Samuel, 44, 201, 215

Smith, Sardius, 95, 102

Smith, Sister, 131

Smith, Sophronia, 201

Smith, Warren, 95

Smith, William, 202; Kirtland home of, 147

Smith family cemetery, Nauvoo (Ill.), 44, 47

Smith farm, Manchester (N.Y.), 6, 164, 166, 170, 176-77, 178, 179, 181, 182, 216

Smith homestead, Nauvoo (Ill.), 47, 52

Smith and Morton (publisher), Salt Lake City, 22

Smoot, Reed, hearings, 4, 9, 16, 152, 154

Snow, Eliza Roxcy, 124

Snow, Erastus, 57

Snow, Lorenzo, 9, 14, 57

Snow–Ashby Duplex, Nauvoo (Ill.), 57

Snyder, Clara, 141

Society of Friends, 167, 170

Sodium hyposulphite (photography), 119

Sorensen, Sister, 115, 123

Southern States Mission (LDS), 27, 160

South Park Commission, Chicago, 116

South Pleasant Street, Independence (Mo.), 30

South Royalton (Vt.), 15, 203

Southwestern Railroad, 65

*Souvenir of Salt Lake: The City Beautiful* (book), 22

Spangenler, George L., 141

Spanish Fork (Utah), 74

Spaulding, Solomon, 106

Spaulding Institute Building, Nauvoo (Ill.), 60

Spence, William Charles, 3, 32, 60

Spotting (photography), 15, 39, 114, 116

Springville (Utah), 10, 19, 20

*Springville Independent* (newspaper), 4

Squire, Mr., 152

Squires, Joseph, Kirtland home of, 147

Stain, Ellen, 133

Standard Time, 162

Star Theater Building, Buffalo (N.Y.), 162

Stark, Elder, 134

*Stars and Stripes* (boat), 163

Stedwell, Mary, 101

Steele, Elder M., 35

Steffe, Frank, 147, 151

Steffe, Rosanne, 147, 151

Stephens, Elder, 132

Stephens, Moses, 45

Steunenberg, Frank, 123

Stevens, Mr., 160

Stevenson, Edward, 76, 78, 93, 219

Steward, Eunice, 84

Stiegall, Mrs. Frank, 75

St. Joseph (Mo.), 64–65

St. Mary's Academy, Nauvoo (Ill.), 56, 60

Stockyards, Kansas City (Mo.), 65

Stone Church, RLDS, Independence (Mo.), 5, 26, 27, 31, 33, 37

Stone, Albert E., 5, 144, 147, 148, 152, 160, 161, 217

Stowell, Josiah, 198

St. Peter and St. Paul Catholic Church, Nauvoo, 42, 53, 56, 61

Streetcars, 8, 34, 39

Strong, Elmer, 31, 35, 39

Strong, W. E., 10

St. Scholastica's. *See* St. Mary's Academy, Nauvoo (Ill.)

Sunday School (LDS), 4, 25, 61; lessons, 113, 120, 131

Surrey (carriage), 45

Susquehanna River, 197, 198

Swart, Alta, 134

Swenson, George, 130

Swope, Maggie C., 35

Tanner, Benjamin, 129, 130, 136

Taylor, John, 41, 48, 81, 137

Taylor, John W., 135

Telephoto lens (photography), 113

Telescope lens, 106

Temple Committee, Nauvoo (Ill.), 52

Temples (LDS). *See individual temples and temple sites*

Tennessee Pass (Colo.), 20

Thatcher, Albert, 31

Thayer and Grandin Brick Row, Palmyra (N.Y.), 171

Thayer, Ezra, Kirtland home of, 147

Thomas, Mrs. E. L., 22

Thompson, James, 76, 78, 123

Thompson, J. L., 78

Thompson, Mrs., 78

Thompson, Virgil, 76

Thompson boys, 76

Thompson River (Mo.), 89

Thornburg, Walter W., 2, 19, 126, 127

Thornstoff, Elder, 134

Three Witnesses Monument, Richmond (Mo.), 70

Time, Standard, 162

*Times and Seasons* (newspaper), 41, 43

Toronto Power Company, 163

Tower Building. *See* Montgomery Ward and Company, Chicago

Tower Hill, Adam-ondi-Ahman (Mo.), 89, 91

Transportation revolution, 8

Trays (photography), 39

Troupe, William Alonzie, 85, 89

Trout, Clyde, 76

Trout, Mrs., 76

Tunbridge (Vt.), 200-202

Turk, Keziah Jenkins, 150, 157, 159, 218

Turk, Mr., 159

Turner Brass Works, Chicago, 136

Twelves, Charles Murray, 74

Twelves, Ruby, 74

Uhlman's Supply Depot, St. Joseph (Mo.), 65

Uintah Railway, 115

Uncompahgre Indians, 21

Union Depot: Denver, 20; Kansas City (Mo.), 27, 39

*Union Jack* (boat), 163

Union Park, Chicago, 121

Union Stockyards and Transit Company, Chicago, 10, 119

United Brethren Church, 109

Utah Apex, 78

Utah Fuel Company, 20

Van Cleave, Josephine Helen Schweich, 70, 74

Van Cleave, Josie, 74
Vance, H. S., 115, 124, 128, 131
VanNoy, T. L., 162
Vegetarianism, 13-14
Veterans Memorial Park, Watertown
     (Wis.), 129
Viall, Fred, 141, 143
Victoria, Queen, 115
View cameras, 3-4
Views (landscape photographs), 20
Virgin Mary (image of), 61
Volker, Mrs., 120
Volker, William, and Company, 27
Volunteers of America, 13, 124

Wadleigh, Mr., 20
Wadsworth, Nelson B., 16
Wallace, Lewis, *Ben Hur*, 74
Walters, George, 214
Wanless, W. L., 123, 130
Ward, Minnie, 131
Ware, Miss/Mrs., 113, 121
*Wareroom*, Anderson's use of term, 162
Warsaw (Ill.), 109
*Warsaw Signal* (newspaper), 109
Washing (photography), 39
Washing and anointing (ordinance), 107
Water and Bain Streets, Nauvoo (Ill.), 52
Water filters, 106
Water Street, Nauvoo (Ill.), 50-51, 52
Waterloo (Iowa), 108
Watertown (Wis.), 128-29
*Wayne Sentinel* (newspaper), 171, 181, 182,
     191
Webb, Chauncey, Nauvoo home of, 110
Webb, Eliza Jane Churchill, Nauvoo home
     of, 110
Webster, Daniel, 20
Weir, Mrs., 132
Wells, John, 95
Wells, John F., 144
Wells, Junius Free, 1, 57, 119, 127, 130,
     207
Wells, Mr., 161
Wells, Salomi Billings, 144
Wentworth, John, 119
Wesport Landing. *See* Kansas City (Mo.)
Western Federation of Mines, 123

Western Health Reform Institute, Battle
     Creek (Mich.), 14
Western States Mission (LDS), 13, 20, 22
Wetherill Collection, Denver, 21
Whiffletrees (wagon part), 113
Whipple, Jennie, 141
Whipple, Jessie, 141
White, Edgar, 76, 78
White, Frank, 101
White, I. N., 80
White, Ike, 95
White, John B., 95
White, Laf B., 95, 101
White City Park, Chicago, 128, 139
Whiteley, Earl, 31
White's home, Haun's Mill (Mo.), 97
White Star Line, Boston, 32, 35, 45, 60,
     64
Whitmer, Catherine, 70
Whitmer, Celia Ann Tattarshull, 80, 85
Whitmer, David, 67, 70, 74-75, 170,
     190, 214, 216; Richmond home
     of, 68, 72-73; Richmond monu-
     ment of, 65; Richmond tombstone
     of, 69, 70
Whitmer, David John, 70
Whitmer, Edwin Franklin, 65, 67
Whitmer, Elizabeth. *See* Cowdery, Eliza-
     beth Ann Whitmer
Whitmer, Harry Elmore, 80
Whitmer, J., 136
Whitmer, Jacob, 65, 70; Richmond tomb-
     stone of, 5, 69, 70
Whitmer, Jacob David Jefferson, 78, 80
Whitmer, John, 70, 78, 82, 213; Far West
     Hotel of, 80; Kingston tombstone
     of, 82, 85, 87
Whitmer, John Christian, 65, 70
Whitmer, John David, 80, 82, 123, 130
Whitmer, Julia Ann Jolly, 65, 70; Rich-
     mond home of, 72-73
Whitmer, Julia Ann. *See* Schweich, Julia
     Ann Whitmer
Whitmer, Mariann. *See* Bisbee, Mariann
     Whitmer
Whitmer, Mary Musselman, 68, 82, 190;
     burial site, 70; Fayette farm of,
     189; Richmond home of, 71

Whitmer, Peter, Jr., 190
Whitmer, Peter, Sr., 70, 82, 190, 215,
     216; Fayette farm of, 189; Rich-
     mond burial site of, 70; Richmond
     home of, 67, 68, 71
Whitmer, Sarah Elizabeth. *See* Kerr, Sarah
     Elizabeth Whitmer Johnson
Whitmer Coal Company, Richmond
     (Mo.), 67
Whitmer family, 7
Whitmerite Church. *See* Church of Christ
     (Whitmerite)
Whitney, Elizabeth Ann Smith, Kirtland
     home of, 157
Whitney, Newel Kimball, 107, 144, 219;
     Kirtland home of, 143, 157; Kirt-
     land store of, 144, 152, 156, 161
Wight, Harriet Benton, Adam-ondi-
     Ahman home of, 90, 91
Wight, Lyman: Adam-ondi-Ahman cabin
     of, 91, 92; Adam-ondi-Ahman
     home of, 89, 90
William Galloway Company, Waterloo
     (Iowa), 108
William Volker & Company, Kansas City
     (Mo.), 27
Willoughby (Ohio), 141, 160, 161
Wilson, R. C., 147
Wilson, Sister, 160
Wine industry, Nauvoo (Ill.), 56, 62-63
*Wisconsin* (ship), 128, 130
Women's Christian Temperance Union, 45
Wood, Wilford C., 14, 53, 170
Woodbury, John B., 103
Woodruff, Asael, 123
Woodruff, Phoebe Carter, Nauvoo home
     of, 59
Woodruff, Wilford, 14, 41, 81, 109, 110,
     152; Nauvoo home of, 5, 59
Word of Wisdom, 13-14, 39, 64, 134
World's Columbian Exposition (1893),
     116, 122, 128, 133, 141
Wright, Jonathan C., Nauvoo home of,
     49, 50-51

Yearsley, David, Nauvoo home of, 62-63
Yearsley, Mary Ann Hoopes, Nauvoo
     home of, 62-63

Young, Brigham, 81, 110, 152, 216; Nauvoo home of, 107; table made by, 176, 179
Young, Clarissa Hamilton, 112
Young, Jane Bicknell, Nauvoo home of, 110
Young, Joseph, 217; Nauvoo home of, 110
Young, Lucy Cowdery, 112
Young, Mary Ann Angell, Nauvoo home of, 107
Young, Phineas, 112
Young, Seymour B., 16
Young Ladies National Mutual Improvement Association (LDS), 64
Young Ladies Retrenchment Association (LDS), 64
Young Men's Christian Association, 21
Young Men's Mutual Improvement Association (LDS), 23, 64
Young Women's Christian Association, 21
*Young Women's Journal* (magazine), 64

Zarahemla Stake (LDS), 41

*George Edward Anderson's 1907 Diary,* courtesy of DUP, shows entries for 13–14 August 1907 when Anderson was in New York visiting and photographing LDS Church historical sites. Along with the bulky glass-plate negatives that so richly detail the sites of LDS Church historic significance, the 1907 diary also richly details Anderson's experiences as he traversed the dew-laden fields, the dusty village lanes and roads, and the busy streets of America's largest metropolitan cities. Both the photographs and the diary preserve a sense of the reality of a now-vanished world.

*Joseph and Lucy Mack Smith Farm,* Manchester, New York, August 1907, Anderson Collection, LDSCA. A view from a hill looking southwest across the Smith family farm. The traditional site of Joseph Smith's 1820 first vision (Sacred Grove) is seen in the distance on the right of the photograph. The "small country lane" leading to the grove is seen in the center of the image. Joseph and Lucy Mack Smith's frame home, which is located on the east side of Stafford Road, can be seen on the left in the trees. Note the rock fences and sheep in the foreground.